ME AND THE DEAD END KID

Leo Gorcey—1945

Leo Gorcey—1965

Me and the Dead End Kid

*Leo Gorcey, the Hollywood Legend
—Leo Jr., His Happy Ending*

by Leo Gorcey, Jr.

Published by *The Leo Gorcey Foundation*
with *Spirit of Hope Publishing*

Me and the Dead End Kid
Leo Gorcey the Hollywood Legend
—Leo Jr., His Happy Ending

Copyright © 2003 Leo Gorcey, Jr.
Published by *The Leo Gorcey Foundation*
with *Spirit of Hope Publishing*

International Standard Book Number 1-929753-15-2

Written by Leo Gorcey
Edited by Jerry Seiden

Printed in the United States of America

For information:
Spirit of Hope Publishing
PO Box 53642
Irvine, CA 92619-3642
Phone & Fax (949) 733-1486
Website: www.LeoGorcey.com

DEDICATION

To Krista, my life-partner and best friend.
To all our earthly fathers, who did the best they knew how.
And most humbly, to our heavenly Father,
whose love for us is without measure.

ACKNOWLEDGMENTS

Jerry Seiden, my editor, publisher, consultant, mentor, encourager, spiritual advisor, brother and dear friend.

Rich Buhler, raconteur par excellence, for making me choose between a bargain-bin biography and a passionate story, even though it meant writing *two* versions. His generosity and willingness to share the secrets of his success, and his unwavering commitment to truth and integrity, have inspired me for over two decades.

To Eden and *Hayley*, my two beautiful daughters, for giving me the gift of fatherhood.

Elizabeth Gorcey, the cousin I never knew I had. You gave me the kick in the pants I needed to face my past and tell a story that needed to be told, by showing your confidence in me.

Robert Evans, whose magnum opus, *The Kid Stays in the Picture*, gave me permission to break the rules and pull no punches.

John Townsend and *Henry Cloud* of Cloud-Townsend clinics. John and Henry taught me that living in reality is far more satisfying than numbing the pain, and that the truth really *does* have the power to set people free.

David Alibran. You convinced me that growing up is worth it.

Arlyss McDonald. You appeared to me like an angel of God. A Divine Messenger of healing. You led me into the epicenter of my pain, where you spoke the words of peace, "It wasn't your fault."

Robin Young, Numero Uno Leo Gorcey fan. Your generous and loving encouragement, in the middle season of *Me and the Dead End Kid*, carried me across the finish line.

Bill Shipman. You helped show me the way. You not only shared your admiration for my father, you openly shared your courageous reconciliation with your own father. When I came out the other end, you were there with a smile and a hug.

Krista Lynn, for holding me through those many dark nights, and drying the tears when the pain of writing about my father threatened to consume me.

Bob Mirtha, my creative writing teacher.

Scott Allen, my recovery 'big brother'. You kicked my butt so often I needed a doughnut pillow to sit down. You made it okay for me to come out of hiding by admitting your own weaknesses. Thank you.

Frank McCourt. You are living proof that a memoir can be every bit as engaging as a novel. You inspired me to *tell a story,* not just write a book.

Julia Cameron, for the precious and practical insights you shared so beautifully in *The Writer's Life.* You rescued me more than once.

Brandy Jo Zeisemer, my little sister with the big heart. Your tireless years of research, interviews, and hours of Xeroxing paid off. You provided the starting point and stayed with me. Love ya, Sis!

Brandy Gorcey (AKA Nurse Betty), my step mom. Bless your heart, Mom! You not only survived nine harrowing years with the *Dead End Kid,* and got healthy, you were the one gleam of hope shining through the darkness. Had you not come along when you did, and stayed as long as you did, I would not have made it.

Denny (Tiger) and *Kathy Latimer,* for being Dad's best friends in his retirement years, and my God-parents. You loved my father for what he was, warts and all. That's what it's all about.

Jimmy Roberts, another Numero Uno Leo Gorcey fan. You did the unthinkable. You obtained copies of over 50 of my father's films and got them into my hands. And you refused to accept a dime. That's *true* love, with a capital L.

To My Two Ex-Wives. Inadvertently, you inspired me to take refuge in Ashland, Oregon for four months. The idea for the book and the first chapters came to me there. I wish you both the best.

Brent Walker and *David Hayes.* For the years of love you two invested into the writing of *The Films of The Bowery Boys.* How you guys did it, I'll never know. But I'm glad you did!

Benny Drinnon, co-founder of the *Bowery Group* at *Yahoo.* You brought me out of my shell and introduced me to thirty beautiful fans of *The Dead End Kid,* from all over the U.S., Canada and the UK. The ensuing correspondence was life-changing. You're a good man, Benny Drinnon!

Kenn Gulliksen. I will love you forever for introducing me to the power of forgiveness.

SPECIAL THANKS!

I wish to thank the following fans of my father, Leo Gorcey. You gave me the encouragement, love, and support I needed during the writing of *Me and The Dead End Kid.* I appreciate your many contributions, responses to questions, and the materials and memoriabilia you sent me in the mail.

THANKS TO: Richard Banta, Cathy Buck, Mark Corl, Benny Drinnon*, Dale Drinnon, Jamie Evangelista*, Terry Fielding (Canada), Karen Guenther, David Hayes, Rob Heiler, Michael Robin Lee Lewis, Terry Lee Lewis, Andrea Meine, Dan Miller, Lauren Miller, Jim Lakey, Lisa, Greg and Beth Milliken, Elaine and Morgan Moore, Harry Moyles, George Flagg Nixon, Ben Ohmart, Vincent Omara, Bonnie Parker, Sherry 'Slip' Post, Jimmy Roberts, John Robinson, James Scott, Derek Shayne, Bill Shipman, Kate Tann (UK), Brent Walker, John Webber, and Robin Young.

May God bless you as you have blessed me infinitely beyond what you would dare to think or ask!

With Love,
Leo, Jr.

*Co-founder of bowerygroups@Yahoo (email to: bowerygroups@Yahoo.com).

Table of Contents

THE FANS

This book was born after a year of labor. Its spark of life was given to me as a gift. I've carried it since childhood. But the nourishment and encouragement to bring it to full-term came from my dad's fans.

I spent untold hours with fans via email. People I had never met inspired me with their love for my father. I caught their excitement about this book. I developed a vision beyond my own. I was implanted with a passion that sustained me through the low times. I tossed in the towel more than once. But Dad's fans picked it up and put it back in my heart. They moved me to give this story life and breath and voice.

I grew close to many of Dad's fans. We shared intimate thoughts about life and its struggles. We talked about the losses we grieve. We discussed the wounds we suffered and the scars we bear—the legacy of dysfunctional families. We mourned the loss of fathers taken before their time. We related to the experience of alcoholic parents—or of parents who were distant in other ways.

Dad's fans and I shared life via email. Philosophies were espoused. Beliefs were expounded. Memories were evoked. Dreams were exposed. And our hopes for the future were expressed.

We banged away on our keyboards and told our stories. We shared our experience, strength, and hope. We chronicled our journey to become our own person. We noted the past that we had embraced. We wrote about those we had forgiven. They did the best they could. They raised us with the little they had. Then their moment passed, and they were no longer with us. It was up to us to let go and choose to love.

Like me, many have chosen a higher path. We love and honor their memories.

Yeah, we talked about a lot—Dad's fans and I. But mostly, we talked about our favorite celebrity—Leo Gorcey, the Dead End Kid.

To all of you, whose names are listed in the acknowledgments, I am grateful beyond words. My heart overflows to the point of tears. I will never forget you.

THE FAN LETTER

This letter—every word—came from Leo Gorcey fans. It is the composite of dozens of emails. Expressions of the thoughts and feelings that fans have for my dad. This is a memorial to my father's life and career. But it is also my tribute to my father's fans. Without Dad's fans this book would never have been born.

I have come to treasure all the emails I received. Every one was printed out and bound with the others. I would love to share them all, but that's impossible. Instead, here are verbatim email excerpts. I changed nothing except to edit punctuation.

The messages express a common experience. They share a connection with the onscreen lives of Leo Gorcey and his various gangs. They relate to the Dead End Kids, to the Eastside Kids, to the Bowery Boys.

Dear Leo Gorcey Jr.,

I've been a Leo Gorcey fan most of my life. I watched them on TV as a kid and couldn't get enough of them.

I've waited a long time for the real story! I think your book is a great idea, and long overdue.

I have a copy of *The Films of The Bowery Boys* by Brent Walker and David Hayes. It was like the Holy Grail of the Bowery when it was released. I've wanted for so many years to learn more about him. Now, it appears, it will finally happen!

Leo Gorcey (A.K.A. Spit, Muggs McGinnis, Slip Mahoney) was an old-fashioned tough guy who knew what he wanted! He was from the Damon Runyan School; the type of low-life who was lovable even though he did things you hoped your own kids wouldn't do.

Even as a kid, watching Leo's movies, I sensed that your dad was a true original. He marched to his own drummer. He didn't have to work at being cool. He had 'existential cool' in large doses!

Though Leo Gorcey stood only 5 feet, four inches

tall, I looked straight up to him.

Experiencing the onscreen camaraderie of Leo Gorcey and The Bowery Boys is like having an extended family of no-accounts show up at my house for an hour. I'm glad I'm not related to them, but I want to be part of the fun.

The whole point of your dad's films was for the actors and the audience to have fun together!

Watching your dad, whether in the Dead End Kids, the Eastside Kids, or the Bowery Boys, was to watch a great actor at work. One who never failed to elicit smiles from me, because he was always trying. He was always himself.

Leo Gorcey possessed natural charisma, passion, and intuitive understanding of character that the best-trained actors in Hollywood could not match.

This is best indicated by the fact that Samuel Goldwyn could not find a Hollywood kid actor to recreate your father's stage role, which led the mogul to import your father and the rest of the Dead End gang from Broadway to Hollywood.

Leo and the Bowery Boys were slackers, but they were noble slackers. They would jump to the aid of a friend, even if it meant risking their own personal safety.

And the Bowery Boys were loyal to each other. If one was in trouble, the others would rally to his side.

Slip Mahoney (Leo Gorcey) may have belted Sach (Huntz Hall) with his hat and slapped him, but woe to the one who was foolish enough to take the same liberties.

I remember the scene in the Bowery Boys film, *Dig that Uranium*, where one of the villains tried to slip Sach a Mickey.

Slip Mahoney jumped up from his table and said to the rest of the gang, "I'll handle Dis! Dere's only two of 'em!"

Leo approached the bad guys. "Dat wasn't very facetious of you gentlemen," says Slip. Then he knocked their beers in their faces and waded into them! What's not to admire about the guy?

As the leader of the Bowery Boys, Leo Gorcey brought a sense of danger as well as shrewdness to his character, Slip Mahoney.

Along with that great face; the half-moon eye-
brows, thin mouth and tiny nose, Leo's voice reso-
nated danger, gravity, and power.

I remember the scene in the Bowery Boys movie,
Jail Busters, when Slip Mahoney is visiting Chuck in
the hospital. Your dad says, "I know yuh ain't in very
good shape, Chuck, but jist tell me one ting. Who done
it to yuh?" You knew that whoever was responsible
was in big trouble!

I've always had the sense that Leo's strength was
real. He was a little powerhouse. When he threw a
punch onscreen, I could feel the wind!

Slip Mahoney could handle anything without
losing his cool. He had the quality Earnest Hemingway
referred to as "Grace under pressure." Gorcey was the
John Wayne of the New York streets!

He was a free spirit.

Though he needed to belong to the gang, he seemed
to be leading the Bowery Boys out of necessity. If Slip
didn't get the gang out of a jam, who would?

I believe your father achieved true comic greatness
with the Bowery Boys character, Slip Mahoney.

Watching your dad's movies has enriched my life
in so many ways. Slip Mahoney always came through,
no matter what kind of trouble he and the gang got
themselves into.

I think about that sometimes when I'm feeling
down. I can just hear your dad, as Slip saying to me,
"Whadd'ya bawlin' fer kid? Get out dere an' woik it
out!"

I love the way Slip Mahoney would give that look
when Sach said something dumb, right before he hit
him with his pinned-up hat. I feel that way a lot!

There was a basic honesty about Slip and the gang
that made me love them.

Leo Gorcey's characters remained true to one
simple theme: If you get in trouble, there's a price to
pay. But amends can be made and wrongs can be
righted.

There was always a moral to the Bowery Boys
stories having to do with keeping a kid on the right
track. At least that's what the Coppers would say!

The thing I love most about your dad's movies, is
that he made me forget my troubles. That's the highest

compliment I know of to pay any comic actor.

Your father was a great and wonderful man.

I still, to this day, love watching the Dead End Kids, Eastside Kids, and Bowery Boys movies whenever I get the chance!

Your dad was "The Bomb." He was "The Man." He was "It."

Leo Gorcey wasn't just a tough guy. He was a tough guy with a heart. He perfected that. He was awesome.

One of the profound tragedies of my life is never having met the man.

When my pal called me on June 2nd 1969 with the news that your father had died, I was in shock. I said to him, "Are you sure it was Leo Gorcey who died?"

My pal answered with sadness in his voice. "Yeah, I'm sure. I heard the radio news anchorman say, The Dead End Kid, and leader of the Eastside Kids and the Bowery Boys...."

I ran to the TV. There was Walter Cronkite doing the obituary. "Leo Gorcey, The Dead End Kid, is dead...."

I just crawled inside myself and stayed there for quite awhile. I can only imagine what you must have gone through. My own dad died when I was twenty, and it left quite a void.

I think it's fantastic that you're writing this book. Maybe this will open eyes (especially at Warner Brothers) about getting the best of the gang on DVD! (I can also visualize Slip and Sach watches, beach towels, coffee mugs, dolls, board games, posters...the works!)

I hope the company that owns the films will see how entertaining the Bowery Boys were and still are!

Whenever I watch your dad's movies (and it's often), it's like visiting old friends!

I want to thank you for the ways in which you are helping us to remember your father. I look forward to reading your book.

God bless you and your endeavors,
The Fans of Leo Gorcey

P.S. I recently made a pilgrimage to the old Monogram studios where your dad made the Bowery Boys pictures. I took a whole bunch of photographs, but couldn't get in to see the place. Guess you gotta know somebody!

WASN'T THERE AN ACTOR BY THAT NAME?

Leo Gorcey was the star of a complex, multi-branched family tree of films in Hollywood's Golden Age. Leo's three film series are (in chronological order) *The Dead End Kids*, *The Eastside Kids*, and *The Bowery Boys*. They included over 70 films produced by *Samuel Goldwyn*, *Warner Brothers*, and *Monogram* (later *Allied Artists*). The production years were between 1937 and 1957. In total, Dad appeared in 90 movies.

The Dead End Kids with Bogart, Cagney, and Garfield (to name a few) reached classic status. *Angels With Dirty Faces* with James Cagney was the signature film of the bunch.

The Bowery Boys were profitable comedy hits all over the world. This in spite of garage sale production values and cold shoulders from most critics. They ranked a permanent place in the pages of Hollywood movie history.

Off-camera, Leo was a one-man cottage industry. His bigger-than-life persona provided the perfect smorgasbord for a nonstop feeding frenzy of reporters, gossip columnists, and journalists: A rebellious youth, the big break, domestic spats, divorces, the battle with the bottle, and the decline and fall.

All my life, I've been accosted by countless strangers who asked, "Are you any relation to Leo Gorcey the ACTOR?"

My father's name is a head-scratcher. When people hear my name (Leo Gorcey, Jr.) or see it in print, they scratch their heads and say, "That name...Leo Gorcey...sounds familiar...."

Seconds later, I hear, "Leo Gorcey...wasn't there a famous ACTOR by that name?"

I answer, "Yes, that's my father." Then faces light up like klieg lights. Smiles appear out of nowhere. They act like I handed them a winning lottery ticket.

"Yeah, Leo Gorcey...he was a comedian, right?"

Then comes the double take.

"Yeah, now that you mention it, you do resemble him."

I make the same joke every time.

"Yeah, especially the receding hairline. Ha, ha!"

There have been hundreds of these encounters over the years. I kept the smile glued on my face. I listened to comments about the good old days. "Yeah, you could see a double feature for a nickel!" the fan pines away. "I loved Saturday matinees with the Bowery Boys!"

I imagine the fan as a being from another planet. He rambles and reminisces about how great life was where he came from. Of course, he later admits that life wasn't that great. But my father's movies made life better. The films provided some comic relief—hilarious shtick to balance life's harsh stuff. A sixty-two minute vacation from all his troubles. And his troubles were many.

I have to be careful. In no time, the conversation can turn. Then I find myself on the Leo Gorcey Memorial Freeway. Exits are few and hard to find. The drivers become guides and experts—they know all the happenings and points of interest. I hear up-to-the-minute reports and schedules for television re-runs of Dad's films. I learn about the most recent airing. The day and time it ran. "It was on channel 12," he declares. Then a hesitation and retraction, "No, I think it was channel 27. You know, that classic movie channel—the one that runs all the old movies?"

No, I don't know. In fact, I hate old movies! I muse to myself. But for the fan's sake, I reinforce the plastic smile and refresh the glaze over my eyes.

"I think it was last Saturday," the fan declares. Then he hesitates and adds, "Or maybe it was Sunday."

You don't need me for this conversation, I fume inside. *I'm just a prop— the straight man for your act.*

"And what was that tall guy's name again? You remember, the tall guy your dad used to slap around?"

"Do you mean, Huntz Hall?" I offer.

"Oh yeah, Huntz Hall—that's the guy." He smiles and nods

his head. "Yeah, he played, uh, er...."

"Sach," I prod.

"Oh yeah, Sach, that was his name! And whatever became of the rest of those guys anyway? Do you know?"

No! And I don't care! I say to myself. *My back is killing me. I can't bend my knees now. And I've lost all feeling in my feet. If you don't stop talking and let me go, I may hurt you!*

But what I say aloud is, "No, I have no idea."

All I wanted was to do a simple transaction with my check or credit card. I wanted to get my receipt and get out of the restaurant or store. But instead, I was held hostage by a Leo Gorcey fan.

Oops! Well, there you have it.

In truth, the fans have always been decent and pleasant people. They loved my father.

I never wanted to be rude. *I'll make my dad look like a jerk,* I thought. *Then I'll be in trouble.*

But for the life of me, I couldn't comprehend what all the hoopla was about.

Whether the Dead End Kid, the Eastside Kid, or the Bowery Boy, I knew this movie star as my distant and scary father. His breath always smelled funny, and his drunken buffoonery always embarrassed me.

My friends had normal fathers. My dad was weird.

I didn't share the warm fuzzy feelings that the fans had about Leo Gorcey. They wanted me to share their adoration. They needed me to reinforce their illusion. They intended to make me agree with their dream—whether I wanted to or not! But I just smiled and wished I had the *cojones* to tell them to bug off.

A certain type of female fan has always baffled me more than bugged me. This type recounted her childhood antics. She was the girl who insisted on playing my dad in neighborhood re-enactments of the Bowery Boys.

I always thought, *Whoa! What's up with that?*

But out loud I say, "Really? Ha, ha, you wanted to be my father?"

The flow of fans on the Leo Gorcey Memorial Freeway

wanted to hear about the hero—the legend. The average fan didn't want to tour the truth. He didn't want to discover the alcoholic. He didn't want to visit Dad's pain. He didn't want to travel to Leo's real dead end.

The enthusiastic fan asked, "What's Leo up to these days, anyway? Is he still making movies?'"

The first time I decided to lose the phony smile and be honest, I said, "No, he's not. Actually, my dad died of cirrhosis of the liver. He drank himself to death. He hated acting. He was miserable in show business. He always wanted to be a plumber."

That was no easy exit off the freeway. In fact, it caused a wreck.

My honesty was like a photo pulled from my wallet. I saw the truth. The fan saw a morgue snapshot—his icon's autopsy.

The fan's face fell. The twinkle left his eyes. A pall settled over him. "Oh. I'm sorry– When did he 'pass'?"

"Many years ago," I answered.

News of his death sank in, but the conversation didn't end. "He was young!" the fan declared.

Yeah, and I'm not gettin' any younger standin' hear talkin' to you. I fussed to myself. *So, are you done asking questions?*

Out of habit, I had to add, "Yeah, he was fifty-two."

"Fifty-two! That's young! How old were you?"

"Nineteen. I was in the Army."

But I said to myself, *Shut up, stupid! Don't offer more than they ask for. Just get off the 'Freeway' before you bash your old man's good name.*

"Well, Leo, you should be proud. Your father was a very funny man. He brought joy to a lot of people."

Finally, an exit ramp. I put on my turn signal.

"Yeah, well thanks. I appreciate that."

Then, I'd scold myself. *Why did you say 'thanks'? That was stupid. You're not the one getting the compliment. You're standing here like an idiot thanking someone for a compliment to your dead father. Can this get any more weird?*

To finish, I said, "Well, it was nice meeting you." Then I turned and walked away.

I could feel the fan's smile biting at my heels like a bloodhound. After a block or so down the street, I'd be able to breathe again.

Usually the truth failed. So I resorted to my dumb act. I just repeated whatever the fans said about my dad!

"...Yup, he was a funny guy alright....Yeah, he was good wasn't he? Lots of people feel that way about him...."

Then I'd cut across the center divider and make an exit. "Well, nice meeting ya. I think I left the ice cream on the front seat. Gotta run."

I never knew what to say when the fan asked, "What was it like living with a famous father? Was he just as funny at home as he was in the movies, or was that just a character he played?"

THE RESEMBLANCE

Don't get me wrong.

Dad had his moments. He could make the whole family roll around the living room carpet in stitches. I loved those times. I used to think, *This guy is the funniest man on the planet!* At times I'd beg him to stop. I had stomach cramps from laughing so hard.

But other memories—not so happy—were mixed up with the good times.

Once Dad passed out in a bowling alley bar. Two bouncers dragged his booze soaked body out to his car. They handed me the keys. I was fourteen years old.

Ahead of me was fifteen miles of country road. It was filled with pitch darkness and pure terror. Dad was passed out in the back seat. The air was foul and full of alcohol.

How do I turn on the lights? I wondered. *How do I make this car move?* I numbed out—whistled through the graveyard. Thirty minutes later, I saw our house. I pulled in the gravel driveway and wondered, *How did I get here? It's a miracle! An angel must have picked us up and dropped us in our driveway! There is a God!*

Still there was much to do. I had to get him out of the car. I had to move him to bed. It felt like another fifteen miles. Some how I figured a way. I moved his dead drunk corpse. I put him to bed.

Those who cherish my father's memory do not want to hear those stories. They are nice people who cling to imagined memories. They think of him like an old friend—a best friend. They reminisce about my dad's movies. They remember how funny he was. They have the Leo they want. My truth only disappoints them.

Most are shocked when I say that Dad banned his movies in our house. I never saw one of my father's ninety movies. He didn't want us kids to get any ideas about show business.

People chuckle at that, but for some reason, no one ever hears the words. Instead, they go ahead and ask more questions about Dad's movies. They expect me to be a walking library on his career. They assume that I am obliged to know all about him because I am his son.

I try to imagine their thinking. *This is as close as I'll ever get to my idol,* they muse. *So I'd better squeeze every drop I can out of this fleeting moment with his son.*

I remember the day I started to hate my name. I tried other names. For a while in high school, I introduced myself as Scott. That failed. I couldn't remember who knew me as Scott and who knew me as Leo. Plus my ID card said nothing about Scott. I was stuck with Leo whether I liked it or not.

In the summer of 1999, Leo Gorcey and *The Bowery Boys* ran on The Classic Movie channel (TCM). The films aired every Sunday morning all summer long. They called it the Bowery Boys Summer.

Millions of cable viewers tuned in to the weekly romps of The Bowery Boys. It was a half-century after the movies were made and thirty years after Leo Gorcey went the way of all flesh. A whole new generation jumped on the Leo Gorcey Memorial Freeway.

Just when I thought I was free from Dad's shadow, I got hit with a new generation of Leo Gorcey fans.

"Did you know your father was on TV last Sunday? I didn't know your father was a famous ACTOR! Come to think of it, you even look like him!"

I often wondered, *What is so astonishing about the fact that I look like my father? Doesn't every son look like his father?*

On the other hand, there was the occasional skeptic. "Turn to the side, let me see your profile. Hmmm. No, you don't look anything like him—not at all," they concluded. I felt like I was accused of fabrication and fraud.

Some times, the skeptics saw my startled and sore look. They caught themselves and tried to recover. "Well, what I meant was...er...you're better looking than he was!"

COUSIN LIZ AND THE BIZ

In the Spring of 2002, I ran into Elizabeth, a cousin I had never met. Our paths crossed on the Internet—by accident.

Our first meeting was in Beverly Hills. And my cousin's first remarks were, "Hey, Leo, let's make a movie about your dad!" I soon discovered that cousin Liz is a documentary filmmaker.

Oh, no! I panicked. *How do I tell her I've never seen any of my father's movies?*

I drove straight home, clicked on to Amazon.com, and ordered *Dead End*, *They Made Me a Criminal*, and some assorted Bowery Boys flicks.

I took a crash course on the 'Old Man.'

I thought, *Wow! This guy is really funny! And he's smart, to boot! I guess all those fans weren't so nutty after all!*

I caught a glimpse of why his fans love him so much.

In his early crime melodrama movies with Warner Brothers, Leo (in the Cagney tradition) threw punches at the system. All the outsiders and underdogs watched him and identified. He spoke for them.

In his later comedy films in the 1950s, Leo served the audience his world of wacky upside-down-cake. He offered IOU's for malts at Louie's Sweetshop. He mixed in several dollops of delicious sarcasm. He tossed in a few salty whacks to the head of Sach, Leo's goofy sidekick. He added an exotic and spicy adventure. And topped it off with a slather of morality tale icing.

Dad repeated this recipe in forty-eight black-and-white Bowery Boys films. He served up slice after slice of comic relief for millions of fans. He brought laughter and lightheartedness to people who needed his nourishment.

Leo's fans loved him because he made them feel confident. He radiated optimism. He demonstrated that everything would work out in the end—no matter how crazy the circumstances.

His very presence on the screen guaranteed that a good time would be had by all.

Leo's characters shouted through a megaphone, *I've got it all under control! Jist do wuht I tell yuh, and everyting's gonna toin out jist fine!*

But I wasn't so sure.

If I agree to take part in a film about my father, I thought, *I'll have to learn more about him—a lot more. And not only about him...about other members of the family...and about myself.*

For weeks, I toyed with the questions. I dribbled them like basketballs. I asked, *What if I uncover more unpleasant facts? What if I find more trash than treasure? Will my discoveries add to my life long fear that I'm destined to repeat his mistakes? Will new knowledge re-injure old wounds? How much do I want to peer into his dark side? How much do I want to get into mine? How is this going to change me? Is there a happy ending anywhere in sight?*

IS THAT YOU, DAVID?

My most vivid memory of my father comes from May of 1969. The scene was a hospital room in Oakland, California. But the story began on a miserable, soggy night at Fort Lewis in the state of Washington.

I was on C.Q. In Army jargon that means I babysat the phone all night. I was stuck at company headquarters. All the others guys were snug in warm bunks.

The office was dank and dreary. A cold gray metal desk was my headrest. My scenery was the off-white, cement block, basement wall. No windows, no art, no life.

I fought hard to stay conscious. The clock was a cruel reminder of my captivity. Solitude and silence stretched the time into torture. I prayed for 6 a.m. to hurry. I could hardly wait to climb the stairs and collapse in my bunk. But my half-opened eyes peeked at the clock and found only disappointment.

Then the phone rang.

The caller asked, "Is this Madigan Hospital, Fort Lewis, Washington?"

"Yes it is," I answered. I tried to sound perky.

"This is Dr. Robbins at Merritt Hospital in Oakland, California." The doctor's voice was somber and serious. "Is there a Private Gorcey, Leo Gorcey, Jr., stationed there?"

It was a Twilight Zone moment.

The guy wants me, I marveled. *And I'm the one on C.Q. duty. What are the chances of this happening? But wait a minute! Why is a doctor calling me from a hospital in Oakland?*

"Uh, this is Private Gorcey!" I answered.

"Your father was transferred here late last night from the general hospital in Corning, California." The doctor droned on in a clipboard monotone. "I'm sorry to tell you that he's in critical condition. He probably won't live for more than a day or two."

My brain went on *tilt*. The words registered, but the message didn't. My head felt light and fuzzy. I talked, but it sounded like someone else's voice. Like somebody from another part of the room stepped up to talk for me.

"Um, well, thanks for calling. I'll see if I can come."

I rested the receiver back on its cradle, but it sounded like I slammed it from the roof. Everything was in slow motion. For a moment, I had no idea where I was. I didn't know how to get back to where I belonged. It was like doing the breaststroke in butterscotch pudding. My heart dropped. I felt light-headed.

What do I do? I wondered. *I can't leave my post. Regulations are clear.* All I could do was wait.

At 6 a.m. I called the Commanding Officer. I hoped that he would understand and not be angry for the early call. He was sympathetic, and by 10 a.m. I was knee deep in paperwork. It would be a ten-day bereavement leave. I was issued a round-trip plane ticket—Seattle to Oakland.

I felt lost and lean. I was alone—cut off. I couldn't connect with anyone. The cab spewed toxic fumes. The airports were full of frigid faces—mine among them.

Then Merritt Hospital. It was stark, sterile, sanitized, and sad. I zigzagged through the labyrinth of squeaky-clean corridors. Around every corner I expected to be met by a feeling. But only more of the same.

I endured the dreadful search. I tracked the room number from desk to desk, from floor to floor. I passed the nurse's station and the carts with food, and then I found his room. I stuck my head in. I saw a bed with crispy white sheets. Then I saw the man that the bed cradled—my dying father.

I entered Dad's room, but he was preoccupied. Dad was in withdrawals. He was in de-tox from his one-shot-of-whiskey-per-hour addiction. He'd been hard at it for 37 years.

His face was droopy and yellow with jaundice. His hair was designed by a light socket. He was disoriented and incoherent—medical terminology for 'scrambled mess.' There he was—my dad, the celebrity.

The air was thick and pungent—the fumes of antiseptic

death. I hated to inhale. The attending physician strode in and tapped me on the shoulder. He pulled me aside and whispered in my ear. "Are you the son?"

"Yes," I answered.

"Has anyone spoken with you?"

"Spoken with me?" I asked.

"About your father's condition?"

"Uh, no...not about his condition."

The physician's voice carried a measure of compassion. He spoke with a polite but hurried cadence. My father was not the only patient dying at Merritt Hospital.

"Cirrhosis of the liver," the doctor continued. He was well practiced in his bedside manner. "His liver has been eaten away by alcohol. His doctors at home ordered a blood transfusion. They hoped to regenerate what little was left of it."

"Regenerate it?" I interrupted.

I thought back to my high school biology teacher, Mr. Ruffner. He told us that the Salamander is the only animal that can regenerate parts of its body. Chop off a leg, and the Salamander will just grow another one! But for the life of me, I couldn't remember Mr. Ruffner saying a word about human livers.

This all went through my mind in a flash. Then I heard the doctor say, "Sometimes we can save the liver if we get to it in time. I've seen some cases where the liver has completely regenerated itself from almost nothing."

I had to ask again, "The liver can regenerate itself?"

"Yes, the liver is the only organ in the human body that can regenerate itself. But in your dad's case it's not working. His body rejected the transfusion. There's not much we can do at this point. I'll leave you two alone."

I was stunned. My brain dangled in space.

Off in the distance, I heard the doctor's rubber-soled shoes squeak out the door.

I slumped down on the edge of the bed and took my father's hand. It was cold and clammy.

Through squinty eyes he gasped, "Is that you, David?"

David was Dad's younger brother. The brother who got Leo the part in the Broadway play *Dead End*. The brother who, without knowing it, changed the direction of Leo's life forever.

I was shocked. "No, Dad," I whispered. "It's not David. It's me—Leo. Your son."

I waited for a hint of recognition. I looked for some foothold on reality. I wanted to grab on to something that would stop the sensation that had me. I felt like my mind was about to slip away from me.

I got nothing but numbness as Dad slumped back into his delirium. He returned to a bizarre wrestling match between him and some unseen force. Like Jacob wrestling with the Angel.

He writhed around and mumbled. Over and over again he said, "Those dirty rats, those dirty rats...."

Who? I wondered. *Who are the 'dirty rats'?*

He had only a few ounces of life left. I wanted him to see me. To recognize me. To talk with me. To say good-bye—or something—anything. Instead, he spilled his strength in a struggle with phantoms that only he could see.

I couldn't watch. I looked away.

NO TIME FOR GRIEF

I stayed at Merritt Hospital for two days.

Snickers Bars, doughnuts, and coffee were my rations. The lounge chair outside my father's room was my bunk. It was on the balcony. The sun gave me comfort and kept me warm.

A touch woke me on the last day. I shook myself and tried to think. *Where am I? I* wondered. *How long have I been asleep? Who's there? Who woke me?*

A nurse in a white dress stood above me. The sun was at her back. I squinted hard till I found her face. Her expression spoke first. I knew what she had to say.

"He's gone," she whispered.

My body felt like it had turned to lead. I hoisted my weight and stood to my feet. The nurse had headed back to his bedside. I followed.

Thank God, it's over, I thought. Then I felt confused. *Now what do I do? Do I stay? Do I leave? Do I have to sign something? What?*

The staff around me launched into action. Two orderlies appeared. Starchy white smocks and straight faces. They positioned a gurney alongside my father's bed. They worked with a snappy, professional cadence. Then one called out, "One, two, three." In perfect rhythm Dad's body was lifted and moved. Then he was gone. All evidence of death had disappeared.

I stood alone and still—a statue frozen in place. A nurse padded in and tidied up the room for the next occupant. She looked at me, but said nothing. The *Do Not Disturb* sign around my neck was hard to miss.

I was numb—struck dumb. I was seized by the thought, *My father was in this hospital room less than an hour ago. He was living and breathing. He was alive, but now he's not.* My head swam—but just the dog-paddle.

The next time I saw my father, he was in a casket. He looked like a department store window display—only horizontal. *He doesn't look like my dad,* I thought. *He looks like something in the Holly-*

wood Wax Museum.

I felt rushed in the viewing line—like my price-check was holding up the checkout line at a supermarket. All the fidgety customers in the express lane behind me were pressuring me and pissing me off. *Hey!* I fumed to myself. *It's my dad in that casket.*

I was desperate to slow things down. *Wait a minute. Is he really gone?* I wondered. *Is that really him in that box? Are they really gonna lower him into a hole? Shovel dirt on top of him? No. Something's wrong with this picture. Something's not right.*

My head felt like it had Jell-O for brains. I had no control over my thoughts. My gelatin brain wobbled around inside my head. Nonsense jiggled every solid question.

What's gonna happen to me now? Is this how **my** *life will end? Is this all there is? Dad, I miss you. I miss what we'll never have. The relationship that should have been. Why now? Why did you have to go now?*

Grief filled my heart and spilled out of my eyes. At last, I felt something. The stone cold emptiness was gone. In its place the sting of loss—the pain of what I could never have.

I started to cut loose and have a good cry. Then one of Dad's friends grabbed me. She jerked me away from the casket and said, "Not now."

I was angry. I felt violated.

If not now, I wondered, *then when?*

SIX FEET UNDER

Monsignor James Casey droned on through the grave-side liturgy. A slight brogue provided the only modulation.

I slouched down in the folding chair. My place was with "the family." We assembled under the shade of a green canvas cabana. That same cover had sheltered hundreds of families. It kept them from the elements while they buried loved ones and said farewell.

I was hot and sticky. There was no ventilation in my U.S. Army dress greens. Perspiration poured from my armpits.

I stared at the casket in disbelief. I didn't hear a word of Monsignor Casey's memorial service. None of it made sense. His black suit and white collar took me back in time. I remembered the visits of the local parish priest. I could see him there in our living room pouring down the cheap whiskey with my father, the Town Celebrity.

At my left was my sister Jan. She followed in my father's footsteps. Unlike Dad she found recovery in her forties. She discovered a 12-step program. But it was too late. Years of alcohol and abuse had stolen her strength and broken her body. She died at forty-nine.

At the end of the row was my silver-haired Grandma Josephine. My father's bootlegging, alcoholic, Irish-Catholic mama. One in a long line of hand-me-down, dysfunctional ancestors. She was dressed in black from head to toe. A pillbox hat and veil concealed her face. Hidden were troubled years etched in hardship and sorrow.

Leo had convinced his mama to move out to California from New York. He was an established star in Hollywood. He promised to support her. And he did—until he died. It was just as he promised himself when he was fifteen-years-old. Grandma outlived her son by seven lonely years.

Next to Grandma Josephine was my father's fifth wife Mary. Dad dialed Mary up out of a *Lonely Hearts Club* magazine. He flew her out from Boston to the ranch in Northern California.

Mary seduced the Dead End Kid into marriage. Nine months before he died she took his name. After he died, she took everything he had.

In the back row stood my father's fourth wife, Brandy. She was dressed in her crisp white nurse's uniform. A starched white hat was perched atop her short, red, curly hair. She left her shift at St. Elizabeth's Hospital to join us at the grave.

Brandy was my stepmother. She was the only sane adult in my childhood.

We all joined in one purpose for one man—to grieve and honor. An assembly of strangers in the rural cemetery fifteen miles from town. Solitary souls cloistered by sorrow. There's nothing more personal than grief. No two of us do it the same way. That's why it's so hard to know what to say—to someone who grieves. I guess the best thing is to say nothing.

As for me, I questioned the whole experience. *Who is the man in that box?* I wondered.

I answered myself, *That's your father.*

If that's true, I puzzled, *then why do I feel out of place? Why do I feel like I don't belong? Why does that man, that corpse, seem like a stranger to me? Who was he? Who was I to him?*

I had lost something. I could feel the emptiness. *But what did I lose that had not already been lost?*

Monsignor Casey droned on. But a parade of private thoughts marched through my brain. I was oblivious to the priest's prattle and patter.

Why am I here? I insisted. *I can't deal with all these people. The casket will fall and they will flock—around me. They'll say how sorry they are. But I'm not sorry—not at all. I just want to get back on the plane and return to Fort Lewis.*

Monsignor Casey stopped.

Now what?

Two cemetery workers approached. They lowered the box into the ground. The mechanics of the descent caught my attention. The system with its straps and pulleys broke my stream of thoughts. For a moment the heaviness lifted. Then the deal was done. Dad with death had reached his depth, and there he would stay.

Now to get out of here!

(Red Bluff Daily News photo by Larry Lowell)
Scanned from newspaper, June 7, 1969

THE ABYSS

The bizarre graveyard day was done. Dad was gone. It was time to put my father out of my mind. It was my turn to take center stage. Like Scarlett in *Gone With The Wind*, I'd "think about that tomorrow."

My tomorrow turned out to be mid-life crisis. Anyone who says that mid-life meltdown is a myth is in denial. And duh Nile ain't just a river in Egypt.

At age forty-two, I found myself in a meeting with a bunch of addicts. I talked about my feelings. Before that afternoon, I didn't know I had any.

"Hi, my name is Leo. I'm addicted to everything—to anything that makes me feel better. One is too many—ten is not enough. When I'm not acting out, life sucks. Thanks for listening."

How did I end up in this church basement with all these losers? I asked myself. *There must be some mistake.*

Up until the craziness, I had been living the American Dream. I had a wife, two daughters, and two new cars in the driveway. I had the perfect job, plenty of green in the bank, and a brand new house in the suburbs. I paid cash for it. Walked right into the escrow office and plunked down a cashier's check for $160,000. No mortgage. No pressure. Man, did I have it made.

Then I crashed and burned. I was neck-deep in solitude in my spanking new Jacuzzi. I bobbed around on jets of warm bubbly water and gazed up at the Southern California night sky. I cast a lazy eye on rose bushes in bloom. The spa's new deck smelled of pinesap. Like the Cabernet I sipped, it was an intoxicating pleasure.

Everywhere I looked, it was Paradise. The lights in the family room glowed soft amber. The glow reached through the slider and touched my spacious, sod-covered back yard.

The house was at peace. My two daughters were asleep. My wife puttered on some craft project. I frolicked like an otter at

Sea World. The bath-temperature water bubbled, and I breathed out a sigh, *This is the life.*

Then, without a murmur or warning, a cavernous abyss yawned open in the pit of my stomach. A void like a monster black hole opened in my soul. The pleasure ended in a heartbeat. My brain tingled and ached. A sense of imminent dread seized me. I felt like my elevator ride to the penthouse was over. In fact, the cable had snapped, and I was on free-fall to the basement. My stomach was in my throat.

What is happening to me? I wondered.

Then another part of me spoke. *Is this it? Is this all there is?* Then an answer loomed in my mind, *If this is it, I'd rather be dead!*

I tried to ignore the dread and dark thoughts. I swirled and splashed. I searched the yard for distraction or beauty. But no. The black and cavernous hole wouldn't close.

It didn't close the next day. Nor the day after that. The abyss consumed many days that followed. All the usual distractions failed to fill the void and close the gap.

I can't go on like this, I told myself. *Ask for help.*

I called a longtime friend—a Ph.D. in psychology. I rattled off a litany of my symptoms and asked, "So what the hell is wrong with me?"

"I have a friend you should talk to," Jerry answered. "Got something to write with? I'll give you his number."

I took down the number and repeated it back to be sure.

"Leo."

Jerry spoke my name like a parent. "Yeah?" I answered. He had my attention.

"Don't put this off."

Put it off? I wondered. *Put what off?* But I said, "Yeah. Sure, Jerry. Thanks." Click.

I had wandered down every path of enlightenment from Baba Ram Dass and *Be Here Now,* to Dr. Janov and the Primal Scream. *What was this guy gonna tell me that I didn't already know?*

THE LIFE RAFT

At my first counseling appointment, Jeff, the therapist, asked me about my father.

"He was an alcoholic," I answered. I rattled it off like page six newspaper copy.

My eyes wandered around his office. His walls held framed diplomas, certificates, and pictures. His family photos were prominent. *I wonder what it would have been like to have a normal family?* I pondered.

Jeff's voice jerked me out of my daydream.

"What brought you here today, Leo?"

"Um, oh— A friend referred me. Um, Doctor Reddix. He's a buddy of mine. He said I should call you."

"So, why are you here?" Jeff asked.

Oh, what the hell! I thought. *I'll just blab it all out to this guy. I'm never gonna see him again anyway.*

I rambled on about the hurt I felt inside. I complained and moaned. "I've got no clue how to stop the pain. I've lost the desire to live. Right now, death seems better than my tilted view of life.

"I'm overshadowed by a cloud," I continued. "It haunts and taunts me. It says, 'Everything you busted your ass for doesn't make you happy. Yeah, there were moments of satisfaction. But they're over and gone.'"

It felt good to talk about it. So I blabbed on.

"I feel like I'm drowning," I told him. "I have nightmares that I'm surrounded by water."

"Water?"

"Yeah. I'm driving along in my Jeep Cherokee, and all of a sudden the road ends. There's water everywhere. It closes in on me. I wake up in a panic. My heart pounds like an African drum."

"What do you do then?"

"Uh, well, usually I'll start to wake up my wife. But then I don't. I'm afraid she'll think I'm crazy."

"Crazy?"

"Yeah. What am I gonna tell her? That I'm scared?"

When the word "scared" came out, I burst into tears. I was embarrassed. I wanted to stop, but it felt so good to get it out. I knew the guy really listened to me. Yeah, I had to pay him ninety smackers an hour to listen. Still, it was good to be heard.

"When's the last time you cried, Leo?"

"I can't remember," I sniffled.

Jeff handed me one of four boxes of Kleenex that flanked both ends of the couch. I thought, *I'll bet this happens often in here.*

I blew hard in a handful of tissues. I mopped up mucus and moisture. I wanted to turn off the emotion, but I couldn't find the valve.

Jeff knew his stuff. He cut to the chase. "Do you want to get better?" he asked.

"Is that possible?"

"I have a question for you," he said.

"Shoot."

"Would you be willing to let me be your life raft for awhile?"

"Life raft?"

"Yeah. Till you can get to the shore on your own."

"Um, yeah, okay." I agreed, but I had no idea what he meant.

Jeff glanced at his watch and announced, "Well, we're out of time for today."

Jeff and I paddled together for over a year. Well, *I'm* the one who paddled. He navigated. He also empathized and encouraged. He was damn good at it.

I knew it was me workin' the oars. Still, it felt good to have Jeff acknowledge my progress. He'd often smile with a supportive look and say, "You did good work today, Leo." He never once said, "*We* did good work today." The guy never broke a sweat.

After four sessions with Jeff, I had two life-changing revelations. I had a suspicion that my future happiness was buried in my past. It was in my father's casket. I knew that I needed to dig up my relationship with dad. I needed to deal with the painful parts. I couldn't run from them. They might be the key to my freedom.

I also came to believe that I was gonna be okay. *No matter what the future has in store,* I thought, *I have a feeling that life is gonna get better. It did—for a while.*

From a visit to my dad's grave in 2002—Los Molinos, California.
It was always weird seeing *my* name on my father's headstone.

TIME FLIES

Ten years after Jeff fished me out of The Sea of Despair, I picked up the trail that started at my father's graveside.

It helped a lot that Leo Gorcey was a well-known celebrity. I discovered endless newspaper and magazine articles about Dad's life and show biz career. The name Leo Gorcey popped up in the biographies of such Hollywood moguls as Samuel Goldwyn and Jack Warner. And he appeared in the memoirs of stars like James Cagney and Groucho Marx.

I also had Dad's old scrapbook. I hadn't opened it in over thirty years. More than once, I faced and fought the temptation to toss it in the trash. It was dust covered and decades old. The tattered and torn black album haunted me with a painful and private history. It was my own childhood reminder of life with the Dead End Kid.

I still have it. And it survived—along with me.

I had Leo Gorcey's self-published autobiography. One hundred and eleven pages of rambling anecdotes. Dad dictated the book to a secretary before he died. He was drunk when he wrote it. Still, a lot of the stories checked out.

David Hayes and Brent Walker published a book called *The Films of The Bowery Boys*. It's a pictorial history of *The Dead End Kids, The Eastside Kids,* and *The Bowery Boys.* The copy highlights the films and updates the vitals on all the key players.

I ran "Leo Gorcey" through Yahoo's search engine. Websites popped up everywhere. The Internet was full of Leo's fans. I started a dialogue with dozens via email.

My journey also took me to Brandy, Leo's fourth wife. I drove up to central California and interviewed her. She filled in a lot of blank spots for me. She spoke of my childhood and her memories of the man she loved. Story after story about my father poured from her heart and mind and mouth.

To all these things, I added my own memories.

Dad's stories—the bits and pieces of his fifty two years—seemed endless. Still, the random tile chips of Dad's life began to form a mosaic. I saw a fascinating portrait of my father—the original Dead End Kid.

To make the puzzle fit, I started with pieces from his childhood. I searched out Dad's relationship with his parents. I traveled back to June 3rd, 1917. I went back to Bernard and Josephine Gorcey. I revisited the apartment in Manhattan—their kitchen, to be exact.

Bernard, Leo's father, was from a family of Russian-Jewish immigrants. He made his living as a Vaudeville comedian. Josephine, Leo's mother, was Irish-Catholic. She immigrated from Wales at the tender age of 14. She worked in the theater as a chorus girl.

Josephine was sixteen when her doctor found her lying on the kitchen floor. It was her second pregnancy.

Bernard Gorcey, my grandfather, in *Abie's Irish Rose* on Broadway—1922.

A STAR IS BORN

Josephine's water broke at 2 a.m. There was no time for the hospital. The family physician made an emergency house call. He found her passed out on the kitchen floor. Leo's father, Bernard, hovered over her and tried to rouse her.

The doctor grabbed her legs. "Quick, help me lift her up on the table. On three!" They heaved and lifted her in place. Then the doctor barked, "Now, quick, boil some water."

The doc plopped some forceps and a scalpel into the pot. Josephine screamed. And thirty minutes later, Leo Bernard Gorcey made his grand entry. Grandma Jo was only four feet, eleven inches tall. Leo tipped the scales at over twelve pounds!

The doctor held Baby Leo and Bernard cut the umbilical cord.

My father grew up in a show biz family. And that family was smack in the middle of the melting pot known as New York City.

It was a tough time, and money was tight. So tight, Leo's mother turned to bootlegging to supplement the family income.

Josephine worried at first that a speakeasy in her apartment might put her and her boys at risk. She didn't want a trip to the Big House and a separation from her husband and children for years.

But she was told, "There are more than thirty thousand speakeasies in this city. The chances of a bust are about the same as getting hit by lightning. Just have your pickups ready on time, and you're as safe as Fort Knox. Safe even from the cops."

The green started rolling in. Lots of it. Josephine had more money and friends than she had common sense. Her comedian husband was on the road. So she welcomed the cash and company.

Grandma had second thoughts about her kitchen, speakeasy operation. She cringed at the occasional bloodbath splattered all over the headlines. And she told her "boss" about her fears.

"Fuggeduhboudit." He waved his hand and flashed his diamond pinky ring for emphasis. "Anybody messes wit you, messes wit me. Anybody messes wit me, messes wit my Capo. And so on— You get what I'm sayin'?"

She got it. Go home and sell more booze. Wasn't prohibition great?

Bootlegging gave Leo's mama ready access to an endless supply of booze. What better way to numb the pain of a hard life? She started to drink when friends came over to place their orders. Then she drank every day—to be social, of course. Just one or two drinks to loosen up and enjoy herself. Then she drank alone.

One day Josephine crossed paths with a "made" guy. Bernard was on the road. She bragged to all her girl friends at the theater about Joey Dominic. "When I'm with Joey, people roll out the red carpet. You should see how they wait on this guy hand and foot! And the way he treats me— It's like I'm the Queen of England!"

"What about Bernard?" asked another chorus girl.

"Listen dearie, I ain't spreadin' my legs fer this dope. It just gets a little lonely with Bernard on the road so much. Me and Joey dinner and drinks. That's it—a few laughs."

"Sure, Jo. That's all there is. What do we know? We were just born yesterday."

"You wouldn't understand," Josephine fired back. "Your Freddie's not in show business."

The next night, Josephine and Joey walked arm-in-arm out of Joey's favorite eatery. The crack of gunfire spooked the crowd. The people on the street scattered. Folks tore at and trampled on each other to find cover.

"Get the hell back in the restaurant. Now!" Joey screamed and shoved Josephine hard. She fell back into a hedge. There was chaos and cries everywhere. Jo struggled to her feet and became a target. A stray bullet found her chest. Blood oozed from the tiny chorus girl.

"Where am I? Somebody...where am I?"

A nurse appeared and took Josephine's hand. "You're a very lucky woman."

"Somebody get Joey. Somebody get the car. Bernard? Where

are my boys?"

"Mrs. Gorcey, you've been hurt...badly...."

"How? What are you talking about? He was just with me...we just...."

"Mrs. Gorcey, you've just had major surgery. Please don't try to get up or we'll have to give you a sedative."

A wake up call, by any other name, is still a wake up call. Josephine didn't hear it. In spite of her gunshot wound, and Joey's bloody demise, Josephine continued to bootleg. But she tightened her social circle to exclude gangsters.

I can live a long time without any more of that shit, she thought.

In 1922 Bernard Gorcey got his big break. He was cast in a starring role in the Broadway hit *Abie's Irish Rose*.

For over three years, the elfin Bernard with the twinkling eyes and the infectious smile, charmed Broadway audiences as Papa Isaac Cohen. He played a dyed-in-the-wool Jewish patriarch who tried to put the *kibosh* on a marriage between a...well...er...a Russian Jew and an Irish Catholic.

Bernard, Josephine, and the three Gorcey boys (Freddie, Leo, and David) lived an enchanted life until Bernard got itchy feet. He gave his notice three years into a five-and-a-half year run. He would return in the fifth year of *Abie's Irish Rose*, to reprise his role and close the show.

Bernard's exit from Broadway and return to the carefree highway was the beginning of the end. But that wasn't the worst of it.

In 1929 came the Great Depression.

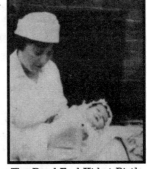

The Dead End Kid at Birth

THE OPERA SINGER

Dad was twelve when his parents divorced. Like most divorces, it was a painful, ugly mess.

One night, when Bernard was on an extended road trip, Josephine brought a man back to the apartment. The boys had never seen any man but Papa in the house with Mama.

"Mama," Leo asked the next day, "who's dat guy yuh brought home tuh de apartment?"

"Oh, he's just a friend...an Opera Singer."

"Wuhdd'ya tink Papa would say about dat?"

"Never mind, Leo. Papa doesn't need to know anything about it. Your mama needs a man around once in awhile fer some laughs. Don't stick yer puss where it doesn't belong. Understand?"

"Yeah, Mama. I unduhstand. Jist bettuh not let Papa catch yuh is all I gotta say."

"That's enough outta you, young man. Do I need to get out the Shillelagh Stick?"

"I didn't mean nuttin' by it Mama. Don' worry, I ain't no snitch."

The opera singer called on Josephine almost every night while Papa was on the road. He brought opera records over to the apartment and they broke out booze from Jo's bootleg stash and sang along with the Victrola. Sometimes, he brought flowers.

When her conscience got too noisy, Jo argued with it. *Why not get a little comfort for myself for all I have to go through?* She thought. *What Bernard doesn't know won't hurt him, and he'll never know. The boys won't make a peep or I'll kill 'em. And why should he care? He's gettin' his comfort. He'd never tell me if he wasn't.*

When Bernard did show up, after a long stretch on the road, he bypassed the customary hugs and kisses for Josephine and the boys. Papa stomped into the kitchen, reached into his overcoat, and took out a crumpled, cancelled check. Papa slammed the check down on the kitchen table in front of his wife and sons and pulled himself up to the full stature of his four feet, ten inches.

"Whose signature is dat?" he growled.

His angry glare was met with squinty eyes and screwed up noses. *Why is Papa asking us whose signature is on the check,* they wondered. It was his signature, of course.

To keep himself from spontaneous human combustion, the red-faced comedian shouted, "Dat's not my signature! Dat's a forgery! Who duh hell forged my signature on dis check?"

The family's curiosity turned to fear as Bernard pounded his chubby fist on the table.

"I asked a question, goddammit! I deserve an answer!" He howled. "Are all of you just gonna stand there wit dose asinine looks on your faces? Am I speaking English? Have you all been struck deaf, dumb, and mute?"

Josephine stared at the check. She thought she recognized a section of scrawl in the forged signature. *Where have I seen handwriting like that?* She wondered.

Bernard whirled around and blew out of the apartment. He slammed the door hard. Two framed pictures popped off the wall and crashed to the hardwood floor.

Josephine broke the silence. "Freddy, Leo, get a broom and a dust pan and pick up that glass before somebody cuts themselves all to hell! Go!"

After the boys were tucked in, Josephine went to the closet. She tunneled beneath a pile of clothes to a stack of shoeboxes. She opened and closed three boxes. "Shit! Which one is it?" she asked herself. "It was the pink one, I think. Oh, it's this one!"

She ripped the lid off the fourth shoebox and pulled out a stack of letters. She didn't have to read very far. The clumsy script on the tacky stationery matched the scrawl on her husband's forged check.

The sappy love letters were from the Opera Singer.

The letters suddenly were repulsive. She wanted to burn them and flush the ashes down the toilet. But someone in the apartment building would smell the smoke and call the fire department.

She knew she couldn't hide the truth from Papa.

Leo's mother shuffled back to the living room and collapsed on the sofa. She shuddered, wept a flood of bitter tears, and finally went limp. She waited in the dark to break her husband's heart.

Bernard staggered in. It was just after one o'clock in the morning.

Jo was startled awake by his noisy entry. She sniffled out her confession in broken sentences and gut-wrenching sobs.

Papa yelled, then cried, then yelled, "I'll kill the cocksucker! I'll blow his fucking brains out! I'll break his arms and chop his fingers off! He'll never sign his name to anuddah piece uh paper again, as long as he lives!"

The shouting woke up the Gorcey boys, but they knew better than to make a peep or show their faces. Besides, they were scared. Papa had never been this angry. All three Gorcey boys pulled the covers over their heads and waited.

After twenty minutes of silence, the boys heard the sound of footsteps. There was creaking over the hardwood floor and sounds in the hall closet. *Is it Mama or Papa?* They wondered.

Papa balanced himself on a chair and wrestled his valise down from the closet shelf. The boys heard Papa growl, "He's a soap salesman! He's no goddamm famous 'opera singer'."

Jo was startled. *How does he know that?* She wondered.

"Did you really think I didn't know? I had a friend at duh precinct check up on duh gigolo sonofabitch. He sells soap!"

With that, Bernard quietly packed his suitcase and left his family.

Josephine would have told the Opera Singer to go to hell, but she was pregnant with her first daughter, Audrey.

Charlie Chaplin and Bernard Gorcey with Paulette Goddard
in *The Great Dictator* (1940)

LIFE WITHOUT PAPA

Leo couldn't quiet his angry thoughts. *It's not fair! Who's gonna take care of us? Why did he have tuh leave us? Why did Mama let that Opera Singer wreck our lives? Why didn't I say sump'm tuh Papa?*

Between ages twelve and fifteen, Leo was booted out of more than half a dozen schools for roughhousing. School became Leo's Rocky Balboa boot camp.

One kid's mother accused Leo of killing her son. The boy died of appendicitis a few days after being pummeled by Leo at the school yard.

Leo's guilt was never proven, but the guilt stayed with him. The accusations and snubbing were enough.

When fights and bravado didn't numb the pain (or made it worse), Leo turned to the bottle. At the age of fifteen he took his first drink and had his first affair.

Alcohol and sex became Leo's self-prescribed medication to treat the gaping wound of a lost childhood.

Leo had deep feelings of conflict toward Mama and Papa. The resentment and rage exploded to the surface in frequent outbursts.

Still, he remained fiercely loyal to his parents.

Somehow, he thought, *I'm gonna make it. Den, I'll take care uh Mama and Papa.*

Was Dad looking to assuage his guilt over a divorce he believed was his fault? Who knows? Leo would make good on his promise.

Mama had lived through worse, and she was determined to do her best to keep the boys' spirits up and make ends meet.

Tough-Guy

THE PLUMBER'S APPRENTICE

When Leo turned fifteen, he quit school to go to work for his Uncle Rob.

Who needs school? Leo groused to himself. *Not me! School ain't puttin' groceries on duh table. Besides, I know all dat stuff anyway*

Rob offered his nephew six bucks a week to work in his plumbing shop. Six days a week, twelve hours a day. Leo took it.

Jeez, thought Leo, *dere are guys on my street dat used to be big shots on Wall Street dat are sellin' apples on duh corner to make ends meet. I'm lucky to be woikin' at all.*

When Leo got his weekly paycheck, he took it home and gave it to his mama. It made him feel good to be the man of the house.

Uncle Rob, Bernard's brother, stepped into the shoes of Leo's absent father. Lots of fun and clowning around. And lots of fireworks when Rob got ticked off. It was home, sweet home—chaotic and unpredictable!

If I woik hard enough for Uncle Rob, Leo reasoned, *maybe I could even be duh boss uh my own plumbin' shop someday. Den I'll have my goil, a family uh my own, and duh respect uh duh neighbuhood, jist like Uncle Rob. And den I can take care uh Mama and Papa.*

Leo got back at his Uncle's penny-pinching by quitting every time he found another job that paid one or two dollars a week more than Uncle Rob. The wayward teenager always ended up begging Uncle Rob for his old job back. And Uncle Rob always took him back—at the same six bucks a week.

Uncle Rob kept Leo on his toes by firing him whenever he thought Leo was getting too comfortable.

After three years, something had to give.

THE LEAKY BATHTUB THAT LED TO HOLLYWOOD

Leo grabbed the sack lunch Mama packed for him the night before and walked over to Uncle Rob's plumbing shop.

He arrived a few minutes early and found the door locked. He peeked through the window. No Uncle Rob.

Shit! Leo griped to himself, *if I only had a key.* After three years, Uncle Rob still didn't trust Leo with his own key to the place.

Each blast of wind through the holes in his sweater caused Leo to shudder like a jackhammer. He stomped his feet hard on the ice-cold New York sidewalk to keep warm as he waited for Uncle Rob.

"Jeez, it's been three stinkin' years," Leo said out loud to himself, "an' I still ain't gettin my own jobs, an I'm still makin' six bucks a week, duh same as when I started, an' I still ain't got no goddamm key!

"An' all dose times I told Uncle Rob I was quittin', an' he said he would gimme a raise, an' I ain't seen a penny of it!"

Leo kicked a can off the curb and continued his soliloquy. "Six months ago he said he was gonna train me to be his partner, and maybe even lemme take ovuh duh business some day, an' here I am, still haulin' pipes up and down duh stinkin' elevator—when it's woikin'. Udduhwise, I'm hoofin' it up an' down duh stairs."

Leo shook his head and stomped his feet. "I gotta find anudduh racket. Dis one's gonna kill me before I'm twenty-five!"

A customer rushed around the corner and up to the door of the plumbing shop. Leo's face turned beet-red. He was thinking, *If dat guy hoid me talkin' tuh myself, he's gonna tink I'm nuts!*

He pulled his shirt collar up around his face. The customer was oblivious to Leo's monologue. He grabbed the doorknob and jiggled the door back and forth.

Leo couldn't resist. "What's uh madduh, can't yuh read?"

The man ignored Leo's wisecrack and peeked through the glass.

"C-L-O-S-E-D. Dat spells closed," Leo continued. "Don' worry, my uncle owns duh place. He oughtta be here any minute."

Just then, Uncle Rob came around the corner in his heavy overcoat, hat and leather gloves.

When they were all inside, the customer asked how much Rob would charge to move his bathtub from the kitchen to the bedroom of his two room apartment.

In the back of Uncle Rob's plumbing shop, Leo was digging out the stuff he would need to assist his uncle on the first job of the day. Hoisting a heavy bag of tools, Leo was trying to figure out how to balance the bag of tools over one shoulder, and carry a toilet bowl on the other shoulder at the same time.

The customer howled at Rob. "Are you nuts? For that kind of money I could have my bathtub moved to Africa! I'd rather take a bath in front of my friends than lay out twenty bucks!" With that, the customer stormed out and slammed the door so hard the doorknob fell off.

Uncle Rob shook his head as he answered the phone. He took an order to fix another radiator leak. He cupped his hand over the mouthpiece and barked, "Leo, make yourself useful and go fix that fucking doorknob!"

Leo fiddled with the doorknob and stared out the window. The stranger was making a beeline for the diner across the street.

"Uh...you wouldn't mind if I run across duh street an' grab a soda before I fix dis, would ya' Uncle Rob?"

"Fine. Go ahead...and don't take all day. Whatever we don't get done today is coming out of your wages! It would be nice to get a decent day's work out of you for a change."

A decent day's woik outta me, thought Leo, *I'm de only one dat does woik aroun' here. He jist shows up fer de easy stuff!*

Leo grabbed a dime out of the register, walked across the street to the diner, and bought a soda. He spotted the stranger alone in a booth with a cup of coffee and a newspaper.

"Excuse me mistuh, remembuh me? I woik at duh plumbin'

shop across duh street."

"Yeah, I remember...you're the one with the big mouth."

"Hey, I didn't mean nuttin' by it...I was jist pullin' yer leg."

"Really? Well, if you don't make yourself scarce, kid, I'm gonna pull your leg. Know what I mean? Now, beat it!"

"I don't want no trouble, honest, I just hoid yuh askin' my uncle about relocatin' yer tub."

The stranger kept his eyes on his paper.

"I thought I made myself perfectly clear to your uncle, young man. I'm not paying twenty bucks to move my fuckin bathtub! Now go back where you came from and tell your Jewish uncle to kiss my ass!"

Leo looked out the window and across the street. Rob was still on the phone.

"Look, I'll make yuh a deal, arright? I'll move duh tub for yuh fer five bucks if yuh can wait till Sunday. Five bucks! We gotta deal?"

The man lowered the paper enough to see over the top. He glared down his nose at the ambitious urchin with the holes in his sweater. "Cuttin' out the middle man, eh, kid? Take a hike."

Leo was antsy to get back before Rob started looking for him. "Look, I ain't got all day, arright? Is it a deal or ain't it?"

The man looked across the street at the plumbing shop, then went back to his paper. "You think I just fell off the turnip truck, or what? Go home and play with your crayons before I tell your Ma you're talkin' to strangers."

"Listen, Al Capone, you need a job done and I work fer a plumber. You ain't gonna find a pigeon anywhere in dis neighbuhood who's gonna move dat tub fer yuh for less dan five bucks! Dis is my last offer. I'll do duh woik for yuh, and if yuh ain't happy wit it, yuh don't have tuh pay me nuttin'! Fair enuf?"

The stranger put down his paper. "Kid, do you ever quit?"

"I'm jist offerin' tuh help yuh out, dat's all."

"If I give you the job, will you leave me alone?"

"If yuh gimme duh job, you'll never see dis mug again as long as yuh live!"

"All right, kid. Five bucks and not a penny more. Tomorrow morning, and don't be late. I've got a lunch date with a real fine dame. Now scram before I rat on yuh to your Uncle Scrooge."

"Tanks, mistuh. I'll do a real good job for yuh, I will!"

That night after work, Leo gathered everything he needed to 'borrow' from his uncle to move the tub. He stuck a pipe wrench and two lengths of lead pipe down his pants and under his sweater.

"I tink I'll call it a night, Uncle Rob. See ya Monday mornin'."

Leo slithered past his uncle.

Rob didn't look up from his bookwork. "Sure. See you on Monday, Leo."

Bright and early the following morning, Josephine went to wake up her sons for church. There were three beds, two boys, and a note on the kitchen table. *Dear Ma, had to do an emergency plumbing job for Uncle Rob. I'll meet you at church in an hour. Leo.*

At last, Leo would prove to uncle Rob that he could do his own jobs. And he would make five dollars, all to himself—almost a week's pay for one hour of work! He could take his neighborhood sweetheart on a real date.

I'm a stinkin' genius, Leo bragged to himself as he lugged his wrench and pipes up three flights of stairs to the tub owner's apartment. The elevator was out of order.

Leo dropped off his load and made the customary, door-to-door announcement to the tenants. "Duh wadduh's gonna be off fer about ten minutes. Sorry fer de inconvenience."

Two hours later, Leo's work came to a grinding halt. He was baffled over how to improvise a makeshift drain from the tub in the bedroom to the sink pipe in the kitchen.

The tub owner slapped on some cologne, turned to Leo, and said, "Hey, kid, I'm goin' out. I gotta hot date. I'll meet you at the diner first thing tomorrow morning and pay you the five bucks. Make sure you clean up your mess! I want that floor spotless when I get back or you won't see a nickel, you understand?"

"Yeah, sure," said Leo. His tone of voice said that he couldn't have cared less.

If I don't figguh out how to get dis drain woikin', Leo worried, *I ain't gonna have tuh worry about cleanin' dis guy's floor...I ain't gonna have to worry about nuttin'...I'll be takin' a long nap in duh morgue!*

He tried to force a joint together for the fourth time. It didn't fit any better than the first time.

Wait a minute, he thought. *I remember at duh job we did at duh school buildin' last week. We didn't have duh right piece fer duh joint, an' Uncle Rob fixed it wit uh sodderin' iron! Dat's what I need.*

Leo looked at the kitchen clock and thought, *Wait...it's Sunday...even if I could figguh a way to break into duh shop and get duh sodderin' iron, I ain't nevuh soddered nuttin' on my own....*

His internal dialogue was shattered by pounding on the apartment door like the sound of a police raid. Seven tenants who couldn't flush their toilets or take showers had formed a fist-waving posse. They were ready to break Leo's skull with his own pipe wrench and string him up from the fire escape if they didn't have running water in five minutes!

"Arright, arright," Leo answered. "Hold yuh horses! I was just about to toin it back on!"

On the way down to the basement, Leo thought, *Well, dat's de end uh dat. I ain't woikin' here no more tuhday unless I wanna end up a moider victim.*

Back in the apartment, Leo scratched out a note. *Please don't use the tub tonight! The water is hooked up, but I need more tools to finish working on the drainpipe. The tub will be ready tomorrow.* He left the note on the kitchen table.

Leo figured, *I'll ask Uncle Rob fer a sodderin' lesson in duh mornin', den I'll sneak back here on my lunch break an' finish duh job.*

He headed down the stairs and wondered how fast he could get home. *Now all I gotta do is figguh out how to keep Ma from talkin tuh Uncle Rob about dis.*

The landlord's husky voice barged into Leo's thoughts.

"Next time you do a job in this building, kid, bring somebody who knows what the hell they're doin! You got me? On second thought, don't come back at all! I'm hirin' a super tomorrow!"

"Yeah, right," Leo muttered under his breath. "I'll get yuh a super, arright! A super fist in yer kisser!"

GEORGE WASHINGTON AND THE CHERRY TREE

The next morning, Leo and Rob got ready for their first job. Rob was about to deliver the punch line of a joke, but the phone rang.

"You have the wrong plumber," Rob said. He started to hang up the phone, but the caller yelled. Rob held the phone at arms length and rolled his eyes at Leo. Then he put the hand piece back to his ear.

"No, we don't do jobs on Sundays. What duh yuh mean a flooded apartment? Two flooded apartments? Yeah...Yeah...he works for me...Yeah...all right, all right, I'll be over as soon as I can get there." Rob slammed the phone down. No more rolling eyes. His face was red and a vein in his forehead was popping up.

"Who was dat, Uncle Rob?"

"I just spoke to a landlord who swears that a boy matching your description did some work in his apartment building yesterday...says you promised to move his tenant's tub for $5."

Leo turned red and stared a hole in the floor.

"When the tenant drained his tub last night, the water leaked out on the floor, flooded his bedroom, then soaked through his floor to the apartment under his, and flooded that one too!"

Uncle Rob came out from behind the counter. "Leo, tell me you didn't go over to that apartment yesterday and try to move that tub by yourself."

Leo's face felt like a Christmas Turkey in a broiler. *Sonofabitch,* he thought. *Duh moron didn't read duh note!*

Uncle Rob stood in front of Leo—arms crossed.

Tink uh sump'm, c'mon, tink uh sump'm fast! Leo racked his brain. He flashed on the image of George Washington. He remembered how George chopped down the cherry tree. When confronted George said, "I cannot tell a lie!"

That's what I'll do, thought Leo. *I'll do what George Washington did! I'll tell Uncle Rob duh truth, and I won't get in trouble!*

"Leo, say something! What the hell is goin' on here?"

"Uncle Rob, I ain't gonna lie to yuh...."

"Well, that's a good start," snorted Rob.

Then Leo blurted out the whole story about how he followed the tub owner over to the diner on Saturday and made a deal to move his tub for five bucks. All so he could prove that he could do a job on his own and earn enough money to take his girl on a real date. He told him how he got up early Sunday morning and left the note for Mama. He said that everything went fine until he couldn't hook up the drain. He explained how he hoped that Uncle Rob would teach him how to solder today so that he could go back to the tub owner's apartment on his lunch break and finish the job.

Leo took a deep breath and braced himself. But in a split second he thought, *Uncle Rob says it takes a big man to apologize...maybe if I apologize....*

"Please don't be mad at me, uncle Rob. I'm sorry. I really am! I'll fix it, I will. And I'll clean up all duh wadduh, and make everyting just duh way it was, an' I'll nevuh do anyting like dat again. I promise! Honest, I do!"

To Leo's surprise, Uncle Rob said nothing. Instead, he walked over to a nearby shelf and picked up a hammer.

"Uncle Rob...diddya hear wuht I said? I said I'm sorry!"

Rob wheeled around and threw the hammer straight at Leo's head.

Leo turned and the hammer bounced off a load of pipes Leo had slung over his shoulder and sailed through a glass windowpane.

"You're fired!" Yelled Rob. "You're fired, goddammit! Now get the fuck outta here. That window is coming out of your pay and so are the damages to the apartment building. Do you hear me?"

Leo was frozen solid with fear. Uncle Rob was a 'yeller', but Leo had never seen him like this.

"Did you hear me? Get the hell outta here...now! Before I knock your fucking brains out with a pipe wrench, you sneaky little bastard...and don't ever show your face in here again!"

Leo clattered out the door, pipes and all, and didn't stop running until he was five blocks away.

The doorknob popped off the door, rolled across the room, and stopped at the toe of Rob's boot.

THE APPLE DOESN'T FALL FAR . . . .

Leo plopped down on a stoop to catch his breath.

His thoughts wandered five blocks away to the Belasco Theater. His thirteen year-old brother, David, was there in dress rehearsal for a play called *Dead End*.

I wonduh how liddle brudduh's rehoisals are goin'?

From there, Leo recalled the talk at the dinner table the night David got the small part as a member of a street gang in the slums.

"Mama, guess what?" David's face lit up like Coney Island. "Papa took me to an audition today an' I got duh part! Papa was so proud uh me. An' I'm gettin' thirty-five dollars a week, Ma! Thirty-five dollars a week! I can quit my job at the cleaners."

Mama didn't turn around from the stove.

"Mama, diddya hear what I said? We're gonna be rich again! We start rehearsals tomorrow morning at the Belasco Theater! Will you come an' see me Ma? Will ya?"

No one went to see David rehearse except for Papa.

Leo thought about how long it had been since he last saw Bernard. Four years, going on a lifetime.

I miss Papa, he thought.

One of the pipes rolled toward the gutter and jerked Leo's mind back to the present.

"Dis is moider," Leo mumbled out loud. He watched the pipe roll into the gutter. He didn't get up.

"I'm sittin' here wit sixty pounds uh lead pipes and no woik. An' my liddle brudduh's making toity-fi dolluhs a week for doin' nuttin'!"

He jabbed at a loose brick with his pipe wrench.

"Maybe if I go back an apoluhgize again tuh Uncle Rob...he'll let me come back tuh woik like he did last time. Aaaah, maybe not. Dat stubborn sonofabitch would cut off his nose to spite his face!"

He jabbed harder at the brick.

"On de udduh hand, actin' ain't no decent racket needuh. Woikin' today, hungry tomorruh.... Dat's fer duh boids!"

The brick came loose and tumbled down into the stairwell that led to a basement apartment.

Shit! I hope dere ain't nobody downnair...dat's all I need!

Leo peeked over the stair rail to see where the brick landed. *Whew, I was lucky on dat one!*

He sat back down on the stoop and continued to think out loud. *I'll pay fer duh stuff I messed up. Den I'll go ovuh an' apoluhgize tuh dat dumb bastid landlord. I'll tell 'im I didn't mean nuttin' by it. Uncle Rob'll cool off aftuh duh floor is all fixed....*

His determination turned to shame. *Jeez, why duh hell did I offuh to move duh tub in duh foist place? Wuht duh hell is a madduh wit me?*

He got up, retrieved the renegade pipe from the gutter and tightened the strap around the bundle.

Maybe Uncle Rob'll at least teach me how to use duh sodderin' iron, an' I can go out on my own an' start my own fuckin' plumbin' business.

What duh hell, Leo thought. *I'll go an' watch my little brudduh rehoise. Maybe dat'll cheer me up! Den I'll go back tuh duh shop in duh mornin' when Uncle Rob's cooled off.*

Though Dad would protest that he hated acting all through his Hollywood career, and into his retirement, the opposite was true. He was president of the drama club in high school.

Dad's papa was a brilliant comedian. His mama was the life of the party. Her boisterous personality and her endless tales of survival, the bootleg business, the mafia, the chorus line, and her romances could fill a dozen pulp novels.

Like his mama and papa, Dad was loaded with bigger-than-life charisma. Leo's schoolmates loved it when Leo spouted off in his brick-chiseling, street urchin accent. They loved his brand of humor that punched back at a society that looked down on all of their kind.

They weren't the decent folk. And they knew it. Leo was fighting back for all of them.

He shot off his mouth like a hair-trigger Colt 45. He fired wisecracks at teachers, cops, parents, priests, the rich, the poor, the pompous, the intelligent, the illiterate, the pretentious, and anyone else who crossed his path.

His smart-alecky ad-libbing in class drew giggles and smirks from everyone except the teachers. His classmates never knew when they would show up and find Leo's desk empty. Not because Leo was ill. But because he had been expelled.

David Gorcey—Leo's Little Brother

LEAVE THE BOY
IN THE BATHROOM

Leo hoisted the pipes up on his shoulder and headed over to
the Belasco Theater. He found his little brother David with another kid backstage. They were in the middle of a dress rehearsal.

"Leo!" David was beaming. "You're just in time to see me go
on!"

"Well, I'm glad duh show ain't cancelled yet," whispered
Leo, "cuz uncle Rob just gave me duh boot! You an' Freddie
may be de only ones bringin' home duh bacon for awhile."

Leo's load of pipes hit the boards with a clatter that drew
unwanted attention from two stagehands.

Just then, the boy sitting next to David swooned, and keeled
over—flat on his face.

"Oh, shit!" David tried to revive him.

"Leo, help me! He's been feeling sick all day. I gotta go on in
three minutes, and this is a dress rehearsal!"

Leo joined David in his efforts, but it was no use. The boy
was out cold. "Dis kid ain't goin nowhere but to dreamland.
He's down fuh duh count!"

Leo stood up.

David turned to his big brother. "Leo, this is a full dress
rehearsal! I can't do my line unless he does his! You gotta help
me! You can read this kid's line. It's easy. You could prob'ly
even do it better than him!"

Leo balked. "I ain't even seen duh script!"

The kid on the floor stirred, stood up, swayed back and forth,
then ran to the bathroom and started to puke.

David begged, "C'mon, Leo. Please!!! We gotta go on right
now! Just stay close to me. I'll nudge you when it's time to say
your line!"

"Arright, arright arready. Just make sure you don't leave me
out dere high and dry."

Pulitzer Prize winner Sidney Kingsley, the playwright, was in the audience.

Leo and David made their entrance.

Leo not only delivered the line, but upstaged David and ad-libbed a few more lines to boot!

Backstage, David was on the verge of tears.

"Shit, Leo! Why couldn'ya just do like I told yuh? You're always smartin' off. Now I'm gonna get fired after I been workin' on this for three months. Papa's gonna kill me!"

"Aaaah, don't worry about it," Leo fired back. "Dat was a stupid line. What I did was bettuh, an' if duh directuh knows anyting, he'll rekanize it! Tanks fuh duh memories. I'm gettin' outta here."

Leo was about to skidaddle through the stage entrance when Sidney Kingsley came barreling backstage.

"David, David, where the hell are you?"

Leo turned when he heard his brother's name.

Kingsley rushed past Leo and did a double take. "What's your name, kid?"

"What's it to yuh?"

David spotted Kingsley with his big brother and scurried over. "Did you call me, sir?"

"Well, it sure as hell wasn't the Ghost of Christmas Past! David, what's this kid's name and what the hell is he doing on my stage? This is a dress rehearsal, son, not an open casting call!"

David cringed. "Yes sir. I know that, sir. But the other boy's in the bathroom tossin' his cookies. I didn't think there would be any harm in havin' my big brother do the line just this one time so I could do my part in the rehearsal, sir."

David motioned behind his back for Leo to leave. Leo slipped out the stage door.

Jeez, dat's all I need, Leo grimaced. *Gettin' kicked outta two places in one day. Now what duh hell am I gonna do wit dis load uh pipes? I'd like tuh lob 'em through Uncle Rob's window....*

Meanwhile, back in the theater, David didn't come up for air. "Please Mr. Kingsley, don't fire me, sir. I swear—it'll never happen again. I promise...."

Kingsley cut in, "Young man, will you pipe down for a minute so I can say something!"

"Yes, sir. Sorry, sir."

"You forget about that boy in the bathroom, you understand? Get your ass out that door and go tell your brother I want to see him in my office tomorrow morning. Screw that other kid, you understand me?"

David was bewildered. "Yes, sir!"

"Well then, what the hell are you waiting for, son?"

Kingsley rushed back out to watch the rest of the rehearsal.

David caught up to Leo in the alley. "Leo, I think you gotta part in the play! We're gonna be in the play together!"

Leo dropped his load of pipes and waved his hand. "Whoa, whoa, not so fast liddle brudduh. I may be unemployed, but I ain't no patsy! I'll do duh part, but I want duh week's pay *up front!* Duh way I figguh, duh show's got maybe two weeks, den you an' me are back out lookin fuh woik, an' I ain't plannin' on gettin' stiffed fer duh dough!"

"Well, that's not up to me, Leo. All I know is that Mr. Kingsley wants to see you in his office first thing tomorrow. I wouldn't be late if I were you."

"Well, yer not me, so get off it, okay? I'll tink about it."

Are there other versions of my father's big break? Yeah. But this one is the one most often cited. And this is the way my dad always told it to me.

Knowing my father, it makes perfect sense. Many doors to success were opened to him because he didn't give a damn. Risk was his middle name.

In show biz, as in life, the one who can walk has the power.

SPIT

The next day, Leo swaggered into Kingsley's office. Kingsley motioned for Leo to sit down.

But Leo shook his head and said, "I'd jist as soon stay on my feet. Dat way I'm closer to gettin' outta here if tings don't woik out."

Kingsley smiled. "Are you always this cordial?"

"Are you always dis nosey?"

"By the way, I didn't get your name, son," Kingsley asked.

"It's Leo. An' by duh way, I ain't signin' nuttin' til I see duh dough, *up front*. Unduhstand? Udduhwise I'm goin' back to my uncle Rob's plumbin' shop tuh get my old job back."

"Okay, okay," Kingsley interrupted. "You're awfully cocky for a kid who hasn't even been hired yet! Now shut the door and take a seat, Leo Gorcey."

Leo's eyes got big, and he gave Kingsley a second look. Then he shut the office door and sat down.

"Now Listen, Leo, before you take over my job, I have a little proposition for you."

"Arright, shoot. I'm all ears."

Kingsley put on his glasses and pulled out a stack of twenty-six pages of dialogue.

"I like what you did yesterday," he started. "I like it a lot. You've got exactly the kind of raw emotion I need to make this show work."

Kingsley handed the sheets to Leo. "I'll pay you thirty-five dollars a week, up front, if you'll agree to understudy the part of Spit. It's the second lead in the gang. By 'understudy' what I mean is...."

Leo broke in, "I know wuht unduhstudy is. Whaddya tink, I ain't nevuh seen a stinkin' script before?"

Leo leafed through the pages.

Kingsley put his hand up. "I'm well aware the Gorceys are a show business family, Leo. Your father mentioned something about one of his son's being in the plumbing business...."

"Arright arready, what's yer point?"

"I'd be glad to get to it if you'd let me get a word in edge-wise, son!"

"Get in as many woids as yuh want. I got all day!"

"Rumor has it the kid playing the role of Spit—Charles Duncan—is leaving for a bigger part in *Red Light*, and I don't want to be left holding the bag, if you get my meaning. I think you'd be a cinch for the part."

Leo squirmed in his chair. "Mr. Kingsley, I don' wanna...."

"Don't worry, son. The kid's on his way out...thinks *Red Light's* gonna make him a star."

"Yeah, arright."

"By the way, son, can you spit?"

Leo curled his tongue, puckered his lips, and landed a perfect wad of spittle on the brim of Kingsley's fedora.

"Uh, that was good kid."

Kingsley picked up his tan fedora off the corner of his desk and rubbed the brim on his pant leg.

"You can pay to have my hat cleaned out of your next check. Now get to work on that script. And by the way, you need to work on your blocking. We open in three days."

"Not so fast, chief," Leo chirped, "Ain't yuh forgettin' sump'm?"

"Oh, of course, your up front check."

"Dat ain't wuht I was talkin' about, Einstein. Yestuhday, my brudduh said you was hirin' me fer a part wit one page uh dialogue."

Leo fanned the pages. "Now yuh want me tuh 'unduhstudy' a part wit twenty-six pages uh dialogue! Dats Twenty-six times more woik, I oughta get twenty-six times duh dough fer it!"

"Are you crazy?" hollered Kingsley. "There are hundreds of kids in New York who could play this role!"

"Yeah, well go out an' find one!" Leo chucked the twenty-six pages in the trashcan and made a beeline for the door.

"Now hold on, Leo! Be reasonable. If I pay you more money, I'll have the whole cast on my back. They'll eat me alive. I have to open this show in three days! I can't afford that!"

Leo pushed out his bottom lip in mock sympathy. "Well, den I guess you'll have to call back dat kid who was pukin in duh batroom. He might be a little easier to woik wit!"

Kingsley got out his checkbook.

"All right, Gorcey, I'll pay you fifty dollars a week and not a goddamm penny more. Take it or leave it!"

"Now yer usin yer brain fer sump'm more dan a hat rack! Yuh gotta deal!"

Leo grabbed the script out of the trash and headed for the door. He turned and rapped the sheaf of pages with his knuckles. "Oh, an' by duh way, dis needs some woik. It's a little stiff."

Kingsley frowned.

Dad didn't have time to memorize his lines by opening night, so he ad-libbed most of them.

Three months after *Dead End* opened, Spit's dialogue had no resemblance to the original Kingsley script.

It was better.

The director complained to Kingsley. "Who the hell does this kid think he is?"

"Leave it in," replied the playwright. "I like it."

Leo Gorcey as "Spit"

THE GANG

David was standing outside the door when Leo swaggered out of Mr. Kingsley's office.

"How'd it go, Leo? What was the screamin' about? Did you get fired already?"

"Well liddle brudduh, I'm a buck in duh hole fer spittin' on Writuh Boy's hat. But udduh dan dat, I just inherited anudduh twenty six pages uh dialogue an' anudduh fifteen bucks a week! But keep it unduh yer hat. Writuh Boy don't want duh whole cast climbin' on his back on accounta duh fact dat I'm gettin' more money."

"No problem, Leo. Let's go backstage to the dressing room and meet the rest uh the gang."

"You mean we all have tuh share one dressin' room? What about dat kid ovuh dere?"

Leo peeked through a crack in the door across the hall.

"All I see in dere is one kid an' his mudduh!"

"Pipe down," whispered David. "That's Billy Halop. He's a big radio star. He plays Bobby Benson, ya know, on that radio serial? He's rich! He plays Tommy in *Dead End*, the leader of the gang. Yuh don't wannuh mess with him."

"Well, if dat's wuht yuh have to do tuh get yer own dressin' room is be a star, den I guess I'm gonna have to be a star."

David led Leo into the gang's dressing room, and over to a thirteen year-old boy with his nose in a book.

"Bernard Punsly, this is my brother, Leo. He's playin' a Second Street Gang boy and understudyin' the part of Spit."

"Hey...*Bernard*...dats my fadduh's name," Leo squealed. "Whaddya readin' dere? By duh size of it, looks like duh history uh duh woild in one volume!"

"Leave him alone, Leo. He's studyin' to be a bacteriologist."

Leo wasn't listening. He'd spotted a kid across the room who looked closer to his own age. He strode over and extended his hand. "I'm Leo Gorcey...David's big brudduh. You gotta name to go wit dat nose?"

David looked the other way as if to indicate he was no relation to Leo.

"Duh name's Huntz—Huntz Hall. An' if I hear one more crack like dat, I'm gonna bust yer ribs!"

"Hey, I didn't mean nuttin' by it, really."

"Never mind," waved Huntz. "Fuggedaboutit. It's not like it's the world's best kept secret!"

Huntz turned to the side and mugged for Leo.

"When my big brudduh first saw dis schnoz, he thawt I looked German. I'm not. I'm Irish. I was born, Henry. But he thawt I looked German 'cause uh duh nose! So he nicknamed me Huntz. He said it means *dog* in German. It stuck. So wuhdd'ya doin' here? We ain't acceptin' no new cast members."

David rushed over to bail Leo out. "Leo's been hired to replace one of the Second Street Gang boys who got sick."

David nudged Leo away from Huntz.

"Leo, you're gonna get yerself a black eye if you're not careful. Some uh these palookas would just as soon knock yer block off as look at yuh. Huntz is a tough guy. Comes from a family of sixteen kids! He's been actin' since he was a baby. So watch yer mouth. Besides, Billy helped him get in here. You don't want 'em on your bad side."

Leo brushed David off. "I tink I'm poifectly capable uh defendin' myself liddle brudduh. I've put more school yard bullies in duh hospital dan you can shake a stick at! Who's duh cherub wit duh baby face ovuh dere?"

David turned to align his eyes with Leo's. "Oh, that's Bobby Jordan. He plays Angel."

Leo laughed. "Well, dey sure cast him right."

"He's only eleven," said David. "But his dad's a car mechanic. The kid's a terror if you get him riled up."

"Yeah? He looks like he's still teething to me."

"Don't let the looks fool yuh, Leo. He's one of those kid models. But I saw him beat the daylights outta one kid fer makin' fun of a book he was readin'. He's a bookworm like Bernard Punsly."

The only other boy that looked close to Leo's age walked over and extended his hand. "I'm Gabe Dell. I play T.B. Mr. Kingsley mentioned you might be comin' back. You're David's brother, Leo, right?"

"Yeah, dat's right." Leo smiled. "Pleased tuh make yer acquaintance. Is 'Gabe' short fer sump'm?"

"Yeah," said Gabe. "How'd yuh guess? Actually, it's Gabriel. Gabriel Marcel Del Vechhio!"

David cringed. At home, Leo was known to hurl racial epithets to get laughs. He prayed Leo would display a rare moment of impulse control.

"I come from a long line of Italian doctors," Gabe continued. "They wanted me to be a doctor. Yuh know, follow in the family tradition. I wanted to be an actor. So, I made my dad a bet that if I got good grades, he'd send me to acting school. So, here I am. I figure now is as good a time as any to change my name to something more theatrical!"

Leo couldn't resist. "Dats pretty funny. Yer dad's a doctuh, an' yer playin' T.B.! I hope yer old man don't get ovuh zealous an' sen' yuh to duh sanatorium!"

Huntz overheard Leo's remark and cut in. "I think you mean *sanitarium*."

As David pushed him toward the door, Leo shot back over his shoulder to Huntz, "I tink if yuh look it up in Webstuh's dictionary, you'll see it's duh same ting! An' while yer at it, try lookin' up duh woid *proboscis*. I'll give yuh a pop quiz at rehoisal innuh mornin'!"

After David and Leo left, Huntz and Gabe smirked at each other.

Gabe thumbed through his paperback dictionary. Under *sanitarium* he read out loud to Huntz. "A health resort. A sanatorium."

"Ahh, dumb luck," wisecracked Huntz, and he went back to a jitterbug step he was working on.

"Wuht does it say unduh *proboscis*?"

DEAD END

Dead End opened on Broadway on October 28th, 1935. Eight hundred and fifty-seat theater. Standing Room Only.

Thanks to Roosevelt's Federal Theater Project, record numbers of depression battered New Yorkers could afford to attend a Broadway show for little cost.

The curtain went up on the debut performance of *Dead End* and the audience broke out in spontaneous applause—for the set! For weeks before the play opened, hordes of New Yorkers knotted up on the sidewalk to gawk at the bizarre spectacle of a wrecking ball demolishing one entire wall of the Belasco Theater.

Norman Bel Geddes, super star set designer, insisted on driving a caterpillar steam shovel onto the stage as a prop. Bel Geddes installed a vast tank of water to represent the East River. (The first body of water ever used in a theatrical production). When the audience walked in, they might as well have been getting off a plane in San Antonio, Texas. The humidity was palpable.

Once seated, the spectators' breath was taken away by the facade of a three-story, crumbling, redbrick tenement slum. It was so realistic that the ushers could have sold hard hats.

The other side of the 'street' was lined with meticulous reproductions of dazzling, ornate gates leading to the luxurious, high-rise apartments of the rich upper class of New York's East 52nd Street.

Bel Geddes had transported the entire theater full of New Yorkers to a floating raft in the middle of the East River. There, they would witness an explosive collision between the "haves" and the "have-nots" taking place on the shore.

The forty-four cast members assembled at curtain call to thunderous applause. When the Kids came out, the audience clamored to their feet for a standing ovation.

Later that week, the critics were unanimous. The Kids were at the center of this firestorm called *Dead End*.

But the Kids were the least prepared for the blinding success that followed.

Leo Gorcey, Billy Halop, Bobby Jordan, Huntz Hall, Bernard Punsly, and Gabriel Dell gathered around the swimming hole in the Broadway play *Dead End*.

BACKSTAGE

The Dead End Kids clowned around in their dressing room after the show. Billy Halop and his mother, a dancer, withdrew to Billy's private dressing room across the hall.

A loud knock at the gang's dressing room door went unnoticed by the giddy boys. The knocking continued, and Huntz Hall finally heard it. He pulled the door open doing his impersonation of a doorman at the Ritz.

"Boys! Boys!" The crusty, lyrical ring of the visitor's voice was familiar.

At first, Leo turned away and tried his best to disappear in the crowded dressing room. But the rest of the kids moved in a big knot toward the door to see what was in the package the visitor had brought them. Leo was exposed in the visitor's line of sight.

When their eyes met, Leo and Bernard had to strain to focus on each other's faces through their tears. Four years had done nothing to dim their affection for one another. Leo felt a jumbled up torrent of happiness, relief, sadness, and surprise.

The rest of the boys tore open the package. It was a brand new radio set! They plugged it in and started to fumble with the tuner. Bernard crossed the room and hugged Leo.

David looked apprehensive.

Bernard's eyes were twinkling. "Son...I heard from David you were down here. So, yuh decided tuh give the stage a shot after all, huh?"

Leo's face was flushed and wet. "Tanks, Papa. I know it's cuz uh wuht yuh done dat David got duh part. How are yuh, Papa?"

"I'm good, son. I'm bettuh now dat you and yer brudduh are woikin! How's Josephine?"

Leo wiped his face with his sleeve. "We're takin' care of her Pop. We're makin' it, arright."

Bernard smiled. "Dats good, Son. Dats good. Well, I gotta

go an' rehoise for duh *Harvester* broadcast over at WABC. I brought dis radio over here so you boys could catch my act as Otto Schneider on Thursday nights before yuh go on! Loosen' yuh up a bit! Well, I'll be seein' yuh boys. Break a leg for me, would yuh?"

Leo walked his papa to the door. "I'll nevuh fuhget dis Papa. You'll see."

Just as Bernard was leaving, Sidney Kingsley and Norman Bel Geddes appeared in the doorway.

"Boys, may I have your attention," Kingsley shouted in his Cornell trained stage voice.

The room grew still, a miracle for a bunch of wired kids.

"Boys, I want to be the first to congratulate all of you on an outstanding performance."

The boys cheered so loud, the walls shook.

"One more thing...."

The kids calmed down.

"I also want to be the first to say, you should all settle down and make yourselves at home. I have a feeling that we're going to be here for awhile!"

The Dead End Kids listening to the radio backstage.

SPARE NO EXPENSE TO SAVE MONEY ON THIS ONE!

(One of Samuel Goldwyn's 'Goldwynisms')

Entertainment was big business during the Great Depression. Millions of unemployed Americans scraped their pennies together and lined up at the box office to escape their troubles. A depressed America kept Hollywood humming.

Samuel Goldwyn was a household name in Hollywood.

Goldwyn, an immigrant from Warsaw, made his mark in New York as a super star glove salesman.

Like many movers and shakers who ended up in Tinsel Town, Goldwyn had come under the spell of the Nickelodeon.

Sam's unprecedented success in the movie biz rested on the foundation of his Goldwyn Touch. He bought the book, he hired the screenwriter, he hired the stars, he hired the director, and he hired the crew. And he made all the decisions.

His secret was the property. "The property is King!" said he.

Goldwyn was a David in a town full of Goliaths. Big studios ruled the roost. Sam took them all on. When the smoke cleared, he was running his own show.

"I'm tired of having to take so much time explaining things to partners," Goldwyn blustered. "I'd rather spend that time making pictures." And so he did.

In 1935, when the play *Dead End* opened in New York, Goldwyn had just forged what would become a legendary partnership with film director William Wyler. Wyler would sign off on Sam's most memorable pictures.

The *Dead End* buzz traveled to the West Coast.

Goldwyn was rooting around for his next great property.

"Villy, I'm looking for a story that starts out with an earthquake and works it's way up to a climax!" Goldwyn blustered over breakfast with his new partner, director William Wyler.

"I couldn't agree more, Sam." Wyler dug into a Denver Omelet. "I directed a picture at Universal a couple years ago—*Counselor at Law*. Killer script—adapted from a Broadway play. One set for the whole production—dialogue to die for...."

Goldwyn interrupted. "Ah— Yes, John Barrymore...brilliant performance. God makes the stars...."

Wyler finished the mogul's sentence. "...And it's your job to find them! I know, Sam, there's not a mogul in town who hasn't quoted you on that one."

Wyler waved his fork at Goldwyn. "I say it's eighty percent script and twenty percent your great stars. There's nothing else to it! You need a great script...something raw...something with guts that grabs 'em by the throat and doesn't let go."

Wyler strangled his linen napkin with his free hand. "Without the *Word*, Sam, your stars are nothing more than cardboard cutouts."

Goldwyn reached into his briefcase and, with a dramatic flare, tossed the entertainment section of the morning paper on the white linen tablecloth.

"Hot off the press! Eleanor Roosevelt has been to see Kingsley's new play, *Dead End*, three times. The scuttlebutt is...it's going to the White House—first command performance of a Broadway show. FDR's looking into a 'slum study' commission because of it! Now that's what I call Show Business!"

Wyler picked up the paper, perused the article, and polished off a strip of bacon.

"Looks good...beautiful set. Bel Geddes has outdone himself. I like the contrast—slums next to penthouses, the dock, the water. Greg could do some great lighting on this."

The Greg was Greg Toland, Wyler's acclaimed cinematographer. But Sam was playing his cards close to the vest. He wasn't offering Wyler the director's chair—yet.

Goldwyn signaled the waiter for more coffee.

"Villy, it's a great story...luxury high-rise apartments go up in Manhattan along the East River on the same street as a slum. I've been to that neighborhood, it's right over by the

Queensborough Bridge. The "Dead End" on the wharf is the kids' home away from home. Like Hell's Kitchen on the west side."

"Great travelogue. Where's the story?"

"I'm getting to it. The upper crust neighbors look down on the kids—like gutter trash, like they shouldn't even be allowed in the street around decent people. But the kids were there way before the hoity-toity crowd. You get me?"

Wyler attacked a large cinnamon roll.

Goldwyn waved his hands in the air like paint brushes smearing wild strokes on an invisible canvas. "It's all there! Conflict between the rich and the poor, corruption, and jam packed with tears and lots of room for pretty faces!"

"Jam packed with tears?"

"Okay, there's an idealist young architect to play the romantic interest and moral conscience. I see Joel McRea. He's got a brother...a gangster named Baby Face. We'll borrow Cagney from Warners. Baby Face is coming home to see his mother and his girl, who's now a streetwalker. But in the end, it's about the kids. What's going to become of these slum kids and their desperate conflict with society? Will they get out or will they become like Baby Face? And with all the hoopla around this thing, it'll sell itself."

Wyler reached in his pocket to pay the check.

Goldwyn caught him out of the corner of his eye and pushed Wyler's hand back from the table, then motioned to the uniformed waiter. "Put that on my tab, Martin, and a buck for yourself. And remember, son, the harder you work, the luckier you get!"

"Yes, Mr. Goldwyn. I'm getting luckier every day! I'll tell your driver to bring your car around, sir."

Wyler grabbed his brief case and said, "I have one question, Sam."

"Fire away."

"Didn't you tell one of your partners once that pictures are for entertainment?"

Goldwyn interrupted, "And 'messages should be delivered

by Western Union'. My exact words. What of it?"

"So why the sudden interest in a script with such a heavy social message...and so preachy at that?"

Goldwyn slid into the back seat of the car. "Villy, America is a generation of immigrants—outsiders. I know the feeling.

"Their story is a story of conflict with society—at every turn. That's what people want to see in the movies. Their lives blown up on the silver screen and dramatized by their favorite glamorous Hollywood stars. We give 'em that, and we never have to worry about where our next meal's coming from! Get me?"

"Hell, Sam, life in Hollywood is no bowl of cherries. Up at five in the morning to shoot at nine. I'm only here for one reason...." Wyler thrust his index finger in the air. "That one reason is to make good pictures. But, I'll tell you straight up, if I don't see it, I don't touch it."

Sam smiled, reached into his coat pocket and pulled out two tickets. "Got 'em in the post yesterday. One week from tomorrow night. If this piece is as good I think it is, I'm prepared to let Kingsley write his own ticket."

Wyler looked skeptical. "What if he doesn't bite?"

"I do not intend to set sail from New York without his John Hancock on the dotted line.

"And by the way, you're going to do a lot better with me than 'make good pictures.' You're going to become a legend— one of the all-time greats. Just stick with me."

Willy smiled. "I'll settle for making good pictures for now, Sam."

"You'll see. I'm not always right, but I'm never wrong!"

"Well, this is all fine and good, Sam. I need to get to work on *Dodsworth*. I'm leaving for New York tomorrow to meet with the producer and writer. I haven't finished packing."

Wyler and Goldwyn got out of the car. Wyler headed for his car parked in front of Goldwyn's offices.

"I'll see you in New York in a week. Say hello to Sidney Howard for me. I think he'd be perfect for the *Dead End* screenplay."

The following week, Goldwyn arrived in New York, accompanied by his wife and son. The night before he sailed on his first trip to Europe, Samuel Goldwyn took William Wyler to see *Dead End*.

The curtain dropped to the roar and cheers of nearly a thousand New Yorkers. Goldwyn turned to Wyler and yelled over the din. "Well, what do you think?"

"It's great, Sam. Great!"

"I'm glad you think so," Goldwyn shouted over the bravos, "because I want you to direct it."

"I'd love to!" Wyler yelled back. He couldn't hide his glee.

"I heard Selznick has already offered $150,000 for the rights," Sam yelled to Wyler.

"So, how badly do you want it, Sam?"

"You'll find out tomorrow."

The next morning, Goldwyn made headlines when he offered Sidney Kingsley $165,000 (in 1935 dollars) for the rights to *Dead End*. Goldwyn wrote out a $25,000 personal check as earnest money to lock-in the deal and sailed off for Europe.

KNOCKIN' ON HEAVEN'S DOOR

Six weeks later, the Goldwyns' ocean liner docked in New York. Sam was ill. An ambulance whisked the mogul to the emergency room at Doctors Hospital in New York.

One week later, Sam's doctor called his wife Frances into his office. "Mrs. Goldwyn, Sam has shown steady signs of improvement—until this morning."

"This morning? What happened this morning? I thought...."

The doctor interrupted, "Well, we're not exactly sure...." Before he could finish, the door swung open. Another physician swept past Frances and whispered in the doctor's ear.

Frances pushed herself to the edge of her chair.

"Doctor, is Sam...?"

"I have to go down to the lab, Mrs. Goldwyn."

"I'll go with you!"

"It would better if you stayed here."

Frances waited, paced in circles, and wrung the blood out of her hands. The doctor returned and Frances exploded, "What is it? Doctor, is he...?"

"Mrs. Goldwyn, Sam is in critical condition."

"Well, is he...?"

"I wish I could tell you for sure that your husband is going to be okay, Mrs. Goldwyn. We've tried everything."

"What do you mean?"

"I mean, barring some miracle, we don't expect him to pull through. I'm terribly sorry."

Mrs. Goldwyn kept watch outside Sam's room. She vacillated between sobs and prayers. Her terrible vigil was shattered. A dapper little man in a suit hurtled down the corridor and shouted her name.

"Frances! Frances!"

"Jim?" Francis stood up.

The Jim was James Mulvey, Samuel Goldwyn's most trusted confidant, and right hand man. Sam had appointed Jim head honcho of the New York office.

"Frances, I'm so sorry to trouble you. How's Sam?"

Frances broke down and sobbed on Jim's shoulder.

"He's...the doctor says they've done everything...."

"I'm so sorry..." Jim comforted.

"What...are you doing here?"

"I need you or Sam to authorize...well, you I guess...."

"To authorize what, Jim?"

"The check. We need a check...."

"A check for what?"

"Well, before you left, Sam wrote a check for $25,000. It was good faith money for the rights to *Dead End*."

"Dead End?"

"I mean, the play *Dead End*."

"Yes. The play...."

The doctor interrupted and grabbed Frances' arm. He pulled her away from Jim and said, "Mrs. Goldwyn, may I speak with you for a moment?"

A nervous Mulvey yanked on a vest chain and fished out his pocket watch. His hand trembled.

"What is it, doctor?"

"Sam might have a fighting chance if we operate and remove the diseased section of his lower intestine. But we don't know how much. There are no guarantees, but it's better than—" He paused.

"Better than what?"

"Well, if we do nothing, he won't make it through the night. You have to sign. We need your authorization to operate."

Frances ripped the clipboard from the doctor's hand. "A pen, I need a...."

"Right here, Mrs. Goldwyn." The doctor thrust his pen into her hand.

Frances signed the paper.

"And again on this back sheet." The doctor turned a page and pointed. "On this line."

Frances took the clipboard back and signed the second sheet.

"Doctor, I...."

"Mrs. Goldwyn, we'll do the very best we can. We have to get him into O.R. immediately."

"Okay— Go!"

The orderlies wheeled Sam to the operating room. Frances sat down and cried. Jim took another look at his pocket watch.

"Frances, I need to have it by noon."

"By, noon? Oh, Jim, yes— What by noon?"

"The balance of the money, Frances. The balance of the $165,000 for the rights."

"The rights?"

"The rights to *Dead End*."

"Yes, of course. *Dead End*."

Francis fell silent. She dug into her purse.

"Frances?"

"I...yes...."

Her hand emerged. She clutched a St. Christopher medal the size of a quarter.

"I, just...uh ...." Frances rubbed the medal between her hands. "Sam...what would Sam do, Jim?"

Jim looked perplexed.

"Frances, Sam's a gambler by nature. I mean—it's what he does every day of his life. And I know you're not."

"Not what?"

"Well, if the check isn't in the bank by noon—"

"What, Jim?"

"Mrs. G., are you okay?"

Frances stared at the St. Christopher medal and murmured under her breath.

"Frances? Are you...."

"Yes, Jim," she interrupted. "He's going to be okay. It's going to be a great picture."

"What is, Frances?"

"*Dead End*. This is not going to end. His life is not going to end. I have faith now—faith in God and in Sam Goldwyn."

Jim broke into a sweat. "Uhm, Frances, it's 11:36...."

"Yes. Write the check for the rights to *Dead End*, Jim."

"O.K. Good. I have to run then. Call me. Let me know as soon as he...."

"Jim, listen to me." Frances grabbed his shoulder and pulled him close to her. She whispered in his ear. "No one must ever know that my husband's life is in danger. No one. They'll take everything we have. Do I make myself clear?"

"Perfectly, Mrs. Goldwyn."

"Good. Now go!"

Jim turned to leave and Frances called out, "And Jim—"

"Yes, Ma'am?"

"Until Sam recovers, *everything* goes through me."

"Everything, Mrs. G?"

"*Everything*, Jim."

"I, uh— I have to...."

"I know," Frances said, "Get going!" Then she watched Mulvey disappear down the corridor.

Several feet of Sam Goldwyn's small intestine were removed. His extended recovery was at the Waldorf-Astoria. Then Samuel Goldwyn was back in Los Angeles and more cantankerous than ever.

Wyler, meanwhile, finished shooting the Sinclair Lewis adaptation, *Dodsworth*, in New York, and he returned to Hollywood as well.

A ROCKY ROAD

Almost a year after Goldwyn dropped 165 grand on the rights to *Dead End*, the project was dead in the water.

The Hollywood Titan's relationship with director William Wyler was fragile, due to the fact that Wyler did not want to direct *Woman Chases Man*. It was a screwball comedy picture that Sam was trying to shove down his throat.

"The script," said Wyler, "is just plain stupid!"

Goldwyn didn't care for the word "No." He suspended Wyler until he could prepare a shooting script for *Dead End*.

There were more problems.

Goldwyn wanted Sidney Howard to do the screenplay, but Howard had just been signed by Selznick to bring *Gone with the Wind* to the screen.

He wanted James Cagney for the part of Baby Face, but Cagney was in a contract war with Warner Brothers. Sam's *Consigliere* warned, "Stay away from the Warner-Cagney battle. It's not worth it for one picture."

Goldwyn and Wyler both tried to pressure George Raft into playing Baby Face, but Raft turned it down. George wanted Baby Face to be more contrite for his sins. Wyler and Goldwyn didn't agree.

The part of Baby Face went to a Hollywood newcomer by the name of Humphrey Bogart.

Lillian Hellman was recruited to write the screenplay. But she complained, "Goldwyn said he wanted me to 'clean up the play'. What he meant was 'cut off its balls.'" Hellman's screenplay was heavily censored.

Finally, there was the problem of casting the Dead End Kids. And the question as to where the film would be shot.

Goldwyn on a set in 1937, the year he produced the movie version of *Dead End.*

THE DEAD END KIDS

William Wyler looked up from a table covered with headshots of Hollywood's finest child actors.

"Sam, how in the world can we cast kids who are supposed to be from the slums of New York using child actors from Hollywood? I've screen tested every one of these kids and there's not *one* I want to cast!"

Goldwyn snarled from behind his newspaper. "Yeah, the Little Rascals won't exactly fill the bill, will they? The Kids are the key to this thing, Villy. If the Kids aren't believable, we're looking at the most expensive flop in movie history...the bigger they are...you get me?"

Wyler got up from the table and picked up the *Dead End* playbill off Sam's desk.

"I spent two weeks scouting locations while I was back East. I want to shoot the picture in New York."

The phone rang. Goldwyn picked it up and barked, "I said hold all my calls goddammit! Now hold all my calls or you'll be holding your last paycheck!" He slammed the phone down.

Wyler chuckled. "Is that how you ran off all your partners?"

"It's not funny. Don't back me into a corner like this, f'crissake. The last thing I can afford is to have Forty Take Wyler shooting my picture on location in New York! Who do you think I am, Rockefeller?"

Wyler was back at the table, thumbing through glossies.

"Sam, if we don't do this right, there's no point...I don't want my name on it."

Goldwyn banged his fist down on his desk.

"Goddammit, I run a tight ship here. That's why I'm the most successful independent producer in town. Everything comes out of my pocket which gives me the right to call the shots, and I'll be damned if I'll abandon all the other pictures in development to go to New York and baby-sit Dead End for two months.

"I'm giving you a million bucks to shoot *Dead End* on the lot! But, you're a big shot director now, right? You can tell me what pictures you will and won't do, right? Well, don't fuck with me on this one, or I swear, you'll never work in Hollywood again."

"Don't be ridiculous, Sam, I'm just saying I think it's a mistake not to shoot it in New York...there's no other way to put the audience in the story...."

"This is not a hill to die on..." Goldwyn picked up the phone.

"Stella, I want Richard Day and every carpenter that works for me to report to my office in one hour. Whoever doesn't show up is fired."

He slammed the phone down.

"Villy, I'm going to build the Dead End set right here. I'll spare no expense to replicate the location on a soundstage, down to the finest detail...now talk to me, and f'crissake tell me the truth, even if it means we never make another picture together! Can you do this?"

Wyler was back at the table shuffling through the headshots.

"What do you want to be remembered for, Sam?"

Goldwyn was annoyed. "What the hell are you talking about? I asked you a question."

Wyler continued, "I think I want to be remembered for directing performances that endure the test of time."

Goldwyn walked over to the table, and pulled up a chair until the two were almost nose-to-nose. "In forty-five minutes, I will be giving orders to a squadron of the best set designers money can buy. This will be one of the most expensive sets ever built on a Hollywood soundstage. I'm laying my reputation, my bank account, and my name on the line. So you can direct a *good picture*. Now, will you please answer my question before I have your ass thrown off the lot?"

Wyler got up from the table. "Goldwyn, you abusive sonofabitch, you can direct this picture yourself!"

Wyler headed for the door.

"F'crissake, Villy, calm down...we need this picture. This picture is our only shot at the Oscars...."

Wyler stopped and turned. "Okay, Sam...here's the deal. You get me a group of actors—pros. I'm not doing any hand-holding, and I'm not giving any acting lessons. You get me a polished group of actors, and I'll shoot the picture on the lot."

Goldwyn took a deep breath. "Was that so difficult? You almost gave me a heart attack!"

Wyler looked at Goldwyn as if to say, *Cut the theatrics, Sam.* But he said, "Are you sure you're not a frustrated actor, Sam?"

Goldwyn thought for a minute. "God makes the stars...."

Wyler cut him off, "Sam, Sam, you're making a parody of yourself! Now, who the hell are we gonna get to play these kids?"

Goldwyn picked up the phone. "Stella, get Sidney Kingsley on the horn. Buzz me when you've got him...and bring me those *Dead End* reviews."

Stella walked in with a pile of newspaper and magazine clippings. Goldwyn took the stack of reviews and passed them to Wyler who was on his fourth tedious round through the headshots of child actors. He wasn't seeing them anymore. Just looking at them. The way a woman leafs mindlessly through a fashion magazine.

"Forget about those, Villy...read these."

Goldwyn paced the width of the plush office, and stared out the window.

"There are over thirty reviews of Dead End in your hands, Villy, what do they all have in common?"

"I'm no good at riddles, Sam. Let's see, they're all in black ink?"

Goldwyn opened the window.

"Look again. Every single review virtually ignores the adult actors and heaps holy praises on the kids. You'd think they walked on water f'crissake! The columnist from the Times says the kids are 'The only ones talked about'. *The only ones talked about!*"

Wyler was leafing through the reviews. "What, Sam. What are you getting at?"

Goldwyn turned around and folded his arms across his chest in a gesture of grandeur. "Villy, I'm going to bring the whole dirty, ruthless, gay, heroic, sadistic crew of Dead End Kids to Hollywood!"

"Sam, they're all minors!"

"Then we'll send contracts to the parents, have them sign as the kids' guardians, and we'll have a judge out here sign off on it. Whatever we have to do to make it legal. I want those kids on a Pullman car to California the day after that show closes."

WELCOME
TO HOLLYWOOD

The Dead End Kids swaggered off the train at Union Station in Los Angeles. They were greeted by an attorney and a member of the California State Board of Education.

The Kids filed past the uniformed conductor. The school representative turned to the studio attorney and cooed, "Aren't they cute? They look like a little band of angels!"

The Kids picked up their luggage and followed their chaperones into a cavernous room. The Kids shouted and laughed at the echo of their own voices.

"Settle down boys. Take a seat."

The attorney assisted the young schoolteacher. They handed out forms and pencils.

"Each of you children must fill out one of these forms," chirped the schoolteacher.

Leo bristled. "I ain't 'one uh dese children.' I toined nineteen in June."

"That's fine, young man. Just show attorney Kennedy your birth certificate. We'll fill out a form to signify that you've reached majority age. We'll request a waiver of your educational requirements."

"Well, I'm signifyin' dat my boit cuhtificate is in New York wit Mama. David, tell dis Dame I'm nineteen, will yuh?"

"Young man, I'm not a Dame. I'm a credentialed teacher and a representative of the California State Board of Education. You boys can address me as Miss Wilkinson."

"Yeah? Well, wit a title like dat, yuh oughtta be runnin' duh friggin' Pentagon."

The Kids cracked up.

"What is your name, young man?"

David spoke up. "His name's Leo. He's my big brudduh."

"Thank you, but I think he's capable of answering for himself." The teacher turned back to Leo. "Well, young man?"

"Like my brudduh said, it's Leo."

"Do you have a last name, Leo?"

"Do you have a foist name," Leo mimicked.

"Young man, there's no call for that."

"His name is Leo Gorcey," the Kids yelped.

"Well, Leo Gorcey," the teacher said—her face was locked in a firm smile, "until you can produce a certified birth certificate, you are required by the laws of the State of California to attend school at the studio."

Leo's cohorts snickered.

"I know you boys don't care to spend time in juvenile hall, do you? That would be awful, wouldn't it? It would surely make your mothers very sad! Now, I expect to see you all in class on Monday."

On the first day of school at Goldwyn Studios, Leo showed up with Bobby Jordan, Huntz Hall, Gabriel Dell, Bernard Punsly, and Billy Halop. Leo was gunnin' for the "Dame."

Before the end of the Dame's first week, Bobby Jordan nailed the inside covers of the teacher's textbooks to her desk. Huntz Hall glued all the boys' answer sheets together after a day-long exam. The Kids spontaneously erupted in spitball parties and ink fights. And Gabriel Dell put steel shavings in the blackboard eraser.

The Dame went to use the eraser and the screech of the metal shavings scraped against the chalkboard. Her last nerve was already stretched to the limit. The prank popped it.

"That's it boys!" The Dame screamed. She was going for the tough love. "You're all on detention for one full week. And if this keeps up, you'll be on detention for a month!"

"Is dat supposed to scare us?" Leo piped up.

"It's supposed to teach you a lesson, Mr. Gorcey."

"We held up de opening of a Broadway Show for ten minutes one night 'cause duh stage hands took duh foiniture outta our game room, on accounta duh fact dat we was bustin' it up!"

"What does that have to do with what I just said, young man?"

"I'll tell yuh wuht it has tuh do wit it. When duh coitain didn't go up, dey put back duh foiniture! So wuht makes yuh tink we're jist gonna shrivel up an' die on account of a little detention?"

The Kids looked at the Dame with their Cagney faces.

"Well, Mr. Gorcey, I think it's time you and I had a little talk with Mr. Goldwyn."

The Kids cheered as Leo cried mock tears and skulked out of the room behind the skirt.

The Dead End Kids - 1: The Dame - 0.

In Mr. Goldwyn's office, Miss Wilkinson let it fly. She broke the dam and flooded the office with her mind. She told the boss just what she thought of this undisciplined band of hooligans from New York. Then she cried.

Sam waved Leo out of the room.

"Now, now," Sam cajoled her back from the edge. "Monday morning, we'll split the Kids up and assign them individual tutors."

"Thank you, Sir. Please forgive my outburst."

"Think nothing of it, dear."

"I hope this doesn't get back to my superior. I've worked so hard."

"Don't you worry. You did the right thing."

The Dame left Sam's office. Then the powerful tycoon straightened his tie, poured himself a Scotch on the rocks, and smiled. He swizzled his Scotch and thought, *I'll handle these kids.*

The Dead End Kids—Leo Gorcey, Billy Halop, Bernard Punsly, Huntz Hall, Gabriel Dell, and Bobby Jordan—showing off at Goldwyn Studios during the filming of *Dead End*.

SYLVIA SIDNEY
AND SLUM CENSORSHIP

In 1959, William Wyler would direct *Ben-Hur*. His magnificent opus would pocket over a dozen prestigious film awards, suck up a dozen Academy Award nominations, and bag 'Villy' his third Oscar for Best Director.

Ben-Hur would reign as the undefeated champion of Cinema Gold until the *Titanic* in 1997. But in May of 1937, Willy had to survive the filming of *Dead End*.

Even before his baptism of fire at the hands of the Kids, there was enough torque on the set of *Dead End* to keep all the big wheels burning rubber.

It started with Silvia Sydney.

Goldwyn considered no other actress to play Drina—the female romantic lead. She got the heavy green (to the tune of $75,000 in 1937 dollars).

Wyler couldn't care less about names or fat salaries. The written *Word* was king. Willy kept Sidney on the verge of tears throughout the entire two-month shoot. He had a nasty rep with the ladies.

"Cut!" Yelled the director. "Miss Sidney," loud enough for the entire cast and crew to hear, "I could get an actress for $150 to do a better job than that! Now, try it again, and this time act! Places, everyone...Scene 9, Take 24...."

Wyler sat on the floor behind the cameraman. He took out a trade magazine and began flipping through the pages. "Cut!" Wyler yelled, without looking up from his magazine. "Do it again!"

The director yelled for take after take, without looking up from his magazine.

"Scene 9, take 37. Do it again, Miss Sidney!"

Before Willy could yell "Action," Sidney spun off the set.

"Wyler, you sadistic sonofabitch. You're not even watching

me!" On came the waterworks. "I hate this goddamm picture!"

"We need make-up," Wyler barked.

"Miss Sidney, if you spent as much time working on your lines as you do in make-up, you'd be working on your next film by now."

"Fuck off, Wyler! Saaaaaammm!"

Goldwyn was on the set. He rushed in to soothe his starlet. "Don't cry, Miss Sidney. Villy is difficult. But he turns out good movies."

"Goddammit, Sam, my nostrils hurt...my head hurts...I'm gonna sue Elizabeth Arden's ass off, I swear...."

"Miss Sidney, that kind of bad ink will hurt us both...you slipped and fell...could be a very nasty court battle...and for what? It didn't cost you a cent."

"I know, Sam, I know. I appreciate you paying me while my face healed. I do."

"Sylvia. Please finish the picture, f'crissake...."

"Fuck the picture, Sam! I'm not doing one more scene for that bastard, Wyler...it's over. I'm finished. I'm not ironing one more shirt in front of the camera. I've played the same damn role...."

"Miss Sidney, look at me. This film is yours! You're going all the way to the Oscars with this one. Think what that'll do for your career."

Sam wiped her tears with his handkerchief. Miss Sidney went back to work. When *Dead End* came out, critics from the Big Apple to the City of Angels would cheer her performance as her best in ten years.

The next morning on the set of *Dead End*

"Villy, this set is filthy!" Goldwyn complained and rummaged around the set of *Dead End* in a three-piece suit and a bowler. He acted like a custodian at Disneyland. He was scooping up every shred of paper and garbage that had been carefully scattered throughout the set by the prop man, Irving Sindler.

Sindler and Wyler had spent hours choreographing the garbage the night before. Wyler was pissed.

"But, Mr. Goldwyn, this is supposed to be a slum."

"Well, this slum cost a lot of money."

"But it's part of what we're saying in the picture, Sam. Right next to modern apartments are all those old crummy buildings with dirt and garbage."

"There will be no dirty slums in my picture." Goldwyn scooped up as much garbage as he could carry and walked off the set.

William Wyler, Richard Day (the art director), and Irving Sindler stared at each other in disbelief.

Every evening, after Goldwyn left the studio, Wyler, Day, and Sindler would dress up the set with garbage for the next day's shoot. Every morning, before cast and crew arrived on the set, Goldwyn would clean it all up.

One day, they all collided.

"Sam! If you take that garbage off the set, I quit!"

"Villy, you don't have to quit. *You're fired!*"

Irving the prop man to the rescue— "Mr. Goldwyn, Mr. Wyler, I have an idea."

"Well?" snapped Goldwyn. "Speak up, Mr. Sindler."

"Well, how about if I wash the debris, Sir."

Wyler was dumbfounded. "Has everyone on this production flipped? This is supposed to be a slum!"

Wyler grabbed some papers out of a leather pouch hanging on the arm of his director's chair.

"Here's a sheet from *Kingsley's* stage directions: 'The East River is covered by swirling scum an inch thick...mucky with floating refuse and rubbish...a hundred sewers vomit their guts into it....'"

"That's enough! I just had oatmeal for breakfast...this is my picture goddammit."

Sindler squeezed between Goldwyn and Wyler. "I'll start scrubbing the garbage right away, sir. There won't be one piece of dirty garbage on the set by the time we start shooting, Mr. Goldwyn. You have my word on it, sir."

Goldwyn put his hand on Sindler's shoulder. "Well, at least one person here has the IQ to know who signs his goddamm paycheck! Wyler, you ungrateful sonofabitch, you're back on the picture."

Mr. Sindler, the prop man, coaxed the armful of garbage out of Goldwyn's arms.

Sam eyed Willy. "Surely you can do another take of something while Mr. Sindler cleans up the garbage. I mean cleans the garbage. I mean...fuck it, you know what I mean!

"And Villy, remember what I said yesterday about getting those obscene 'city noises' off the soundtrack."

"Yeah, sure, Sam. Why don't we just change the setting to Central Park?"

"Villy? What the hell is this fishing pole doing over here?"

"Uh, we're using it in place of a mic boom."

"No one told me anything about a shortage of booms!"

"That's because there is no shortage."

"Well, then, what the hell...?"

"Dick didn't leave an entrance onto the set, Sam. He didn't want to disrupt the continuity of the scenery."

"You're all crazy!" shouted Goldwyn on the way out the door.

"I don't give a shit if you dangle the mics from toothpicks. Just get me the Oscar, Villy! I'm countin' on this picture. It's all we got!"

He was gone.

"Okay, folks," said Wyler. "Get the fresh vegetables in the river and assemble the cast for the first shot."

William Wyler (director), Lillian Hellman (screenwriter), and Greg Toland (cimematographer) on the movie set of *Dead End*. Wyler would get an Oscar nomiation for his turn as director.

REACH OUT AND TOUCH SOMEONE....

"**H**ello, operator?" Gabe Dell was on the phone.

"Huntz, get yer stinkin' hands off duh moichendise," Leo scolded Huntz. "Dis is Wyler's office. Yuh want tuh get us all sent up tuh duh joint?"

Leo turned to Gabe Dell who was still hollering for the operator.

"Hang up an' try again, Gabey. An' dis time, make yer voice more like Willy's."

"Hello? Hello? Yes, Operator—"

Leo and Gabe exchanged the *here goes nothin'* look.

"Yes, operator, this is Mr. William Wyler speaking. Uh, would yuh gimme Hillcrest 7-4066, please?"

Huntz Hall winced when Gabe slipped from his impersonation of Wyler back into his New York street urchin accent.

Leo whispered, "Well, did she buy it?"

"She's puttin' me through," smiled Gabe.

"Arright, Huntz, get ovuh here. Gabe, when his mudduh answers, hand Huntz duh phone."

"Hello, Ma? It's Huntz, Ma."

"Arright, Angel, get ovuh here. Yer next." Leo barked.

One by one, the Kids talked to their mothers for about an hour each, while Wyler shot scenes with the principals on the set of *Dead End.*

Two weeks later when Goldwyn got Wyler's phone bill, he went through the roof. He marched over to the set and rounded up the Kids. "You Kids are in way over your heads," shouted Goldwyn.

"Dat's funny," Leo whispered to Gabe and Huntz, "we ain't shootin' no water scenes tuhday, are we?"

The Kids smirked.

"Well, you can wipe those silly grins off your faces, boys. Every dime of that phone bill to New York is coming out of your paychecks. You each talked an hour. So it cost each of you one week's pay!"

The Kids were shocked.

"But Mr. Goldwyn..." Gabe piped up.

"Don't waste your breath, son. Now, get out of my sight. All of you! You're suspended from the lot for three days while we do principal shooting."

Goldwyn started to leave the set. He turned around to call to Wyler and saw the Kids frozen like sticks in mud. "Aren't you Kids gone yet?" he hollered. "I said go! Shoo! Off the lot! And don't come back until Monday!"

"Hey, Huntz," Leo said, "I got an idea...." They talked and shuffled toward the main gate.

Monday morning on the set.

"Places, Kids!" Wyler hollered for the first scene marker on Monday. "I said PLACES! Kids! Get your asses in front of the camera!"

The Kids were hunkered down outside the stage door.

"Will someone get those little felons in here and get them in their places?"

"Sir," The assistant director whispered to Wyler.

"What, son. What the hell is it?"

"Mr. Wyler, the Kids say they're on strike, sir."

"Speak English, son."

"The Kids, sir. They refuse to report to the set. They insist on speaking with Mr. Goldwyn, sir."

"Then get Sam f'crissake! What the hell is this, a nursery? Do I look like a wet nurse to you, son?"

Sam stormed onto the set. "This better be important, goddammit."

"Sam, the Kids want to talk to you."

"What the hell are they doing back here? I thought I suspended the sadistic bunch of brats!"

"Sam, it's Monday. You suspended them until Monday, and I've got an idle crew milling around waiting to shoot a picture."

Sam fumed outside the stage door. He found the Kids. They were tossing coins up against the soundstage wall.

"Kids, Mr. Wyler would appreciate your presence on the set."

"Mr. Wyler can jump in a lake for all we care," Huntz wise-cracked.

"Excuse me? What did you just...."

"You hoid wuht he said," Leo interrupted. "We ain't goin' back tuh woik til you promise not tuh touch a penny of our dough!"

"Yeah," piped up the other Kids. "Not a penny!"

Wyler came out the stage door as Goldwyn came unglued. "You filthy little bastards! Do you know who you're talking to?"

"Sam," Willy called.

"What, goddammit, what?"

"Sam, walk with me."

Sam walked with Willy out of earshot of the Kids.

"Sam, this is not a hill to die on. Shooting on the set is saving enough dough on this picture to fill Ft. Knox."

"What are you suggesting?"

"I'm suggesting we leave the boys' paychecks alone and shoot the picture, Sam. I've got more than enough headaches. I don't need to be watching my back twenty-four hours a day."

"What the hell are you talking about, watching your back? They're kids f'crissake!"

"Sam, for the love of Pete, just take the money out of my check and let's go back to work."

"Fine, Villy. It's coming out of your check. I'm sure as hell not paying for it. But when this picture's in the can, I'm person-ally kicking every one of those defiant little sons-a-bitches down to Union Station and shipping them right back where they came from. I'm not running a Warner Brothers Gangster Training Academy here! I don't need this shit!"

For the remainder of the *Dead End* shoot, Wyler and the Kids became buddies. He often brought his motorcycle to the set and let the Kids take turns riding it around the lot. In turn, the Kids showed up on time and performed flawlessly for Willy. After all, they had done over 650 performances of *Dead End* on Broadway.

But their new found friendship with Wyler didn't stop the Kids from wreaking havoc everywhere else on the Goldwyn Studio lot.

THE DEAD END KIDS VS. THE PRINCE

Humphrey Bogart was fresh off a hard-earned success as Duke Mantee in the film *Petrified Forest*. But he was a long way from *Casa Blanca*.

The suits at Warners didn't see Bogey as a leading man. "He doesn't have the face," they complained. "And he sounds like a fairy with that lisp."

In *Dead End*, Bogey's characterization of Baby Face would be a thumbnail sketch of his yet-to-be-realized Picasso—the classic, hard-nosed gangster in the trademark fedora and Dick Tracy trench coat. The guy who sticks his neck out for no one.

One day, after the Kids pants-ed Bogey (held him down and stripped him of his trousers) for ignoring them, the Prince did the unexpected. He invited the Kids to join him for lunch at the commissary. Bogey was taking them on.

Huntz threw out the bait.

"We're bored, Princey," Huntz whined to Bogart as he ripped into a mustard covered hot dog.

"Bored?"

"Yeah," chirped Leo. "We duhn about everyting we can tink of tuh dese lugs, an' we still ain't been kicked off duh picture! We're all out uh doity tricks!"

"Doncha' think yer pushin' it, boys?" asked Bogey.

"Pushin' wuht?" asked Huntz with mock innocence. "We ain't been dat bad! Duh picture'll be in duh can in a week, an' we ain't gonna be nuttin' but a memory tuh dese kingpins!"

"Oh I doubt that. Let's see, you boys completely destroyed an entire sound stage...."

"Dat was because de gas pedal on duh truck got stuck! Dat wasn't our fault!" Huntz protested.

Bogey narrowed his eyes. "Oh? So what about you boys costin' the studio a pile uh dough when you set off the sprinklers and flooded the whole wardrobe department? I suppose yer gonna claim it was the sprinkler's fault!"

Leo's turn. "But Bogey, we was jist testin' duh new sprinkler system. An' besides, duh five fire engine drivers thawt it was funny!"

Laughter all around. A chuckle from the Prince.

"So, wadd'ya boys want from me, the Congressional Medal of Honor?"

Back to Huntz. "We don' want no medal, Princey, we want ideas! You must have some tricks up yer sleeve! You been in dis racket longuh dan we have!"

"Yeah," piped up the other Kids. "Show us yer bag uh tricks, Princey!"

The bait was too good.

"Ok, boys. I set fire to a guy's newspaper once...while he was readin' it!"

The Kids exploded with laughter. Leo took the lead. "We ain't nevuh done nuttin' like dat!"

"Oh, that was jist fer starters," Bogey bragged. "When I was workin' on my first picture, me and this other kid, we slipped into this actor's trailer and nailed his slippers to the floor. When he tried walkin' in 'em, he fell flat on his kisser!"

Over to Huntz. "Oh, Daaat's a good one, Princey!"

"Listen, if you boys are serious about causing a ruckus, sneak up behind Willy Wyler and pour water into the seat of his canvas chair!"

"Now yer talkin', Princey!" yelled one of the kids.

Confident that he was now in with the Kids, Bogey got up from the table. "Well, boys, I'm goin' to saw some logs before we go back to work."

"Hey, Princey," Huntz slapped Bogey's shoulder. "Tanks fer duh hot tips!"

"There's more where those came from. Now, stay outta trouble, yuh hear? I'd like to get off this picture in one piece. And if anybody asks, we never had this conversation. Is that clear?"

Huntz smiled. "Clear as a bell, Princey!"

The Kids chimed in. "Yeah, clear as a bell, Princey!"

Ten minutes later, the Kids heard snoring outside Bogey's trailer window that was loud enough to wake the dead.

"Well, light 'em up Leo!"

"I'll light 'em arright, Gabe, but I ain't trowin' 'em in."

"I'll trow 'em in," offered Huntz.

"Arright, who's got duh torch?" squealed Leo.

Gabe pulled a pack of matches out of his trouser pocket. Leo lit the bundle of firecrackers and handed it to Huntz. Huntz pitched it through Bogart's partially opened trailer window. An ear-splitting crackling, machine gun sound filled the air. A cloud of gray, puffy smoke wafted out of Bogey's trailer window.

Then Bogart's angry howl. "You Kids'll pay fer this! You're all gonna pay fer this!"

Bogey's threat from behind his trailer door caused the Kids to scatter for cover. When they were out of sight of the trailer, they stopped to catch their breath.

"I tink we jist lost anudduh friend," Leo muttered with regret.

"We shouldda thawt uh dat ten minutes ago." Huntz sounded a bit remorseful himself.

"Ahhhh, shuddup, Cyrano. I didn't hear you firin' no warnin' shots. You trew duh sticks innnair yuh moron!

"Losin' friends is gettin' to be a bad habit wit us." Leo lamented.

But it was too late for apologies.

A thoughtless gag cost the Kids their friendship with Bogey. Bogey wasn't the only one. Sam's patience with the Dead End Kids was wearing paper-thin.

The Prince—autographed picture "To Spit...."

THE PAPER PASSES TO JACK

Dead End harvested a bumper crop of accolades from the critics and knocked 'em dead at the box office.

Goldwyn's genius, combined with Wyler's sure hand, Tolman's brilliant cinematography, and Lillian Hellman's faithful screenplay made *Dead End* a near perfect picture.

Dead End was nominated for four Academy Awards. Best Picture, Best Director, Best Supporting Actress, and Best Art Direction. But it wasn't to be Sam's year. He lost the Best Picture Oscar to a Warner Brothers entry: *Life of Emile Zola,* Jack Warner's first Oscar for Best Picture. But it was Sam who would have the last laugh.

When *Dead End* wrapped, Sam didn't kick the Kids down to Union Station. He came up with a better idea. He sold the Dead End Kids' contracts to his competitor, Jack Warner. Warner now had three migraine headaches: Bogart, Cagney, and the Dead End Kids.

Warner Brothers employed more gangsters than the mafia. Jack had Bogart, Cagney, Raft, Garfield, and Robinson. Box office gold—all.

Why all the interest in gangsters? Some say it was because of Baby Face Nelson. Baby Face Nelson made a name for himself knocking over banks during the Great Depression.

Millions of Americans lost their life's savings when the banks went bust. The banks made the perfect collective villain in the unfolding of the American Crime Melodrama.

As newspaper reporters and the Pinkertons tracked the notorious bank robber from hold up to hold up, Americans cheered for their new hero, Baby Face. That is, until Baby popped too many caps. On cops. Cold-blooded killer, he was.

Even so, America's love affair with Baby Face Nelson rammed the nation's fascination with gangsters into overdrive.

Jack Warner built an empire bringing the bad boys to the big screen.

The Dead End Kids provided the perfect ingredient to throw into the mix with stars like Humphrey Bogart, James Cagney, and John Garfield.

Caught between the sincere and the sinister, would the little angels choose the straight and narrow? Would they bargain with the devil and follow their icons to the electric chair? Or would they face death at the end of a gun barrel?

Warner Brothers shot six features with the Dead End Kids. *Crime School*, with Bogart; *They Made Me a Criminal*, with John Garfield and Claude Rains; *Hell's Kitchen* and *Angel's Wash Their Faces*, with Ronald Reagan (yes, the 40th President of The United States); and *On Dress Parade*. And, last, but not least, the movie that became a classic in the gangster genre, *Angels With Dirty Faces* (directed by Michael Curtiz of *Casa Blanca* fame) with Bogart, Cagney, Ann Sheridan, Pat O'Brien, and of course, the Dead End Kids.

The Lion's share of film critics favored Leo Gorcey as the standout among the Kids. Leo got more ink than all the other Kids combined. He was winning his battle with Billy Halop for leadership of the gang.

Leo enjoyed living big. It worked for him. It worked for the press. It worked for the studio.

Did the patriarchs at Warners ever take Leo aside and give him friendly suggestions as to how he might screw his head on straight? Why would they? Leo's antics were getting gallons of free ink and miles of headlines in all the local rags and mags. Stokin' the star makin' machinery behind the popular flick.

By way of example, when the brass at Warner Brothers discovered Leo had plans to marry, the suits cautioned the young star. "Slow down, Leo. If you reform too soon, it'll be bad for business."

The Dead End Kid's response? Leo chartered a plane and eloped with his sweetheart.

SPEED

Like most adolescents in America, the Dead End Kids fell in love with the automobile. Hormones and wheels. The perfect combination.

Oh, did I mention booze?

Hormones, wheels and booze. A recipe for disaster. And more free publicity than any studio could afford.

None of the Kids came anywhere close to my father's adrenalin-pumping passion for putting the pedal to the metal.

The Kids wanted wheels. They pooled their money together and paid $90 for a Model 'A' Ford. Wow! $19,910 under invoice!

Of course, Leo was elected (or he elected himself) to drive. None of the Kids knew how to drive, least of all Leo. On their first outing, they crashed. The Kids scattered—as in *left the scene of the accident.*

The victim was Gary Cooper. He was taking his new $9,000 Dusenberg out for a spin when the Kids rammed him! Mr. Cooper was in a good mood and didn't press charges.

But Dad's luck on the road was not about to get better!

After the accident, Leo hired a mechanic to do more than repairs. He had him convert the Model 'A' to a Hot Rod. Top speed, 105! Then he bought out all the other Kids' interests in the car.

The stage was set for a truly spectacular exhibition. In eighteen months at Warner Brothers, Leo racked up twenty-six speeding tickets! He was issued a subpoena to appear in court, but thought, *Duh judge prob'ly just wants to meet a movie star. It won't be de end uh duh wold if he don't meet me.*

With that flawless logic, Leo paid a city official $50 to fix the subpoena. The next day, the city official took off with Leo's $50 and $200,000 of the city's money! Leo had no choice but to appear.

The bailiff's voice echoed off the courtroom walls. "All rise! The Honorable Judge Byron J. Walters presiding."

"Thank you bailiff. You may be seated." Judge Walters shuffled through some papers, looked over his glasses and down his nose at Leo. Then he said, "Leo Bernard Gorcey, would you approach the bench."

Leo sauntered up to the bench, still convinced that the Judge just wanted to meet a movie star.

"It's nice of you to join us today Mr. Gorcey. It seems you had a difficult time finding your way here."

"Actually, once I got trough duh front door, it was a piece uh cake!" Quipped Leo.

Judge Walters couldn't help himself. He grinned. Leo grinned back.

"Officer Jack Bigham."

"Yes, Your Honor."

"Are you the arresting officer in this case?"

"Yes, Your Honor."

"You want to tell me what happened?"

"Your Honor, I clocked this young man going over sixty miles per hour at Santa Monica Boulevard and Gower Street."

"*Sixty* miles per hour, Officer Bigham?"

"Yes, Your Honor. Mr. Gorcey pulled over, but then, as I was walking up to his car, he took off again in an effort to escape."

Leo grinned, the judge didn't.

"He was traveling over 55 miles per hour the second time I clocked him. I finally managed to run him into the curb and give him the citation."

"Is that all, officer?"

"Yes, Your Honor."

"Mr. Gorcey, is that what happened?"

"Yes, Judge, dat's exactly wuht happened!"

"You'll address me as Your Honor, young man."

"Yes, Yer Honor."

"Mr. Gorcey, I have here in front of me your complete record from the California Department of Motor Vehicles. It includes twenty-four citations, not counting the two you were arrested for by Officer Bigham."

Judge Walters read off the list of citations. It took fifteen minutes. "...And finally, Mr. Gorcey, you received a ticket prior to Officer Bigham's arrest, for traveling at *ninety* miles per hour down Wilshire Boulevard."

Leo waited patiently for Judge Walters to ask him for his autograph so he could go back to the set of *Crime School*.

"Well Sonny, what do you have to say for yourself?"

"Judge...."

"You will address me as Your Honor, son."

"Yer Honor, dat report is a little longer dan most novels I've read!"

The judge collapsed back in his leather chair, slapped his knee, and let loose with a hearty belly laugh.

Dat's it! Leo mused. *Dis courtroom must get real boring. Dey just brought me down here to liven tings up a bit! I'll give Yer Honor my autograph an' I'll be back on duh Warner Brudduh's lot in 20 minutes!*

"Son, you have a wonderful sense of humor!"

"Tanks, Yer Honor. Now if yuh would be so kind as tuh arrange fer my dismissal, I got a picture to shoot at Warner Brudduh's wit Humphrey Bogart. You mightta hoid of 'im."

"Oh yes, son, I've heard of him all right." Judge Walters stopped laughing and leaned over the bench.

"Young man?"

"Yes Yer Honor."

"Upstairs, in the Lincoln Heights County Jail, we have a mess of prisoners that really love to be entertained. I'm going to give you the privilege of spending five days telling them jokes!"

"Wait, Yer Honor, yuh can't put me in duh slammer. I'm woikin' on a picture!"

"Bailiff, take Mr. Gorcey into custody. By order of this court, Mr. Gorcey is remanded to the County Jail for five days. Court adjourned!" Down came the gavel.

This real-life courtroom scene was incorporated into several of Leo's later movies over at Monogram.

Noah Beery Sr. did the turn as the judge in two of the East Side Kids films. In both films Leo is charged with a multitude of infractions.

When Leo returned to the *Crime School* film set, five days later, Huntz and Gabe were loaded with questions.

Old Newspaper–Caption Reads:
LEO B. GORCEY, 20 (above), who played the juvenile gangster in the film "Dead End," yesterday was sentenced to five days in jail when found guilty of speeding on Santa Monica boulevard. Motorcycle Officer Jack Bigham told the court he clocked the actor traveling at 55 miles an hour. —Daily News Photo

CHRISTMAS IN THE JAILHOUSE

"**L**eo, wuht was it like in duh joint?" mugged Huntz. "Diddya get room soivice?"

"Shuddup, yuh muttonhead. Dat jail was drier Dan duh Sahara Desert! Even duh guards couldn't be bribed for uh shot uh wine!"

Gabe piped up, "Wasn't it boring innair?"

"Well, we did have a little entuhtainment. Aftuh breakfast on Sunday mornin', the sheriff announced dat he had arranged some entuhtainment fer us. When we got back tuh duh tank, dere was dis piano just inside de entrance."

"Well, diddya play it Leo, diddya?" Huntz asked.

"Well, if yuh shuddup long enough, boid brain, I'll tell yuh! Like I was sayin', two guards escorted duh pianist intuh duh tank. We prisoners applauded and started hollerin' for special requests like *Minnie duh Moocher, Tea for Two, It Was Christmas in duh Jailhouse*, stuff like dat."

Leo brought his voice down. "Den, duh pianist says in dis very quiet voice 'Now, gentlemen—we will sing some hymns.'"

A shocked look from Gabe Dell. "Yuh didn't sing hymns, diddya Leo?"

"Wuhdd'ya crazy, Gabe? Uh course I didn't sing no hymns!"

"Well, den what happened?" Huntz was beside himself with suspense.

"All hell broke loose, dat's wuht happened! Duh boo's and duh Bronx cheers wouldda raised duh dead! One uh duh guards growled, 'Quiet, you bastids. Don't be sacrilegious.'

"Duh guys got quiet, den, anudduh guard came in wit a box, set it on duh floor, and growled, 'Arright, you guys, come and get yer chocolate bars.' Like a bunch uh suckuhs, we crowded around duh box. It was full uh hymn books! Duh pianist made a short speech about duh evils guidin' our destinies, den sat at duh piano and started to bang the keys."

Gabe was busting at the seams. "Leo, please tell us yuh didn't sing no hymns!"

"Huntz would yuh put yer hand ovuh Gabe's kisser til I'm done?"

"Yeah, shut yer trap, Gabe, an' let 'im finish!"

"So anyway, de inmates, in attemptin' tuh sing duh hymns, sounded like a bunch uh wild hogs at mating time! Dat was the woist ting dat evuh happened tuh me. Not duh piano, or duh hymns, but duh fact dat jails don't soive liquor! I ain't nevuh speedin' again! Evuh!"

Jack Warner walked on the set.

"Leo?"

"Yeah, Pop?"

"This gentleman brought your jalopy...says you need to sign this paper to get it back. Seems the Department of Motor Vehicles installed a governor on your car."

"Wuht duh hell? Which state?"

"Which state?"

"Yeah, Pop, governor of which state?"

"Goddammit, Leo, not that kind of governor! It's a control device attached to your carburetor. Keeps your car from going over a certain speed."

"Wuht duh hell speed is dat?"

"Well, says here, 40 miles per hour."

"40 miles per hour? I know people wit polio dat can walk faster dan 40 miles per hour. I'll be duh laughin' stock uh duh boulevahd!"

"Just sign the goddamm thing, Leo. I've got a bevy of frustrated actresses mobbing my office. I don't need this shit!"

Leo signed the release. Jack gave the original to the DMV representative, and Gabe grabbed the carbon.

"Ok, boys. Get the hell back to work before I suspend the lot of ya'." Jack walked off.

The Kids razzed Leo. Huntz picked up a prop. A hat with feather plumes sticking out the top. "Leo rides wit a Governor!

Leo rides wit a Governor!" Huntz sat down in the passenger seat of Leo's Tin Lizzie. Faking an English accent. "I'll be your Governor, Ole Chap!" Losing the accent. "And yuh can ride around wit me in duh car!"

"Get oudda dere yuh big ape!" Leo barked.

Gabe was reading through Leo's paperwork from the DMV. "Hey, Leo, says here yuh gotta have dis govuhner on yer jalopy fer *ninety* days!"

At this point, my father claims he had an epiphany. A flashback of his father, Bernard, trying to teach him to respect the law. Dad wrote in his wobbly memoir, "Never again did I try to ridicule an officer or a judge."

Well, that's all fine and good about the ridiculing part. But, as far as I know, my father never learned how to drive.

The best thing I can do is to give you an example from my childhood. We'll call this episode, A drunk behind the wheel, by any other name, is still a drunk behind the wheel.

This incident took place when I was thirteen-years-old. I remember it like it was yesterday.

Okay...maybe like it was last week.

Leo's Movies Mimicked His Real Life

THE HOLSTEINS

It's a warm Spring day in 1962 up at the ranch in Northern California, where my father retired at the ripe old age of thirty-nine. From acting, not from drinking.

I'm thirteen, my sister is eleven, my stepbrother is nine.

Dad's taking us for a drive in his brand new Mercury sedan. The monogrammed silver flask of Hill & Hill whiskey is within easy reach on the front seat. All us kids are in the back seat. No seatbelts.

My retired comedian father is trying out some new jokes on us when a rust-red pick up with wooden racks and a shot gun mounted in the rear window almost runs us off the road.

Dad cuts loose. "Red-neck, son-of-a-bitchin', sheep stealin', cocksuckuh, bastid!"

Dad made a serious avocation out of creating run-on sentences of nothing but epithets. The less sense the sentences made, the more laughs they got. "That Leo. He's a character, isn't he?" was the typical response following such a display of prolific profanity. As a kid, however, it didn't feel good being on the receiving end of one of Dad's abusive tirades.

Anyway, the Dead End Kid reached under the seat for his .44 magnum pistol. "I'm gonna blow that bastid's ass off!"

It was too late. By the time Dad got his piece out from under the seat, the pick-up was long gone. Thank God.

But now, Dad's all pumped up with nowhere to go.

Then, out of nowhere, Muggsy belts out, "I can drive a car backwards better dan most people can drive forward!"

Us kids yelp with laughter.

Dad howls back, "Oh, yuh tink I'm kiddin?"

Did we say we thought he was kidding? Doesn't matter now. We tumble to the floor as Muggsy slams the Mercury into reverse!

One by one, we hoist ourselves off the floor and onto the back seat. Six pairs of little eyes peer out the rear window to see the Mercury fishtailing backwards at 40 miles per hour!

Now it's *Mr. Toad's Wild Ride* at Disneyland.

Screeeeeeeecccchhhhh!!! PUPH-UMP!!!

The shiny new Mercury slams to a halt in a massive cloud of dust. The dashboard is facing the treetops. We're laughing so hard our guts hurt.

"Do it again, Dad, do it again!"

Dad stumbles out of the car, bewildered. *Not a scratch!*

He kneels down and stares at the rear end of the sedan, wedged into the bottom of an irrigation ditch. Strands of barbed wire circle around the rear bumper. The turn signal clicks on and off to the rhythm of the flashing red light, which is submerged in six inches of water.

Back to the car to take a *belt* from his flask. "Well if dat don't beat all," Leo mutters to himself.

By now, he's forgotten anyone else is in the car with him.

Two Holstein cows amble over to stare at us. We hear the sound of an approaching 1950-something, Ford tractor. The Holsteins stare at the Mercury in Gary Larson fashion as the red and gray tractor stops a few feet in front of us.

A sinewy old cowboy with leathery skin climbs down and hikes through the soccer ball-size dirt clods to get a closer look at the disabled hunk of shiny blue metal poking up out of his irrigation ditch.

"By the looks uh things, I'd say yuh banged her up purdy good."

People in the country have a congenial way of stating the obvious.

"Well, I reckon we'd best get her outta that ditch or y'all ain't gonna be goin nowhere!"

Every piece of machinery in rural America is a *her.*

The old cowboy Samaritan in the sweat-stained straw hat and the filthy-dirty boots pulls a logging chain out of a big metal box welded onto the back of his tractor, wraps it around the front axle of the Mercury and eases Dad's war-torn sedan out of the irrigation ditch like he's poppin' a marble out of a birthday cake. AAA couldn't have done it better.

Always the actor, Dad thanks the cowboy in his Bowery Buckaroos western accent. "Much oblahged to yuh naybor," Muggsy drawls, as he tips his Stetson to the cowboy on the tractor.

"Think nuthin uv it."

The cowboy collects up his logging chain and rides off into a dirt field that looks like it goes on forever.

We pile into the car to the sound of Dad's million-dollar, Washington Heights accent. "Not a woid uh dis to yer mudduh or I'll whack yuh one, ya unduhstand?"

If Dad had been wearing his pinned up fedora, he would have smacked us all over the head with it!

I didn't realize it then, but incidents like these would foreshadow my own experience with cars. I ended up totaling out six cars. The sixth at the age of forty-three.

The Apple never falls far from the tree. I acted out my anger at the wheel, just like dear old Dad. In fact, just like Dad, I left the scene of my first accident. The accident wasn't even my fault. I was scared, so I ran.

My dad was no Gary Cooper. He reported me to the cops and we played out the same courtroom scene my father had played out when he was my age.

I didn't go to jail, but I lost my license for two years.

PRETTY WOMEN

Did I mention, my Dad had a thing for women?

Not some women. All women.

Leo envisioned Hollywood as the Big Rock Candy Mountain, where every touched-up centerfold he had ever laid eyes on would come to life!

Leo's imaginary bevy of beauties would be waiting for him in Hollywood. They were heaving and craving for one thing—one thing only. To fulfill Leo's every erotic fantasy.

I guess most young men fall for that illusion—the anonymous encounter with the *Playboy* centerfold of the month—an evening of torrid, adrenalin-pumping, casual sex with the girl of our dreams—no strings attached.

That was the fantasy of the Dead End Kid. A lonely young teenager from the streets of New York, gazing out the window of a speeding Pullman car at nothing but endless miles of uninhabited wilderness and daydreaming about Hollywood.

But what was Leo really looking for? Love? His mother's affection? Revenge? Power? Or was he just looking for someone to listen, and understand. Someone to *get* him, and be his partner?

Whatever it was, he never found it.

He died alone, after being married five times. *But Why?* I wondered, *What kept my dad from finding love? He was handsome, gifted, successful, wealthy, and funny.*

To answer that question, I'd have to answer another question. What kinds of relationships did the flamboyant Leo Gorcey have with his many wives? And what did the ex-wives think of him?

Was there some common thread that ran through Dad's relationships with women that would reveal the secret of his loneliness? *What could I learn from his mistakes?*

Fortunately, there was a small ocean of ink on Leo's wives. And I knew four of them personally. Kay—Dad's first wife;

Amelita—my mother and his third wife; Brandy—my step-mother and his fourth wife; and Mary—his fifth wife.

I began with wife number one.

No Shortage of Pretty Women in Leo's Movies

KAY

Catherine Marvis was on a tour of Warner Brothers Studios with her mother. Her mother was along because Kay was fifteen.

"Is this the set you were looking for, dear?"

"Is this where they're filming the movie with the Dead End Kids, Mama?" Kay inquired of her mother.

"I think so, sweetheart. I see some kids over on the set. Are those the ones you're looking for?"

"Yes. Those are the ones, Mama."

Kay was a head turner. Easy to meet people when they're staring at you before you open your mouth.

"You must be Billy Halop," Kay cooed.

"Jist plain Billy to you, sweetheart! You got a name to go wit dat gorgeous face?"

"Kay. Kay Marvis."

"Where yuh from, Kay Marvis?"

"Hollywood, now. I'm a Goldwyn Girl. I'm originally from Georgia!"

Halop feigned a swoon.

"Now I unduhstand where dey get duh sayin' Georgia Peach! Maybe if you ain't busy latuh, I could show yuh around."

"That's so kind of you, Billy, but I'll be going soon. I have a drama class this afternoon."

"Well, wuht about...."

Kay politely cut in.

"Billy, would you be so kind as to show me where I might find a boy by the name of Leo Gorcey?"

"Oh, yuh got it bad fer Spit, huh?"

Kay put on a calculated blush.

"Well, you ain't de only dame dat's got it out fer Leo. He spends at least two hours a day writin' tuh five dolls in New York. It's all dose fan magazines. He's shootin' a scene right now...an' anyway, Leo don't talk tuh no dames when he's woikin'."

"Is that him over there, Billy?"

"Yeah, dat's him all right. But good luck tryin' to talk to 'im."

Each of the Dead End Kids caught the scent of Kay Marvis as she made the rounds on the set of *Angels With Dirty Faces*.

Leo was inaccessible.

Huntz Hall suggested Kay talk to Leo's Agent. It worked.

Leo's agent caught a whiff of the Georgia Peach, smiled ear-to-ear and happily introduced her to Leo.

"How nice to meet you, Leo. I'm Kay Marvis. I'm a Goldwyn Girl—a dancer and an actress. If it's not too much trouble, could I get you to sign my autograph book?"

Leo thought for sure Kay could see his knees knocking.

"Uh, sure, yeah, I mean I ain't got nuttin' tuh write wit."

"Oh, I have a pen in my purse."

Kay handed Leo the pen, casually stroking the back of his hand with her silky-soft, slender fingers. The fresh coat of red nail polish screamed, *Aren't you burning with desire for me?*

"Places, everyone!" Yelled director, Michael Curtiz.

Not now, was the solitary thought in Leo's mind. Her sparkling blue eyes locked onto his like two heat-seeking missiles. Leo's heart pounded like a metronome on cocaine. A thousand butterflies took flight in his stomach. His eyes fell from the curls adorning her face and neck, to her full, firm breasts, outlined by her translucent white cotton blouse.

A distant echo. "Quiet on the set! Places, everyone!"

Rivers of adrenalin dried up Leo's saliva, rendering his tongue useless. Her thighs...her legs...her ankles.... *My God!*

Kay teased her ruby-red lips into a smile, then parted them ever so slightly, exposing the tip of her moist tongue, pressed against her perfect white teeth.

"Oh, I'm so sorry, Leo."

Kay slid a silky hand over the devastating curves of her waist and hip, and down the length of her pleat covered thigh.

"I'm keeping you from your work. See you again?"

"Uh, yeah...I, uh, I gotta go...."

"It was nice meeting you."

Huntz came over. "Nice goin', Leo. Jack's on duh way ovuh."

"Jack who?"

"Jack Warner, who d'yuh tink? Curtiz had tuh shoot anudduh scene on accounta you weren't dere."

Leo wasn't listening. He collapsed in a nearby chair, higher than a kite.

SEX CAN BE FUN....

Sex can be a lot of fun when you're not fighting
...but most of the time you are.

—Leo Gorcey (1968)

When news of his daughter's celebrity squeeze reached Kay's daddy, back in Georgia, Old Man Marvis threatened by phone and Western Union to annul any attempt on the part of the lovebirds to hook up.

Was that wisdom? Probably so. But Kay was in Hollywood. And Daddy was in Georgia.

Leo chartered a plane and the lovebirds lifted off for Yuma, Arizona, to get hitched.

Leo and Kay repeated the wedding scene at the Blessed Sacrament Catholic Church in Hollywood. This time, for Kay's Ma.

The two ceremonies made a bad idea legal.

In the black trunks, Leo Gorcey—Dead End Kid.

In the white trunks, Catherine 'Kay' Marvis—Goldwyn Girl.

ROUND 1

Leo's marriage to Kay makes headlines in the local rags: Hollywood Tough Guy Goes Soft.

"Leo, I understand your bride is from Georgia."

"Yeah, dat's right."

"Have you ever been to Georgia, Leo?"

"Nah, I nevuh been downnair."

"Are you and Kay planning to go back for a visit?"

"Nah, I wouldn't go. Nuttin' but lazy ex-slave owners."

"Lazy ex-slave owners?"

"Yeah. I read *Gone Wit duh Wind.* I wish I'd a-been livin' downnair den. I woulda been a woise general dan General Shoiman. I'd a-shown dose lazy southerners plenty."

Kay came out swinging.

The black and white photo above the interview copy shows Kay rubbing shaving cream in the wise guy's face. The look on

her face? Her glare could have turned Old Faithful into a stalag-
mite.

A publicity stunt? It didn't matter. The contempt was no
act.

ROUND 2

Leo and Kay were taking a bath together. A romantic idea,
right? Sure it was, until the Dead End Kid cupped his hands
together and squirted water in Kay's eyes.

"What the hell did ya do that for? You got soap in my eyes,
ya crazy son-of-a-bitch!"

Kay hauled off and spit in Leo's face.

Like the flammable cars of a derailing train, each reaction
exploded into the one before it. The damage was exponential.

Leo fetched a glass of cold water and threw it in Kay's face.

Kay was in shock.

"Two can play dat game!" Leo sneered, bloated with bravado.

"You mean-tempered, abusive bastard!" She ran, naked, out
of the bathroom.

Fuck her, thought Leo, *I'm finishin' my bath.*

Before Leo could raise himself out of the warm water to
investigate the jostling sound at the bathroom door, he was paralyzed by a freezing cold flood. Kay had fetched a large bucket
and filled it with ice water.

"There, ya sonofabitch! Serves ya right. Now ya know how
it feels."

Leo flew out of the tub in a flurry of bubbles, water flying
everywhere. Kay retreated to the bedroom, threw on her bathrobe, and locked the door. She grabbed for the phone to call a
friend. The door crashed open, splinters flying.

Leo aimed the garden hose at Kay. It was on full force. Kay
let out a blood-curdling scream and leaped over the bed, skid-
ding on her stomach, on the soaking wet carpet, to the doorway.

Leo chased her through every room in the house like a fire-
man on LSD. "Don't ever spit at me again, goddammit! Don't

you ever spit at me again!"

Kay escaped into the street.

Leo's anger spent, he climbed in the car and fishtailed down the driveway. He aimed the hood ornament on his jalopy toward the nearest watering hole for something to medicate the pain.

Kay had to dive into the bushes to avoid being run over.

For a fleeting moment, Leo was stung by the realization that repairing the water damage to his home would set him back thousands of dollars.

Fuck it, he thought. *It was worth it! She'll nevuh spit at me again, dat's fer sure!*

Besides, in a few minutes, he'd be too drunk to care.

ROUND 3

"Hey, Leo!" Huntz came up from behind Leo and slapped him on the back.

"Hey, Durante, easy on duh threads, will yuh?"

"Didd'ya hear duh news?" asked Huntz. "We're goin' on tour!"

"Why don't yuh go on a *detour* an' leave me alone. I had anudduh fight wit Kay. I ain't in duh mood fer company."

"Maybe yuh jist need to get out an' have some fun wit her! Why doncha' bring her along?"

"Because, Doctor Freud, we'd end up killin' each udduh, dat's why!"

"Ahhh, Leo, dere yuh go exaggeratin' again. I tink it's a lovely idea!"

"*You* tink it's a lovely idea! You ain't even married. Wuht duh hell do you know?"

"An' I ain't nevuh gonna be after wuht you been trough."

"Get outta here before I rip yer nose off an' use it fer a pogo stick!" wisecracked Leo.

"Hey, no need gettin' violent, chief, I'm jist sayin' maybe yuh oughtta give it a whirl. You been woikin' day an' night fer two months straight. Maybe duh broad jist needs to get outta duh house!"

"Yeah. Arright, Cupid. But if it don't woik, I'm puttin' you in duh trunk uh duh car and pushin' it off a cliff. Yuh got dat?"

"Yeah, Yeah, whatevuh you say, Chief."

Two weeks into the personal appearance tour to promote the Warner Brothers' Dead End Kids pictures, Leo and Kay left the theater in search of a nightclub.

They were arguing.

The other Kids wanted Kay to join the stage act they all performed before meeting the fans and signing autographs. The Kids figured the Goldwyn Girl would be a real showstopper. They figured right.

Leo didn't agree. He argued that he wanted to protect Kay from the evils of show business.

Was he competitive or just insecure? He was certainly threatened.

His fear that the Kids would out-vote him put Leo in fight-or-flight mode. He needed a drink.

Leo walked ahead of Kay and followed the sound of lively music to a hole-in-the-wall bar. He spouted a shrill complaint to the bouncer about the high cover, then peeled the bills off the wad he carried in his silver money clip.

"Don't spend it all in one place," he cracked to the guy who collected his money.

Leo and Kay drank, and argued, argued and drank, and drank some more.

"What's the harm in it, Leo? It would be fun!"

"No wife of uh mine's gonna work, and dat's final!" Leo spouted.

"But, honey, it'll help you."

"It ain't gonna help me 'cause it ain't gonna happen!" yelled Leo.

The music went up. A stripper mounted the stage, looking like she just stepped out of a centerfold. Leo was mesmerized. Kay was disgusted. She turned away and left the bar in search of a sympathetic ear.

When the stripper came strutting out of her dressing room,

Leo pushed his way over to her and struck up a conversation. She recognized him.

"Hey, aren't you part of that Warner Brothers thing going on over at the theater?"

"Yeah. We're promotin' our latest pictuh, *Angels Wit Doity Faces* wit Jimmy Cagney."

"You know *Jimmy Cagney*?"

"Do I know 'im? I'm in duh pictuh wit him!"

A tap on Leo's shoulder. Leo turned around. Kay kicked a field goal through his groin. He dropped to the floor in exquisite agony.

"It was your performance, sweetie," spit Kay. "It was a knockout!"

With that, Kay bolted out of the club and back to the theater, hoping to find one of the other Kids hanging around the dressing room.

The Dead End Kid stumbled out into the street and followed her. He found her back at the theater in the dressing room alone. Kay knew the look.

Leo battered her face, slapping her into the wall.

Kay reached over to the prop table, grabbed a large hatpin and jabbed it into Leo's ass.

"Get away from me, you animal! I'm callin' the cops. They're gonna lock you up and throw away the key, you abusive bastard!"

"Yeah?" screamed Leo. "How yuh gonna call duh cops after I bash yer fuckin' brains out?"

Leo grabbed a chair and swung at Kay's head. Kay ducked. The chair bounced off the wall and broke Leo's nose. It was a bloody mess.

Kay's eye was turning black and her face was swelling up.

Did the Dead End Kid apologize to Kay? Did he ask her forgiveness for napalming her self-esteem? Did he walk away, realizing he had it coming? Did he ask for help? Not in this lifetime.

But he swore off throwing chairs against walls. So he said.

ROUND 4

Leo's eyes popped open.

Wuht duh fuck was dat? He thought.

It was two-thirty in the morning. Leo reached for the Smith & Wesson .38 caliber he kept loaded on the nightstand. His hand came up empty.

The light switched on. Leo spun around.

Kay had the .38 in her right hand, pointed straight at Leo's head. In her left hand, she was dangling a handkerchief with lipstick on it.

"What the hell is this, lover boy?"

Leo tried to think.

"It's not wuht yuh tink, sweetheart. If yuh jist lower duh piece an' calm down a second, I can explain," mumbled Leo.

"You can explain now, before I splatter your brains all over the headboard!"

Kay wasn't kidding. Leo was too drunk to be scared.

"Yer mudduh came by duh set today. She was worried...."

"Don't tell me this is my mother's lipstick, you lyin' sonofabitch."

"Dat's exactly wuht I'm tellin' yuh! Now put down duh piece."

Leo lunged for Kay. Kay pulled the trigger. Nothing happened.

"Yuh dumb fuckin' broad. I always keep duh foist chambuh empty in case somebody gets duh drop on me."

Kay burst out sobbing.

"An' inci-dentally, fer yer infuhmation, yer mudduh happens to be more demonstrative dan you evuh were!"

"Goddamm you, Leo, I hate you! I never know where you are. The only reason you come here is to to sleep. I go to dinner parties with you. You entertain everyone at the party for hours, and all I end up with is your drunk carcass gasping for breath at two in the morning!"

Leo emptied out the gun, put the bullets under his pillow, took a shot out of the ubiquitous silver flask of Hill & Hill, and passed out.

"Did you hear a single word I said, Leo?"

Kay plopped herself down on the foot of the bed, her face a mess of tears and mascara.

"Who lives like this? You disappear for days at a time and don't even have the decency to tell me where you've been f'crissake! Leo...LEO!"

He was already snoring. Kay grabbed a pillow and started punching it.

"You're a child, Leo. Can you hear me? When are you gonna grow up?"

Kay jumped up, slammed the bedroom door, cried her way into the living room, picked up the phone and dialed her mother's number.

"Mom...yeah, I know it's late. I just wanted to ask you something...."

Honeymooning with Kay

EARLY MARKSMANSHIP TRAINING

Did I mention, Dad had a thing for guns?

The Dead Ender's fascination with firearms began innocently enough. Much like many young boys.

Leo's parents were out for the evening. An adult Christmas party. Kids not invited. Leo was eleven.

"Dey're gone!" Leo whispered to his brothers, Freddie and David.

Trading off with one BB gun, the Gorcey Boys blasted every ornament on the Christmas tree to smithereens.

Bernard and Josephine couldn't believe the mess.

Bernard spoke first. "Wuht duh fuck happened here? Dose hooligans! I'm gonna...."

Josephine grabbed Bernard. "Calm down, Papa. You don't know if the boys are...."

Bernard pushed past Josephine and tromped into the Boys' bedroom. They were sound asleep. Not a creature was stirring, not even a mouse.

By morning, Josephine had cleaned up the mess and dressed the tree with more ornaments. No one ever spoke of the incident.

When the Dead End Kids went on personal appearance tours for Warner Brothers, they were paid for their stage performances in cash.

After a performance in Philadelphia, Billy Halop spoke up in the dressing room. "Hey, you guys. I'm worried about our dough. We got ovuh six thousand bucks in cash here. Wuht if we get rolled?"

Huntz piped up. "Silly boy, if we get rolled, it ain't duh dough I'm gonna be worried about!"

"Wise up, Huntz! If we lose all duh dough, we ain't got nuttin' to live on, yuh moron!"

Leo, the gang treasurer, stepped in. "Arright, Arright all you geniuses. Listen up. Dis is a very simple problem."

"Shoot, Leo."

"Well, Billy Boy, all we gotta do is mosey on down tuh duh pawn shop an' poichase a piece. We can take duh money outta duh till."

"Good idea, Leo." Halop smiled. "I saw a pawn shop about six blocks from here. We'll do it foist ting in duh mornin'."

Next night after the performance, Leo called the meeting to order in the dressing room, unwrapped the pistol, and placed it on the table in front of the gang. The boys crowded around.

"Wow!" Huntz reached down to pick it up. Leo slapped his hand.

"Get yer hands off duh moichendise, Schnozola. It's loaded!"

Huntz mimed a Tommy gun. "da-da-da-da-da-da-da-da...."

"Shuddup, Al Capone. Dis meetin's called tuh order," barked Leo.

"Dat's how I got duh part in Dead End yuh know," Huntz bragged. "Sidney Kingsley came tuh de audition and asked if any of us could make a sound like a machine gun."

Billy Halop cut him off. "We've hoid it a thousand times, Huntz. Give it a rest. If it woin't fuh me, yuh wouldn'a been at dat audition."

"Arright, arright arready!" Leo cut in. "Enuff uh duh bickerin'. Now, boys, we gotta test dis ting tuh see if it woiks."

"How we gonna do dat, chief?" Huntz puzzled.

"I'll tell ya' how, Huntz, my boy. Everybody follow me."

Leo led the boys into the backstage bathroom. He said, "Arright. Cover yer ears. I'm gonna fire duh heater down duh commode."

When the smoke cleared, water was trickling through a crack in the toilet bowl, forming a small puddle on the bathroom floor.

"Shit, Leo, yuh blasted duh goddamm toilet in half!" yelled Halop.

"Don' worry about it, boys. Once a plumber, always a plumber. I'll glue duh bowl innuh mornin'. It'll be jist like new."

A few weeks later, Martha Raye performed at the same theater, used the same toilet, and had to have stitches in her butt.

Much like the bathtub, Leo tried to hook up while working for Uncle Rob—the toilet bowl repair was left unfinished.

THIS WAS DONE BY AN EMPTY GUN

By the time he retired to Northern California, Leo Gorcey had a gun collection Charleton Heston would die for.

The man who parted the Red Sea recently told Michael Moore in the film *Bowling for Columbine*, "I never expect to have to use a gun to defend myself."

"Never?" Moore asked.

Heston shook his head and smiled. "Never!"

The Patriarch of the NRA insisted he owns guns, not to defend himself, but, well, because it's his constitutional right.

No such poppycock for the Dead End Kid. Leo Gorcey couldn't care less about his constitutional rights. He didn't need the constitution. I'm certain Leo believed he could have ad-libbed the constitution better than our forefathers scripted it.

No, my father owned guns because of the high. The power high—to be exact. And the adrenalin rush he got from shooting 'em off. And the fantasy that he was an undercover FBI agent. That is, when he didn't think he was working for the Mafia.

Think *A Beautiful Mind*.

The retired actor actually leaped out of bed one night at his Northern California ranch, and fired nineteen rounds into the side of his blue Mercury sedan.

Dad feared the mafia was out to whack him.

In all the confusion of the gun battle, the Dead End Kid failed to recognize that he was firing at his own car.

From age thirteen on, I was allowed to grab a gun pretty much anytime, and go out shooting squirrels, jackrabbits, and other small game. I don't recall if Dad decided I was old enough, or if he was just too drunk to notice.

Either way, it wasn't long before I screwed up. One afternoon, while Dad was out, I got curious and took an inventory of his firearm collection.

I counted off twenty-two firearms in all. Here is a partial list of small artillery I found in Muggsy's gun cabinet:

30 ought six rifle

30-30 carbine

.22 caliber rifle

.22 caliber pistol

Beretta pistol

.38 caliber *Midnight Special* (Leo's favorite to conceal in his belt.)

.44 magnum handgun (Dad called this one *The Cannon* and often carried it under the driver's seat of his Mercury sedan.)

.410 gauge, double-barreled shotgun

.12 gauge, double-barreled shotgun

I picked up the .410 gauge, double-barreled shotgun. What started as an eerie reverence, turned to careless tinkering.

I poked my forefinger around the trigger guard. Then inside the trigger guard. Then I fingered the trigger. Then I pulled the trigger.

I was frozen solid by an ear-splitting explosion.

Fear Brain spoke first: *Your little sister and brother are wandering around here somewhere. There's no way you didn't kill one of them. On second thought, you don't want to know. Let's just stay put.*

Like the proverbial deer, I was frozen solid in the headlights, my mind racing too fast to decipher my own thoughts.

Critical Parent Brain spoke: *How could you be so stupid...to pull the trigger of a shotgun without checking the chamber?*

Defense Counsel Brain leapt to its feet: *How could Dad be so stupid...a stockpile of loaded guns sitting right out in the open...not even a lock to keep me from just grabbing a gun and shooting it into the wall. What a moron!*

Child Brain immediately censored the word, "moron."

You know very well it's forbidden to call our dad a moron. He'll kick yer ass. Which means he'll kick my ass. And I'm sick and tired of getting my ass kicked. Besides, you still need his approval!

Executive Brain cut everybody off: *Attention all nerves and muscles. The coast is clear! You can move now! Proceed with caution and watch for blood.*

I slogged through the avocado-green shag carpet, down the hallway, past the walk-in closet, toward Dad's master bathroom. The direction the gun barrel was pointing when I pulled the trigger.

Fear Brain was back: *Get ready to see a dead sibling on the floor...came through the door right before you pulled the trigger....*

Executive Brain took over: *Everybody stay off this frequency until we get to the bathroom!*

I could hear a pin-drop. The board meeting in my brain had fallen silent. I poked my head inside Dad's bathroom. No bodies.

Rational Brain finally decided to show up at the meeting: *All right. Let's all just calm down here. No blood. No bodies. No dead siblings. This is good news. The worst is over. It's all downhill from here.*

Cut off by Fear Brain: *Look at the size of that hole in the wall!*

I spot the six-inch pattern of buckshot imbedded in the door molding.

Rational Brain: *All right, let's just calm down. It's not that bad. We could've hit the antique mirror. Damage control may still be possible.*

Fear Brain shoves rational brain out of the boardroom: *Listen, you schmuck, this is a major disaster, okay? We're talkin' catastrophe here. You might as well put your head between your knees and kiss yer ass good-bye! You're TOTALLY screwed, okay? You'd better just run like hell!*

But where could I run where Muggsy wouldn't find me?

I was completely exhausted from the hormone lollapalooza, never mind the craziness going on at the Synaptic Convention in my brain.

I put the gun away and took a long walk to the far corner of our almond orchard. I sat there among the dirt clods until I heard my dad hollering for me in the distance. Why did I have to go back to the house? Why couldn't I just keep walking? To the next town? To the next state?

Why? Because I was thirteen years old, that's why. I was still dependent on a crazy alcoholic for my survival.

It took Muggsy about three minutes to find the mess of buckshot and shredded pine in the molding of his bathroom door. One trip to his bedroom, one trip back to the kitchen. There it was. Bigger than the planet Jupiter. My Master Screw-Up.

The thing about living with an alcoholic is, ya never know. There's just no way to predict what the crazy addict in the family is gonna do next!

Fear Brain had fully prepared me for the beating of my life.

I didn't even bother to act surprised. In a catatonic state, I rattled off my best stupid defense. Rational Brain could have come up with something so much better. But Fear Brain had chained the boardroom door from the inside, locking Rational Brain in the waiting room.

"I thought the gun was empty," I whimpered.

Shame Brain jumped up. *What a loser. Is that the best you can do? Can't you stand up to this old drunk? Look at yourself! You're three inches taller than him!*

After a half-hour of thunderous hollering, Dad pushed his face up into mine until I could feel the heat of his breath on my cheek. Spittle was running down his chin. He raised his hand to punch me.

I didn't move. Not because I was taller than him, but because I was scared shitless.

He froze, his fist in the air, an inch from my face. I don't know how long he stood there.

Then the Dead End Kid lowered his fist and left the room. He emerged from his office, minutes later, with a 12-inch square piece of cardboard. On the homemade placard, Leo had penned this clever bit of poetry: THIS WAS DONE BY AN EMPTY GUN!

He fastened the cardboard sign directly over the spot where the shotgun blast had blown part of the bathroom door to smithereens.

He never repaired the damage. When his friends dropped by for drinks, he paraded them into his bathroom to gawk at the mess.

In his finest Slip Mahoney Brooklyn squeal, "Dis is duh hole my son put in duh wall wit' an EMPTY GUN!"

Each time, the onlookers reacted with appropriate shock and laughter on cue. Me? I wanted to shrivel up and die.

My father never touched me again. Maybe he thought that wall full of buckshot was too close for comfort.

Dad Cleans the "Empty" Gun

TARGET PRACTICE

It started out as a harmless idea, and ran amuck from there.

Muggsy got a rush from shooting things.

He hunted deer, pheasant, and quail. But that wasn't enough. He couldn't hunt game every day. But he wanted to shoot every day.

He started out with the traditional soup cans balanced on fence posts and tree stumps. Boring. Cans didn't do anything. From a distance, he couldn't even tell if he hit a can or not, except for the anti-climactic motion of the can rolling lazily onto the ground.

"Did I hit duh goddamm ting, or did it jist roll off duh fuckin' stump?" Leo would ask, ordering me down-range to inspect the can.

Dad put his thinking cap on and rattled his brain to invent a better target practice mousetrap.

One summer morning, the announcement came. "Hey Mastuhmind, cancel yer plans for Satuhday. I need your help all day."

I had been planning to visit a friend.

"What do you need me for, Dad?" I whined.

"None uh yer fuckin' business! Just be dere!"

I don't know why I bothered to ask.

Saturday morning, Dad ordered me to dig four postholes. I hated digging postholes. I got back at him by taking forever.

"Why duh fuck ain'tcha diggin' duh postholes?"

"Gotta let the water soak in, Dad. Dirt's too hard."

"Well, come an' get me when yer done. I need a drink."

I piddled around with those postholes for half a day, then we sunk four redwood posts, one on each corner of a six-foot square. We nailed up a continuous roll of chicken wire around the outside of all four posts. I held the wire stretcher while Dad drove the staples over the chicken wire and into the redwood.

He wielded a hammer with the vengeance of Thor himself.

Large drops of sweat trickled down his broad forehead and plopped to the dirt. Sweat stains spread slowly through the fabric of his cowboy shirt.

Dad worked to forget.

I can't wait to be like Dad and wear cowboy shirts with sweat stains and a Stetson, I remember thinking, *and own a bunch of guns I can shoot off whenever I want.*

I even wanted to smell like him.

The chicken wire rose four feet above the ground on all four sides.

As he drove the last staple, Dad announced, "Dis is duh Bull Pen!"

The Bull Pen? I thought. *Right. Okay, then...what now? Do we round up a tiny little bull and....*

Dad cut in. "Now we're gonna fill it up wit empty whiskey bottles."

Whoa. Way too big, I thought. *We coulda built it one quarter that size, and I could have gone over to my friend Mark's place and hung out in his tree house.*

I was wrong.

The Bull Pen overflowed with empty whiskey bottles in less then three weeks.

Good-bye, cans. Hello, bottles.

Dad sent me out to the Bullpen to gather up fifteen empty whiskey bottles. "Yer job is tuh line up dose bottles on de edge udduh river bank!"

At thirteen, all I'm thinking is, *Is that all I get to do, is line up the bottles? What about me shooting the guns?*

I lined up all the bottles on the edge of the bank of the Sacramento River. Which happened to be in our front yard. All the while, I'm thinking. *Maybe, if I do a good enough job lining up these bottles, he'll let me shoot off a round or two...or maybe not. Not if he's still pissed at me for shooting up his bathroom with the shotgun.*

The Dead End Kid carted three pistols and three rifles from the gun cabinet and laid them out on our front lawn. A box of matching cartridges next to each gun.

"Got dose bottles ready, Mastuhmind?"

"Yes, sir." Chances of me getting to shoot: Fair to good.

Dad started shooting. His silver flask was in his cowboy boot, handy for the emergency *nip*.

The transformation was complete: From Hollywood to the Ponderosa. From Dead End Kid and Bowery Boy to Billy the Kid and Ben Cartwright. From actor and producer to undercover FBI agent and part-time Mafia Capo.

My celebrity father had given me a valuable lesson on how a person goes about reinventing himself. They don't teach survival skills like that in school.

No one could deny it. Drunk or sober, Leo had *cojones* like nobody's business.

Leo's Brand

THE CANNON

No doubt about it—target practice with bottles was a winner! This was the kind of action that could entertain the Dead End Kid for hours on end! All that noise, glass shattering, bottles exploding. Muggsy was in Hog Heaven.

That first afternoon, Leo shot the hell out of those bottles from three in the afternoon until after dark. Cases of cartridges spent.

"Now police up dose casings, Mastuhmind." (Dad was fond of military jargon. A throw back to the Bowery Boys Armed Forces comedies).

Muggs reloaded for the next volley and swaggered up to the firing line to "...shoot duh livin' shit outta dose bottles."

He paused between reloads to take a *belt* from the ubiquitous silver flask of Hill & Hill. Back to the firing line for the main attraction—the .44 magnum.

"Dis is duh fuckin' Cannon. Dis is duh biggest handgun dey make!" slurred the Kid.

"Can I shoot it once, Dad?"

"Are you crazy? Duh kick would take yer fuckin' arm off!"

The master marksman showed me how to compensate for The Cannon's 'kick.'

I was in awe of the .44 magnum. I was in awe of my father, Leo Gorcey. The Gunslinger.

A true cowboy, I thought. *I can't wait to be like him. Then I can buy my own Cannon and shoot it off whenever I want, without having to get permission. That'll be a glorious day.*

Four more shots and one whiskey bottle explodes, blasting a thousand shards of glass into the dusky air. Then a strange sound.

"Dad...Dad! Did you hear that?"

"Did I hear wuht?"

Three more shots ring out. No hits.

"That! It sounds like someone yelling!"

Muggs wasn't listening. His eyes blazed, his face distorted with all the urgency of a gunfighter on his way to the O.K. Corral.

His devilish opponent? A tall Seagram's Gin bottle.

"Dad?"

"Not now, goddammit!"

He squeezes the trigger and misses by a mile. Dad's aggravated. He hears the yelling and it's breaking his concentration.

"Who duh fuck is dat?"

"I been tryin' to tell ya, Dad. I think there's somebody down there on the river!"

"Well, get downnair an' find out who duh fuck it is!"

I run to the edge of the bank and peer down. It's about thirty yards to the blue-green water below. Water temperature's in the fifties, and it's a long way across the river. Too cold for most people to swim it, especially with the current being over five knots.

If you fall overboard in the Sacramento River, even with a life jacket, you're in a world of trouble.

I race up from the edge of the riverbank. "Dad, there's a man in a boat down there!"

"Wuht's a madduh wit 'im? Don't he hear duh stinkin' gunfire? Wuht duh hell is he doin' just sittinnair?"

"Fishing, I think...."

"Well, get back downnair an tell 'im if he don't wanna get his fuckin' head blown off, tuh get duh hell outta dere! He's not gonna catch any ting downnair anyway."

"But, Dad...."

"I said fuck 'im! Now, get back downnair an take some uh dese empty bottles witcha'."

Thank God the fisherman was leaving when I got back to the riverbank. No way I was gonna tell him to "get duh fuck outta dere!"

Leo was reloading The Cannon and cursing the fisherman under his breath. "Wait'll I'm finished wit dat little cocksucker. I'll sink his fuckin' boat, den we'll see who's yellin' at who. Duh crazy bastid...."

Another *belt* from the flask of Hill & Hill.

The shrinking fisherman's tiny outboard buzzed off down the Sacramento River, just in time to clear Muggsy's next volley.

The fisherman was looking back at us, shaking his fist and howling at the top of his lungs. "I'm callin' the Sheriff on you, you crazy sons-a-bitches!"

Oh no, I worried, *the guy's gonna report me? I didn't even do anything! I didn't get to shoot the gun once and I'm being reported to the sheriff!*

Muggsy drooled, "Fuck 'im."

The Cannon exploded with fury. Whiskey bottles burst and glass flew everywhere.

It was getting dark. I couldn't figure out how Dad could hit anything. I couldn't even see!

Bleary-eyed, Muggsy retired to his living room cocktail bar, while I stayed behind in the dark and shoveled shards of glass over the edge of the riverbank.

"Can I do it tomorrow?" I had asked, when he told me to "Clean up."

"No, goddammit," he'd barked. "I want it done now!"

The surviving bottles went back to the Bull Pen.

SHERIFF ERNIE

The motion detector triggered a light switch, and nine 150-watt floodlights lit up our driveway like a night game at Angel Stadium.

Dad installed the floodlights so we could play shuffleboard at night. And to foil the Mafia and the FBI, in case either of them attempted to sneak up on him.

The vehicle responsible for triggering the floodlights belonged to the town Sheriff. The townsfolk knew him as Sheriff Ernie. The Dead End Kid knew him simply as, Oinie.

Ernie's rugged looks matched his profession. Six feet, solid as a rock, jet-black hair and mustache, both neatly cut. Not a speck of dirt under his nails. The resonance of his deep voice left no doubt as to his authority to enforce the law. The uniform did the rest.

Fear came over me at the sight of the black-and-white cruiser, the uniformed Sheriff, the badge, the guns, the handcuffs. Sheriff Ernie could kill me or strip me of my freedom at the drop of a hat.

I worried. *I'm going to jail with Dad for attempted murder.*

Ernie smiled easily and waved a friendly hand. I exhaled a sigh of relief. *Whew! Guess if he'd come for me, he wouldn't be so friendly.* I waved back—a feeble smile on my face.

Why do I feel so damned guilty when I haven't even done anything? That's a question that would haunt me well into adulthood.

Dad popped through the screen door and extended his hand in a cheerful welcome. He was oblivious. I'm sure he thought Ernie was just dropping by for a drink.

Ernie followed Dad into the house. The screen door slammed itself behind them.

Dad loved that gas operated gizmo that slammed the screen door. Kept the flies out. But Dad could never seem to get the gizmo adjusted quite right. So the screen door never just closed. It slammed.

I followed Sheriff Ernie through the door at a safe distance, pretending to have something important to do in the house so I could go in and eavesdrop on the conversation.

The screen door slammed itself behind me.

Once inside, Dad offered Ernie a *belt*. Sheriff Ernie bellied up to Dad's custom-made cocktail bar.

The knotty pine panels making up the front of the Town Celebrity's bar, were emblazoned with authentic cattle brands. When Leo was customizing the house, he had invited all his rancher friends over to fire up their branding irons and smolder their Bar-T's and Rocking R's into the front of the bar. The cattle brands across the front of the bar made Leo's rancher friends feel right at home.

The Dead End Kid was nothing, if not an affable host.

In the background, Pat Boone was crooning *Love Letters in the Sand* on the Hi-Fi.

I prayed to myself, *Please, please don't let Dad say, 'Go outside and play!'* I was dying to see how he was gonna get out of this one!

God answered my prayer, or Dad was too drunk to notice. Who knows which? Either way, this would be a better show than *Zorro*, which I was gladly missing, just to listen in on this conversation.

Sheriff Ernie hooked his thumb around his black leather gun belt until it made that crunchy noise, like when a cowboy is shifting around in his saddle.

This is it, I thought. Here we go!

Ernie: "Leo, I gotta call on the radio...dispatcher says a fisherman called in about five minutes ago from LeBaron's Fishing Camp...claims you were shooting at him. You can't shoot at fishermen, Leo."

Leo: "I wasn't shootin' at duh stinkin' fishuhman, Oinie! I couldn't even see him downnair! How duh fuck could I be shootin' at him?"

Ernie: "Well, he says he yelled up at you several times and you just kept shooting! You can't do that, Leo."

Leo shoved a Chivas on the rocks across the bar, and toasted the Sheriff.

"Downna hatch!"

Ernie knocked back a slug of his favorite scotch. Leo always had a bottle on hand—he never drank the stuff himself.

Dad vanished for a minute and reappeared behind the bar with a short-barreled rifle. The kind you see stuffed in the saddle scabbards on all those old westerns.

"You're not gonna shoot me, are ya, Leo?"

Was he kidding? I couldn't tell. I sure didn't blame him for asking.

"Shoot you, Oinie? Hell no! I wouldn't last a week in duh slammer. It's dry as duh Sahara Desert in dere!"

I thought I heard the Sheriff let out a sigh of relief.

Leo set the rifle down on the bar in front of Ernie like some people spread out snapshots of their grandkids.

Leo: "Hey, Oinie, getta loadda dis beauty I picked up de udduh day from Whitey Disher."

Ernie: "Hey, what is that, a 30-30...a Winchester? Lemme see that."

The Sheriff knocked back another drink. The ice cubes clinked as he set the empty glass down on the bar. He lifted the lightweight carbine to his khaki-covered shoulder and focused his right eye down the barrel, his whiskery cheek hugging the stock.

Ernie: "Damn. This is sweet, Leo."

Leo: "Yeah, why doncha take it out and give it a whoil?"

Ernie: "I think I'll take you up on that."

Leo: "I'm havin' anudduh drink."

Leo refreshed both glasses; Hill & Hill for himself and another round of Chivas for Ernie the Peace Officer.

Ernie balanced the carbine on the bar stool next to him so he wouldn't forget to take it with him.

Ernie: "Hey, where's your dart board, Leo? You up for a game?"

Leo: "Comin' right up."

After a lively dart throwing contest and another round of drinks, the Sheriff forgot all about the Fisherman who almost got his boat sunk and his head blown off by Leo's .44 magnum Cannon.

Ernie: "By the way, Leo, can I get you to autograph one of your pictures for my daughter-in-law? She's up from Sacramento. She's a big fan of yours. She'll be thrilled!"

Muggsy tottered away and emerged from his office with a headshot of himself sporting the famous Bowery Boy pinned-up fedora.

It had slipped Leo's mind to return the now-famous hat to the wardrobe department one day, after using it in a scene. He just started wearing the floppy fedora around everywhere. The next thing ya know, the hat became his trademark.

Leo: "What's her name?"

Ernie: "Donna."

Leo scribbled furiously and shoved the glossy across the bar.

Ernie, reading out loud. "To my friend Donna. Love and Kisses, Leo B. Gorcey.

"That's great, Leo. Donna will go crazy over this!"

On the way out the screen door, a slightly buzzed Sheriff Ernie tendered a jovial note of caution to the Town Celebrity.

"Now watch that target shooting, Leo. Just check and make sure it's all clear down there before you start shooting next time, Okay?"

"Okey Dokey, Oinee. Tanks fuh duh dart game. I'll practice up a little fuh next time."

"Anytime...hey, thanks a million for the picture, Leo. I owe you one."

I couldn't believe my ears. I owe you one?

Slip Mahoney had damn near killed a man, and the Town Sheriff was leaving the house smiling and chortling, "I owe you one!"

It was just like a Bowery Boys movie! And Dad was whacked out of his mind, to boot!

When I look back now, I think, *No wonder Dad never got help. He was surrounded by star-struck fans who protected him from the very consequences that could have saved his life.*

I recall something Leo's sidekick, Huntz Hall, once said. "Leo always wanted to be protected."

Dad's custom made cocktail bar at the ranch in Northern California. The long plaques hanging on the wall are copper engravings—one for each of Leo's movies!

A DEAD END FOR THE DEAD END KIDS

Leo and the Kids raised plenty of hell at Warner Brothers. But that's not why Jack Warner tore up their contracts.

One day, Leo was summoned to Jack's office.

"Leo," Jack blustered, "we have a motto here at Warner Brothers." Jack pointed to a banner on the wall.

"Good Citizenship with Good Entertainment."

Leo squirmed in the overstuffed leather chair.

Jack pulled a letter out of his desk drawer. "Got this from the mail room this morning:

Dear Mr. Gorcey,
I am the governess of a little boy. He likes your pictures. But every time he comes home from one, he spits in my eye. Will you please write him and tell him you only act like that in your pictures?"

Leo smiled with embarrassment. "Pop, I...."

"This is not the first. I've got the Youth Authorities climbing up my ass on this, and I'm fighting a battle with the Production Code twenty-four hours a day, seven days a week. The Brits gave *Hell's Kitchen* their 'X' rating, f'crissake. And on top of that, I've got these goddamm congressional hearings to contend with."

"I could ansuh dese lettuhs if yuh want."

"I wish it were that easy, son. It's too late for that. I have no choice. I'm canceling all the Dead End Kids' contracts."

"But, Pop...."

"Don't worry, son. I'm keeping you and Bobby Jordan under contract. I can use a mug like yours around here for young dramatic roles."

"But wuht about...."

"I've made my decision, son. That's where it stands. You've made your last Dead End Kids picture on this lot. Take some time off. We'll be in touch."

CIRCLING THE DRAIN

Over the next year, Leo got little screen time at Warner Brothers. But he did get paid. $10,000 for two days work.

For the first time in eight years, Leo had downtime. There were endless hours to think. And drink. And think some more.

The hollow of his brain echoed like a broken record. *Why duh hell didn't I jist stay in New York? Why duh hell did I evuh get on dat train?*

I knew it. I knew it. Dis is exactly wuht happened tuh Papa. Dis is exactly why I didn't wanna be no fuckin' actor. I knew dis was gonna happen. An' gettin' hitched tuh dat gold digger, Kay...wuht duh hell was I tinkin'?

Foundering in a vicious whirlpool of alcohol and self-pity, Leo circled the drain.

In the bars, there were women struggling to swim against the suction of their own shipwrecked lives. Some were drowning. Some came on to the men with a seductive fury that veiled their rage toward the opposite sex until it was too late.

Leo reached out to these broken women, mistaking them for life preservers.

Kay's anger erupted into homicidal impulses. She tailed her husband one night. Caught him swaggering out of a bowling alley cocktail bar with a fawning hussy on each arm.

Kay tried to run Leo over, pumping the gas pedal with the fury of a woman scorned. Leo and his floozies came inches from being turned into road kill.

"Bitch!" slobbered Leo. "She could at least stop tuh see if she fuckin' killed anybody!"

As I re-lived this period in Dad's life, I ran headlong into a brick wall. I was stuck. I couldn't write any further. *Damn writer's block,* I thought.

By now, I knew better.

Out of my depression, a scary thought took shape. *How have I handled boredom in my life?*

Like scarlett O'Hara, I wanted to "Think about that tomorrow." But I knew I couldn't climb any further up the mountain without exploring this cave.

Better now than later, I reasoned.

A few hours of scary self-examination, and the verdict was in. *I was, indeed, a chip off the old block.*

I too had dealt with boredom by carousing, drinking, drugging, partying, and chasing women. Like my Daddy before me, I was oblivious to the consequences.

"Yuh know," I said to a friend, "all my life I've been afraid that I was doomed to repeat my father's mistakes. That it's in my genes. In my blood. That no matter what I do, I'm doomed to repeat my family's pattern of self-destructive behavior."

No band of angels appeared to reassure me that it wasn't true.

Instead, God appeared as a blanket of sadness, draping himself around me as I reluctantly allowed my mind to be led into a painful reverie of all the people who'd been hurt by my fear and cowardice. By my impulsive choices to numb out, shut down, and scream like a baby for the instant gratification, instead of dealing with my stuff.

The pain I caused my own two daughters by running away and hiding in alcohol, workaholism, and affairs.

But then something flip-flopped in my brain. Instead of feeling revulsion toward my father, I felt closer to him.

By admitting to myself that Dad and I were cut from the same cloth, that I made all the same mistakes my father made, that it wasn't Dad's fault that my life got screwed up, *but because of my choices*, I began to identify with Leo Gorcey from a fresh point of view.

For the first time, I felt empathy for my father.

I whispered the words, "I love you," as if my father were in the room.

THE EASTSIDE KIDS—
LIFE IN THE WOODSHED

After Warner Brothers, the Kids scattered. Some were drafted. Other studios tried to capitalize on the Dead End Kids phenomenon. Nice try, but no cigar.

A few of the Kids, including Huntz Hall, went to Universal, where they made a series of films called the *Little Tough Guys*. The critics panned the pictures as "indigestible."

Leo rejected the idea of languishing in Jack's stable as a Warner Brothers Once-Was. He walked off the Warner Brothers lot one day, and never came back. Jack let him go.

Then, Leo's phone rang.

"Leo, dis is Bobby Jordan."

"Angel, whadd'ya know?" crowed Leo, slipping easily back into the Dead End banter.

"Whadd'ya know yerself, Spit? Hahdly evuh see ya' round anymore."

"Well, yuh know," Leo pattered, "duh show must go on an' all dat jazz!"

"Yeah, right. So Leo, I'm ovuh at Monogram. Duh suits ovuh here are lookin' to form a gang. Dey wan' to call 'em duh Eastside Kids. I'm in wit duh producuh ovuh here—Sam Katzman. I even got my own managuh now—Jan Grippo. Anyway, I tole Sam I'd give yuh a yell an' see if yuh was intrested."

"Yeah? So, wuht's duh catch?"

"Well, duh money's not as good, an' duh pictures ain't like wit Bogey an' Cagney or nuttin' like dat, but it sure beats starvin'!"

Leo joined Bobby at Monogram. The next step was for Katzman to convince Gabe Dell and Huntz Hall to come over from Universal. He did, and they came.

Sam Katzman produced twenty-two Eastside Kids pictures

for Monogram Studios. All moneymakers.

Leo Gorcey and Huntz Hall emerged as the main attraction. The rest of the Kids dropped into the background. Leo was now snatching top billing on the lobbies and theater marquees. The sky was clearing. The sun would shine on Leo again.

But the fantasy-come-true of top billing wasn't doing it for Leo. He was still a peon. An employee of the studio. A clocker.

Leo learned at Warner Brothers that an actor's life was cheap. Somehow, he had to stack the deck in his favor.

The man who once said as a boy, "If bein' a star is wuht it takes tuh get yer own dressin' room, den dat's wuht I'm gonna be," couldn't lie down peacefully with the idea that his destiny was held entirely in the hands of the house.

Leo was a gambler. A novice, but a gambler nonetheless. Once he determined to stay in Hollywood, it was to beat the odds, not to live by the house rules. He could go home to Uncle Rob's and do that.

Nope. Leo had come too far. Made too many promises to himself. Not least of all, the promise to take care of Mama and Papa.

He had to live up to his expectations of himself, or pack it in for good. And he sure wasn't going back to New York with his tail between his legs. That might have flown after the filming of *Dead End*, but not now. There was no other option now, but for The Kid to become his own boss.

Leo tested the waters with Bobby.

"Did it evuh occur tuh you, Angel, dat Monogram's makin' a killin' off uh us, an' we're still gettin' paid peanuts?"

"Leo, I tink you an' Huntz oughtta siddown wit my managuh, Jan Grippo. He's got some smaht ideas about us Kids slicin' off a bigguh piece uh duh pie fuh ourselves. Says we might even be able tuh woik our own deal, bein' as if it woin't fer us kids, dey would'n have nuttin'."

In his mind's eye, Leo could see the piles of chips sliding across the felt, to his side of the table.

"Yeah," Leo chirped. "Let's have a little pow-wow wit dis guy, Grippo, an' surveil duh lan'scape!"

Lobby Poster for *The East Side Kids*

"I DON'T LIKE GORCEY GRABBING ALL THE GIRLS AROUND HERE!"

—Groucho Marx, 1943

In 1943, Dad had a steady gig at Monogram, churning out the Eastside Kids pictures.

Then came radio.

Leo got a call to do a guest spot with Orson Welles on a radio show called *Pabst Blue Ribbon Town*. The host? Groucho Marx.

Leo was not as comfortable on radio as he was in front of the camera. Though he often muffed his lines with Groucho, Leo was invited to co-star on three shows.

Groucho needled Leo on the air. "Sounds like ya had a little trouble with that line, Leo!" sniped Groucho on one program.

Then *Blue Ribbon Town* went off the air. But not before the short-lived program made Groucho a household name.

Feeling like he was back in the driver's seat, Leo got cocky. He sounded off to *Radio Life* magazine, "Radio ain't a bad racket! I not only get Groucho's girls, but I get a salary for it! Leaves me aphonous!" (Aphonous is a *moidered* derivative of a word meaning "speechless.")

Kay tagged along to the WABC studio while Leo taped the shows with Groucho. The Goldwyn Girl had been reduced to a blubbering basket case. She was down for the count.

While Leo and Groucho clowned around, Kay blubbered her little heart out to Groucho's daughter, Miriam.

Miriam was six years younger than Kay. Being celebrity daddy's girl, she grew up fast. Fourteen going on forty.

Miriam went to Daddy Groucho and sweet-talked him into offering Kay the equivalent of an upscale battered woman's shelter at Groucho's place in Westwood. Groucho opened up his home to Kay.

Leo objected. Objection overruled. Groucho would not be intimidated by Leo's blustering.

One morning, Miriam tidied up around the Marx residence and noticed that no one had slept in the guest room bed the night before.

Kay moved in. Miriam moved out.

Groucho and Kay married in 1945.

Leo scribbled off a note to the famous comedian. "Dear Groucho, since you're a millionaire, would you please intervene and persuade Kay to agree to give up her community property rights. I need the money more than you do!"

Groucho wrote back. "Dear Leo, I cannot interfere in this matter. Kay's money is her money and my money is my money."

Leo got the last laugh. When Kay and Groucho divorced, Leo published, "Little did Groucho know that when Kay ran out of my money, she was going to dip into his money even more than she had dipped into mine!"

When Leo and Kay made their last public appearance together in divorce court, Kay told the judge pretty much the same thing she'd been telling Leo all along. "He drinks too much, he carries a gun, he goes AWOL for days at a time with no explanation, and he refuses to grow up. Leo has never outgrown his role as Spit in Dead End!"

Divorce granted.

Leo and Groucho

AS AN ACTOR, YOU STINK!

The truth about my father as an actor is that no one ever really knew when he was acting and when he wasn't.

I could never tell, that's for sure. And I lived with the guy.

Looking back on my life with the Dead End Kid, I suspect he was always acting. I can't say I ever got to know the real Leo Gorcey.

Even today, I can't tell the difference between the guy I'm watching on the Bowery Boys movies, and the guy who hollered at me from the kitchen when I was fifteen years old. "Yuh want tuh get yer drivuh's license? Whadd'ya, fuckin' nuts? De only ting yer evuh gonna drive, is to drive me crazy!"

Most of his buddies agree, Leo hardly ever knew his lines.

They also agree that Leo's ad-libbing was far superior to the third-rate dialogue he was given to work with.

Some of Leo's directors are adamant that Leo was not sloppy. That he discussed script changes ahead of time with the directors.

Either way, Leo's fellow artists fell into two categories. Those who thought he was competent to brilliant, and those who thought he stunk.

The majority of Leo's fellows, and the critics, fell into the first category.

The director, Anatole Litvak, fell into the second category.

Litvak once crowed, "If I shoot a hundred takes of a scene, I am Litvak," implying that if he only shot it once, he was a hack.

Opposing Litvak was William "One-Shot" Beaudine, who directed several of the profitable Bowery Boys pictures. He trusted Leo's instincts and shot good pictures. He knew his craft. He had that rarest of gifts. He could edit in the camera.

Years before Litvak directed Bette Davis, Ingrid Bergman,

Henry Fonda, and Errol Flynn, he directed Leo Gorcey in a gangster film called *Out of the Fog*.

Leo went on loan to Warner Brothers to join fellow cast members Eddie Albert, John Garfield, Ida Lupino, and Paul Harvey.

Early one morning Leo dragged himself onto the set of *Out of the Fog* to shoot a scene with John Garfield.

"I gotta hangovuh," Leo announced. "So let's get dis in duh can. I need a drink. One shot."

"Fine, Mr. Gorcey. You do your job, and I'll do mine!" snapped the Hungarian director.

Litvak showed Leo his mark behind the bar. "You're serving Mr. Garfield a drink. Your line is 'One Bourbon coming up!'"

"Arright, let's shoot it," barked Leo.

Litvak assumed his post behind the camera, "Quiet on the set! Places! Action!"

"One Boibon, comin right up," chirped Leo.

"Cut!" yelled Litvak. "Feed him the line, please!"

Script assistant, dryly, "Sir, the line is 'One Bourbon, coming up.'"

"Thank you. Quiet! Places! Action!"

"One Boibon, comin' right up!"

Litvak spun around, grabbed the script from his assistant, and walked over to the bar. He slammed the script down in front of Leo. "Mr. Gorcey," he growled, "the line is, 'One Bourbon, coming up.' Please deliver the line as it's written. Thank you."

After the twelfth take, Litvak yelled, "Cut!" Then in a voice loud enough for all the cast and crewmembers to hear, he screamed, "Mr. Gorcey, AS AN ACTOR, YOU STINK!"

Leo staggered out from behind the bar, stalked up to Mr. Litvak and stuck his nose as close to Litvak's face as he could without getting burned by the cigarette dangling from the director's mouth.

"DON'T EVER SCREAM AT ME! DON'T EVER, EVER SCREAM AT ME! DON'T EVER, EVER, EVER SCREAM AT ME AGAIN!"

That thunderous performance made Leo thirsty. He walked

off the set.

The assistant director, a *Dead End* fan, followed Leo off the lot, and down the block to one of Leo's favorite watering holes.

"Gimme a shot uh Hill & Hill, Eddie," growled Leo.

The assistant director parked his carcass on the stool next to Leo's, shaking his head.

"Leo...please...do us all a favor and come back and finish the scene."

"Fuckin' Hungarian directors." Muggsy knocked back a shot.

"Leo...."

"Let 'im read duh goddamm line himself. I could shoot a whole fuckin' picture wit dat many takes f'crissake!"

"Leo, Jack has the power to make your life miserable. Don't fuck around. This could hurt you."

"Go back an' tell dat crazy Hungarian he can use one uh duh twelve takes he's arready got. I arready wasted two hours wit dat sonofabitch when I coulda been drinkin'. (To the bartender) Gimme annuduh shot, Eddie."

"Leo, grow up. You're not a kid anymore. Jack Warner doesn't fuck around with actors. He'll have you blackballed so fast it'll make yer head spin."

Leo paused, staring off into space as the alcohol kicked in.

"Hell," Leo smiled, "one ting's fuh sure. If I can't drink in peace, I might as well go back an' finish duh goddamm scene! (To the bartender) Eddie, I'll see yuh in twenty minutes."

"Good choice, Leo," sighed the assistant director.

"Yeah. Just keep dat crazy fuckin' Hungarian away from me. I'll take dat cigarette he's got danglin' from his kisser and shove it up his ass!"

When Leo and the A.D. walked back on the set, you could hear a pin drop.

The Hungarian shot five more takes.

After the fifth take, Litvak dropped his cigarette to the floor, ground it out with the toe of his black loafer, and walked over to Leo.

Motioning to Leo to lean closer, he whispered in his ear. "Gorcey, as an actor, you still stink. And I'm not screaming."

PENNY

Leo's first divorce didn't scare him. He went off to tour the saloons for a rich, young, Catholic. "Instead," Dad says, "I met a goil who was not rich, not Cat-lic, and not young."

The ink was hardly dry on Kay's divorce papers when Dad tied the knot with actress Evalene Bankston. Leo called her Penny.

When Penny decided to dabble in religion, she didn't go to catechism classes. Instead, she became a Rosicrucian.

One evening, after a rigorous day of sparring with his wife, Leo invited Penny to a Hollywood party.

"Screw you, Leo, you bastard. Go by yourself."

Leo grabbed his coat and flew out the door, *Fuck her*, Leo thought. *Who needs dis shit?*

Somewhere around 1:30 a.m., Leo stumbled through the front door of his house, mumbling something about the CIA bugging his phone.

"You stink!" scolded Penny. "Get yer ass in the shower and sober up, you stinkin' bum, or you can sleep on the couch!"

At the bedroom door, Leo stopped cold in his tracks. On the bedroom wall opposite the doorway, there hung a tacky, orange picture frame. In the center of the frame was a large three-dimensional, plastic eyeball.

Leo gaped at the eyeball. The eyeball 'stared' back. Leo moved to another part of the bedroom. The eye 'followed' him. No matter where he stood, the eye appeared to be 'looking' right at him.

Leo: "Uh, Penny, wuht duh hell is dis fuckin' eye doin' on duh bedroom wall?"

Penny gave Leo the cold shoulder. She grabbed a pencil and scrawled on a piece of scratch paper, *This eye is the symbol of my new Rosicrucian religion.*

She crumpled the note and dropped it at his feet.

Leo was swaying back and forth like he was standing on the

deck of one of his chartered tuna boats. He leaned over—ala W.C. Fields—clutched the note and unfolded it.

After reading the last word out loud, Leo paused, as if struggling to arrange his thoughts.

Leo: "Well, I don't like it. I don't like dis sonofabitchin' eye followin' me aroun' duh room watchin' every move I make! Take it off duh fuckin wall or I'm gonna give it a sharp right hook an knock duh shit outtuv it!"

Penny shot a glare of contempt at Leo. She fanned her hand in front of her nose to waft away the smell of Leo's whiskey breath.

Leo: "Penny, did yuh hear what I just said? Yuh got ten seconds tuh get dat eye off duh wall or I'm gonna knock duh livin' shit outtuv it!"

Penny tossed the hem of her bathrobe in the air and stomped out of the room.

Leo assumed his Sonny Liston stance in front of the eye.

Leo: (to the eye) "Arright you bastid, yuh can't say I didn't warn ya."

He pummeled the intrusive eyeball with a sharp left jab, followed by a right cross. The eye shattered into hundreds of shards of cheap plastic. The intruder lay defeated on the bedroom floor, knocked out cold in the first round.

Penny broke her silence, "You dirty sonofabitch!"

Leo whirled around and delivered a roundhouse punch, dropping Penny to the floor with the remains of the Rosicrucian Eye.

Penny

Penny moved out the next day. Leo's marriage to Penny landed in divorce court less than thirty-six months after the pair said, "I do."

There was more money to fight over this time.

Penny tailed Leo with two private eyes. *If I can catch him in bed with another woman,* she plotted, *I'll nail his ass for adultery, and I'll get the settlement I deserve from the sonofabitch.*

She didn't have to wait long. Amelita Ward, my mother, was already in the wings.

Penny and the two PI's followed Leo and Amelita home and waited until they were sure that Mom and Dad were doing the nasty.

CRASH! KABOOM!

The two PI's smashed Leo's door down with a sledgehammer.

What happened next? You guessed it. Off the nightstand came Leo's Smith and Wesson .38 pistol.

KABLAM! KABLAM! KABLAM! Leo fired three shots at Penny and the two private eyes. Smoke filled the room.

Though he fired three times at point-blank range, Leo didn't hit a damn thing. He was drunk. It's a good thing. The Dead End Kid might have spent the rest of his life making license plates at Folsom.

Amelita, my mother, bolted out the window naked, vaulted over a six-foot fence, and hid in the neighbor's garage.

Penny and the PI's scrambled out of the house, running for their lives.

Twenty minutes later, Leo's house was being searched by the local police, Penny, and the two PI's. Flash bulbs popped and pens raced across notepads.

Finding only high heels and nylons under Leo's bed, Penny exploded at having come so close and yet come up empty handed. She attacked Leo and kicked at his shins until she drew blood.

Leo was arrested, booked, and released on $1,000 bail.

The illegal entry turned out to be the greater evil. Penny was ordered to pay Leo $35,000 in damages. That ended up making it a little easier for Leo to pay Penny the $50,000 settlement she was awarded in divorce court.

In full view of the judge and a bevy of reporters, Leo listened as Penny voiced a playback of Kay's grievances, almost word for word. "Leo drinks to excess and carries a gun," Penny told the judge. "My thirty-one-year-old husband can never forget the role he played as Spit in Dead End as a teenager. He's never stopped playing that role."

MOVIE TOUGHIE LEO GORCEY BOOKED IN GUN ROW
His wife ducked three bullets in Gorcey's Valley home

Arrested—
But Feeling No Pain

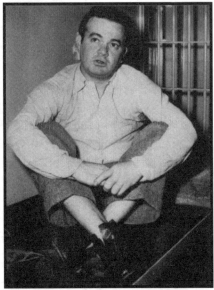

Jail Time—The Bars Are Real!

FINDING THE COURAGE TO CHANGE

As I sifted through all the newspaper and magazine articles about my dad's second divorce, the bullets flying, the adultery, the crazy making, I started thinking about my own two failed marriages.

Ten years after my first therapist, Jeff, had fished me out of the Sea of Despair, my life had become unmanageable for the second time. My second divorce brought me into contact with my second therapist, David.

I met David in the parking lot in front of his office. I put out my cigarette and shook his hand. "Hi. You must be David. I'm Leo."

David's balding head added ten years to his 30-something age. The casual look of his comfortably baggy clothing was topped off by the obligatory pair of brown loafers—soft Italian leather and worn without socks. His shiny black BMW betrayed his $90 per hour fee. And his three month-long waiting list for new clients seemed to justify it.

I followed David into his office. He sat in his chair, and I took my place—the couch. Blabbing my secrets was second nature to me now.

"Secrets make you sick," Jeff often told me. And he was right. The more secrets I blabbed out, the better I felt. It was like magic. Once out in the open, secrets lost their power to control me.

Once I realized I wasn't the only screwed up adult with abusive, alcoholic parents, the world took on a whole different feel. Not so hostile. Not so scary. My feelings, once overwhelming, had become manageable.

But now, ten years later, the demons were back with a vengeance. So I blabbed to David about how my second marriage hadn't worked out any better than my first. (Another coincidence: my second marriage was half as long as my first. Just like Dad's.)

"I'm having an affair." I blabbed out.

David spoke in soothing and affirming tones. He validated my feelings. That's what I loved about talking to these therapists. Not a lick of judgment in their tone. Years of schooling had trained them to be the perfect, non-critical parent figures.

"What are you getting from the affair that you're not getting from your marriage," David asked, with practiced detachment.

"She adores me. She laughs at my jokes. She listens to me."

Then David said something I'll never forget.

"Leo, the root of almost every emotional problem is the unwillingness to let go of childhood. The little kid hangs on and refuses to grow up."

David had a big long word for it. *Narcissism.* He made it all seem simple and clear. The answer was obvious—to him. David asked me to give up my narcissism as if he wanted me to pass the salt.

It wasn't so easy to me. I thought about my dad's fractured love life. I was flooded and overwhelmed with thoughts of my own. *I'm doomed to be like my father,* I thought. *Why am I even trying?*

I started to cry.

David handed me the Kleenex box.

"Do you want to grow up, Leo?"

Uh, oh. Another one of those 'life raft' questions, I thought.

"Uh, not really," I answered. I preferred the bare honesty of denial to another seven boxes of snot laden Kleenex tissues.

"Can't we just leave that one teeny, little area alone?" I whined.

"Well, Leo," David recited calmly, "the alternative is to see you back here on my couch in two years, with your affair partner. You'll have all the same pain you're dealing with now—only worse. It happens all the time. Would you rather do it that way?"

David was not only a good therapist, he was a good closer.

"Honestly, David, no, I wouldn't. I'm too old for this shit!"

I met with David on a regular basis. I blabbed to him about my pain and my problems. I told him how I killed pain and solved all my problems through overworking, carousing, drinking, and chasing women. Just like my famous father before me.

"Who was your father?" David asked.

"Leo Gorcey," I muttered hoping he wouldn't recognize the name.

"You mean Leo Gorcey from the Bowery Boys? I love those movies! I used to watch your dad all the time when I was a kid! I just saw one of his movies here the other day."

No! Goddammit, No, you don't! I thought. *I'm not paying $90 an hour to answer questions about my father!*

I gave David a look that said, *Ask me questions about my dad's movies on your own time.* He got it and backed off.

I smiled and blabbed on. I told David how Jeff had fished me out of the Sea of Despair. But I complained that I was back to my old tricks. When my second marriage hit the skids, I lost it.

"Leo, no amount of power, sex, alcohol, or controlling other people will make up for what you lack in the way of maturity."

This guy was heavy.

"You think you'll die if you don't let your kid run the show. But it's just the opposite. You'll be free to live."

"Free from what?" I asked, trying to keep up.

David made me feel like a sixth grader who had accidentally walked into a Quantum physics class.

"Free from spending the rest of your life trying to get what you never got from your parents. Free to be your own adult, Leo. Being yourself is enough."

"And you can show me how to do that?"

"If you're willing to do the work."

I knew what *the work* meant. *Signal the forklift driver to drop off a pallet of Kleenex boxes,* I thought. *We're doing the work.*

During my time with David, I realized how I had followed in my father's footsteps with women as well as addictions.

I controlled women with my anger. It was abusive and wrong. Just like dear old Dad, I basically scared the shit out of women to get what I wanted. *And what did I want?* I wanted them to make me the center of their world. I wanted them to be Mommy. And the rest of the time, I wanted them to just leave me alone and let me watch TV. In a word: *I wanted whatever I wanted, whenever I wanted it.*

All hell broke loose when the women in my life didn't co-operate. So life wasn't working real well. And I wasn't getting any younger.

David and I paddled through my crisis together. I broke off the affair. Lucky for me, she wasn't a stalker. Then eighteen months later, my second marriage was legally dissolved.

Divorce is terribly painful. Even if it's a bad marriage.

A friend once told me, "Divorce is like having your head chopped off." I agree. I had mine chopped off, grew it back, and had it chopped off again.

But, in spite of the death of two primary relationships, I was a happier person on the inside. Now I knew that I didn't need someone else to make me happy. I had the ability to choose happiness for myself. I didn't need to make someone else re-sponsible for it. And I didn't need to constantly hurl headlong into crisis to feel alive. I could just *be* alive! That was enough.

As a bonus, I learned that I was hanging on to things that were making my life miserable, time and time again. I was do-ing the same things over and over expecting different results. I learned that's the definition of insanity.

Back at the support group meeting: "Hi, my name's Leo, and, goddammit, yes, my life is unmanageable. Again. Thanks for listening."

I waited for a drum roll, or for everyone to get up and leave the room, or for someone to politely ask me to leave. Nothing. They all just sat there. Not one person in that circle of folding chairs made me feel anything less than human.

"Right on!" cheered a guy with scraggly hair and an earring. He looked at me and smiled—like we had been friends in a past life.

I had a lot more to get off my chest. And I did. I discovered I actually had the choice to let go of all this crap!

"It takes courage to let go of being a kid," David told me, "but the rewards make the risks look like small potatoes."

Right again. These therapists were rackin' up the points like crazy. *How do they know so much,* I wondered. *And how come nobody ever told me this stuff before I screwed up half my life?*

It didn't matter. I was getting it now. Better late than never.

At the end of my time with David, I had discovered the possibility for change, and I found the courage to change.

My new motto? *I want to grow up before I grow old.*

4-F

Like many male actors in the forties, Leo's number came up just when his career in Hollywood was about to take off. Uncle Sam wanted a few good men. My father was one of them.

Leo Gorcey was given ten days to wrap up his affairs as a civilian before becoming the property of the U.S. government for two years.

He was not happy about it.

Were the following events Freudian, or just a coincidence? You be the judge.

A few days before reporting to the induction center, Leo was flying down Ventura Boulevard on his Indian motorcycle. The rear tire blew, and Leo's body flew through the air like a circus performer shot out of a cannon. Only there was no net.

Dad slammed into the unforgiving pavement. He broke both arms, fractured his skull, and broke four ribs. His whole body was bruised and cut. But he didn't die.

When the surgeons arrived at Valley Hospital, Leo was in a coma. He came out of it weeks later, but Dad couldn't move for some time. He was in a full body cast.

Almost a year later, Leo checked out of the hospital completely recovered. Except for one reminder—a laterally displaced heart. The condition earned him the coveted 4-F classification: *Not fit for military service.*

Some way to dodge the draft, huh? And just to think, I volunteered!

Dad was scared to death of narcotics. He refused to take the pain pills prescribed to him by his doctor. Instead, he drank more to ease the chronic pain caused by the motorcycle accident.

That decision would have nasty consequences.

4-F

THE BIG 'A'

The day his divorce from Penny was final, Leo Gorcey and Amelita Ward, eloped to Ensenada, Mexico to get hitched.

Why? Amelita was pregnant with the Dead End Kid's first and only son. Me!

Dad called Amelita, The Big 'A'. And rightfully so. The Big 'A' had more moxie per square inch than Dad's first two wives combined.

The first crisis arose when the great State of California refused to issue me a proper birth certificate because they didn't recognize my parents' South of the Border wedding as being legal.

So, when I was nine months old, Dad and The Big 'A' invited a Catholic priest and a couple of friends over to the house in Hidden Hills, all on the QT.

Mom and Dad, the two hambones, couldn't pass up the irresistible shtick of making me the ring bearer!

It got a little tense when the priest eyed Mom with an Irish twinkle of suspicion and asked, "And who might this cute little lad be?"

Mom's friend, who had agreed to appear as one of the witnesses, piped up, "Oh, he's mine!"

And with that, Dad and The Big 'A' made it legal. Nine months after I was born, Mom and Dad were issued a Delayed Certificate of Birth officially recording my entrance into the world.

By 1949, Leo Gorcey, the Bowery Boy, was a star. He could afford to shower his new RKO actress wife with everything her heart desired. As long as she would agree to stop working and stay home with the kids.

But Mom had other ideas. Mom's first official act, after her emancipation from show business? Hire a nanny to take care of Little Leo!

She was out to match the Dead End Kid, blow for blow, drink for drink, affair for affair. Dad was sleeping with his nemesis.

Wife #3—The Big "A"—Mom,
in front of the house in Hidden Hills.

ESCAPE FROM THE CRIB

I did not respond well to being left with a nanny. I got in trouble a lot.

Trouble, I learned, was a spectacular attention getter. I got way more attention when I was in trouble than when I was good. So trouble became my middle name.

Things came to a head when I reached the ripe old age of four-and-a-half.

My parents followed a primitive model of child rearing, common at the time. I was confined to a large crib until I was almost five years old. The problem was that I kept climbing out. Not just climbing out. Climbing out and causing trouble. Breaking windows and trying to smother my little sister with her pillow.

One day, Dad announced that he had "had it up to here" with my antics. "Here" was a place near the top of his throat.

I didn't know what antics were.

Dad got out his power tools.

With his flask of whiskey within easy reach, the Great One grabbed his Skill saw and cut a sheet of plywood the same size as the top of my crib. Then he attached the sheet of plywood to the top of my crib with hinges. Then he had another *belt* from the flask and surveyed his work. It was like Dean Martin doing *Home Improvement*.

I watched this flurry of activity around my crib with intense interest.

Out came the power drill. Within minutes, there was a shiny, stainless steel latch on the lid. I stared in wonder.

Now Dad was ready to play "lock the toddler in the crib."

I was hoisted into the crib, the plywood lid came down on its shiny new stainless steel hinges, KACHINK, went the latch.

I was locked in the crib! But I didn't realize I was locked in the crib. I thought my Comedian father was playing some sort of game with me. Challenging me to solve a puzzle.

Besides, he was making jokes about it.

With hours of time on my hands, I figured out how to undo the latch in a couple days. I thought my father would be proud of me. But all I got was a sore butt.

Once again, the air was filled with the high-pitched whining of the power drill. Now there was a new silver thing dangling from the lid on my crib. A padlock. *Why are they doing this?* I wondered.

The padlock slowed me down.

I spent hours confined to the maximum-security crib. I was allowed out only when there was an adult around to monitor my every move.

I sat there on the plastic covered mattress, as toddlers often do. My little baby fat covered legs crossed, I quietly stared. I stared into space. I stared at the red, white, and blue toy soldiers on my curtains. I stared at the light bulb, then the light switch, then back at the light bulb, trying to figure out how the light could be switched on from so far away.

I stared at the doorknob and I stared at the hinges on my bedroom door, comparing them with the hinges on my security crib.

I stared at my crib. The bars on the crib. The legs of the crib. The wheels of the crib. The screws. The screws? There were screws in my crib? Were they holding it together?

My little toddler brain stared at the screws. *Where had my little eyes seen those screws before?*

The slide projector in my little toddler brain flashed a series of snapshots of my dad working in the garage. One of the snapshots was of a tool he called a screwdriver. I even had a little video in my little toddler brain. A video of my Dad taking screws out of things with the screwdriver. When the screws came out, I remembered, things came apart!

Over the next few days I got very interested in watching Dad fiddling around at the workbench in the garage. He told Ruby, the nanny, "You don't have tuh stay out here, I'll keep an eye on 'im."

Good things come to those who wait.

After guzzling a flask of whiskey, Dad forgot I was in the garage. He shuffled into the kitchen to refill the flask. That was long enough for me to snatch a screwdriver, cart the slender little tool into my bedroom, and hide it under the pillow of my crib.

The next day, Ruby (the nanny), strolled into my room and found my crib lying in pieces on the floor. A rail here. A panel of bars there. Two sets of hinges. And the lid.

"Oh my God," shouted Ruby. "Leo Jr.'s gone! Leo Jr.'s gone!"

Dad issued an all-points bulletin.

"Don't just stand there, f'crissake, go find duh little sonofabitch." Then he ambled over to his bar for a drink.

Ruby found me. I was out in the garage returning the screwdriver.

I got the beating of my life, but they stopped locking me in the crib. Maybe they were afraid. They had good reason to be.

Nearing the end of my Wonder Bread years, I had stuffed enough anger toward my two alcoholic parents to be potentially postal.

The more the Dead End Kid and the RKO actress ignored me and threw me to the nannies, the harder I worked at shocking the hell out of them.

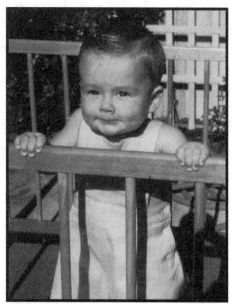

Little Leo, Jr. in "Duh Crib"—a Chip off the Old Block!

PYROMANIA

It was a full-time job eking out my emotional survival on the scraps of attention tossed to me by my Hollywood celebrity caretakers.

But then it got worse. One day, they brought another baby home.

That was the straw that broke the camel's back.

When my little sister was born, two years after me, Mom didn't want her. "She's ugly!" The Big 'A' snarled at the doctor. "I don't want her. Just pinch her head off." Amelita checked out of the hospital and Dad drove her home. Without my new baby sister.

Leo's mama, Josephine, who was now living in Santa Monica, took my baby sister home. Jo, and her daughter, Audrey, raised her on formula until she was seven months old.

My mother finally decided to let my seven-month-old sister come home.

My Dad named her Jan, after Jan Grippo, the producer who made Dad rich.

When Jan started to crawl, I stepped on her fingers. But that backfired. I only got spanked. Hard.

Then, when I was six years old, I hatched a simple plan to rid myself of my competition forever.

One morning, when Mom and Dad had gone out for the day, I tiptoed into my little sister's bedroom. Jan was taking her afternoon nap.

I struck a match and lit her curtains on fire.

My parents pilfered pocketfuls of matches from all the cocktail lounges and spilled them all over the house when they stumbled home in the wee hours of the morning. So matches weren't hard to come by.

My plan was to cremate my sister before anyone caught on. The plan had merit. The fire should have blazed through all the frilly stuff hanging from my sister's walls, and roasted her to ashes in a matter of minutes.

But the nanny smelled the smoke and came running. She had a big red thing that shot white stuff all over the curtains. And the fire went out. *Rats!*

The nanny staggered out of Jan's room hacking and coughing up a fit. Then, for no good reason, she picked up the phone and dialed the fire department.

Then she got the Dead End Kid on the horn.

My father raced into our Hidden Hills driveway, battling two fire trucks for a parking place.

I hid behind a huge chair in a dark corner of the living room and listened to the adults parade in and out for the rest of the afternoon, wondering where the hell I could have possibly wandered off to. I didn't come out until dark.

My Dad was too drunk to look for me.

That night, I heard a lot of yelling and screaming through the walls of my parents' bedroom.

The next day, no one in the house said a word about the fire.

What are they up to? I wondered. I went outside to play, and waited for the other shoe to drop.

The house I nearly burnt to the ground in Hidden Hills, California
—now occupied by actor Powers Booth, his wife, Pamela, and their family.
The guy standing out front was our Greek gardener, Pat.

DRESS PARADE

A week later, my father ordered me into the car and drove me to Desmond's in downtown Los Angeles. Not a word about why we were going there.

I had never been to Desmond's. As we pulled up to the curb, I spied a parade of mannequins in the windows—an entourage of waxy looking doctors, nurses, airline pilots, stewardesses, and waitresses. They were all in uniform, and they were all frozen in Stephen King like positions.

Inside, I stared up at a gargantuan cavern of separate stories, all visible from the center of the ground floor. We floated on the escalator up to the third floor.

After Dad signed an autograph for the department manager, they disappeared for a long talk.

I slipped away to examine the escalator, trying to figure out where on earth those steps disappeared to.

Dad hollered at me from across the store.

Two hours later, we left the clothing store with four large bags of military uniforms. Two bags of Khakis, two bags of dress greens.

The next day, my father dropped me off at my new home. Ridgewood Military Academy in Woodland Hills.

I was starting the second grade, and my number was up. I was drafted. No motorcycle accident spared me from my induction into military school. Whatever the Dead End Kid had gotten away with, he had no intention of letting me get away with anything.

I lived at the military academy during the week, and got to come home on the weekends. I stayed at Ridgewood for a year.

At military school, I learned how to march. All that patriotic music made me a little misty around the eyes. I actually felt proud of something. But that was short-lived.

All the other kids' parents showed up at the parade grounds for the annual Ridgewood Military Academy Dress Parade. The proud moms and dads stood in the bleachers, hoisted their Browning cameras, and snapped shot after shot of their disciplined little men, marching in perfect step to John Phillip Sousa.

My parents were nowhere to be found. They were probably home with hangovers, too unconscious to show up and give me one hug. One smile. One pat on the back. Take one picture.

So I took refuge in the familiar. I got myself in trouble.

The week following the Dress Parade, I threw sand in another kid's face and wrote dirty words on the sidewalk with colored chalk. I also created magnificent chalk frescos of ocean liners on the sidewalk, but Major Sprague wasn't impressed.

"Bend over and touch your ankles," droned the Major, with a tinge of the Marquee DeSade in his voice.

THWACK! THWACK! THWACK! The sting of the thick, plywood paddle made me cry out.

I guess I was lucky. My bunkmate, the kid who incited me to join him inscribing the profanity on the sidewalk, fared worse.

The Major ordered him to pull down his trousers and lay across his bunk while he lashed the kid with a leather belt, insisting that all the other boys in the barracks gather round and watch.

After that, I stayed at the barracks on weekends. Stranded there with a few other kids the adults had branded as *disciplinary problems*.

The Dead End Kid said he thought military academy would make a man out of me. But why was he trying to make a man out of me in the second grade?

I wonder, *Was Dad trying to make me the man he wasn't?*

Pre-Military School Days. The plastic handcuffs around my ankles were to keep me from sticking my feet in the toilet.

THE SANTA FE SUPER CHIEF

On my eighth Christmas with the Dead End Kid, I bounced out of bed at 6 a.m. and bounded over to the Christmas tree. The floor beneath the seven-foot-high pine tree was knee-deep in red and green wrapped boxes. Almost all of them had my name on the tags.

I was in hog heaven. No Dad, no Mom.

The nanny was overseeing the feeding frenzy of wrapping paper and ribbon, filling up the trashcan at the rate of a foot per minute. My sister sat nearby with a lost look on her face.

"Open your presents, Jan," I shouted.

"They're all yours," she whimpered.

I yanked a gigantic, red and gray Santa Fe Super Chief electric train engine out of the first box. After the engine, I ripped open an endless parade of rectangular shaped boxes. A coal car, a cattle car, boxcars, and a funny looking red car with the strange name, *Caboose*.

I was so excited I was about to burst. Dad knew I loved trains. Now, if I could just get Muggsy to help me set up the tracks and show me how to work it.

Dad shuffled into the den, his hair all mussed up, his eyes so puffed up, they were reduced to tiny slits in his head. His breath smelled funny.

"Let's set up the trains, Dad!" I yelled, jumping up and down.

"Yeah, sure, we'll set up duh trains. After I take a little nap fer about twenty minutes."

All I heard was "Blah, blah, blah...I'm going to sleep for days...blah, blah, blah...forget about the trains...blah, blah, blah."

I watched the clock like a hawk. The big hand was on the two. Twenty minutes seemed like an eternity. Finally, as if by some miracle, the big hand crawled to the middle of the six.

I tiptoed into my bedroom where the sleeping giant, Gulliver, had toppled onto my Lilliputian bed in his boxer shorts.

I poked a finger at his naked shoulder. "Dad?" Nothing. Another poke. The movement was too slight to tell if he was waking up, or just twitching in his sleep.

My anxiety was turning to terror. What if he gets angry? I wondered. What if he yells at me or hits me?

But the anticipation of setting up the train set was killing me. I poked him again. "Dad?"

The sleeping giant sprawled to life and yelled at me. "I'm hung ovuh, goddammit. Leave me duh fuck alone," he drooled. "I'll get up when I goddamm well feel like it...." Then loud snoring.

I wondered when he would feel like it, and I felt a knot growing in my stomach. My stomach was keeping score. A running tally of disappointments. Disappointments rising, one-by-one, to the brim of a trunk of emotional baggage that would barrel over me like a runaway freight train thirty years later, and make me want to kill myself.

I wanted to ask Dad, "Why are you treating me like I don't matter? Don't you know how much it hurts to see you lying there for hours, acting like I don't exist, on the most exciting Christmas morning of my life?"

But I didn't dare utter a word. No one ever talked back to my father. He'd jump up and crack me across the mouth, or yell at me so loud I'd be a trembling mess for hours.

Instead, I took out my anger on Dad's Christmas gift.

While Gulliver slept, I hauled the transformer to the train set into the back yard and attacked it with a screwdriver, taking it apart screw by screw, prying at things that wouldn't come loose.

I squeezed the pain out of my guts as I pried, poked, and pulled at every screw, wire, and thing-em-a-bob that would come loose from inside the transformer.

The smaller pieces got lost right away in the dirt. *Now, I'm in big trouble,* I worried. That's the only kind of trouble I got into anymore.

After age seven, I never heard, "Leo, you're in trouble." It was always, "Leo, you're in *big* trouble. Wait until your father gets home."

There was no turning back now. The messy bundle of screws, wires, and switches would never go back together the way it was before—all shiny and sleek and ready to command the wild and stately Super Chief with all of its freight cars and its red caboose. Without the transformer, the train set was a worthless heap of metal and plastic. I had withdrawn and isolated, vented my rage by destroying the sleeping ogre's gift.

Now it was just me and my feelings of impending danger. The state of flight-or-fight had the power to shoot the adrenalin into my system to make me feel alive. But I was already losing the battle for my soul. The Dead End Kid was too powerful.

Dad finally roused himself and came looking for me. When his bloodshot eyes found the first few pieces of the transformer he yelled, loud enough for the neighbors to hear, "Yuh little bastid, yuh break everyting yuh get yer fuckin' hands on. Wuht duh hell is duh madduh wit you? You're a real fuckin' mastuhmind!"

That became my nickname: *Mastermind*. I realized years later that *Masterminds* was the title of one of Dad's Bowery Boys movies. My dad had officially initiated me into his gang by nick-naming me, Mastermind. The moniker stuck until I left home to go to college.

To punish me, Dad didn't replace the transformer. The train set gathered dust in the attic until twelve years later when all us adult children showed up to divvy up what was left of the Dead End Kid's estate.

The dilapidated old Super Chief disappeared into oblivion, just like the relationship I never had with my movie-star father.

Me and my "troll" Santa on Christmas morning,
eking out a smile for the *paparazzi*.

HALFTIME

I had a rough time picking up the second half of this story after completing *The Santa Fe Super Chief.*

Why? Well, when I realized the extent to which Dad had emotionally checked out by the time I reached the age of seven, it knocked the wind out of me.

I needed a quick pick-me-up, so I went back and read and reread the many fan letters I had received since starting *Me And The Dead End Kid.*

Knocked on my back by a sadness that hit me like an unexpected punch in the breadbasket, I gave way to a thought, which carried the finality of death itself.

Dad's fans, I thought, have clearly seen and enjoyed a part of my father I'll never know...precisely because I am his son. I would never know the side of my father that moved one of his young fans to pay $650 for a copy of the skimpy collection of self-published anecdotes my dad referred to as his autobiography.

After having spent his entire savings to purchase the small hard-back from a book searching service, the fan proudly emailed, "My daily rations for the next month were red potatoes, one small hamburger patty, and water. But every night as I got into bed hungry, I read and reread Leo Gorcey's book. I was a very happy clam indeed. One of the profound tragedies of my life is never having met the man."

I emailed back that I myself had never met the man, even though I grew up with him. I would have given anything to know my father the way his fans did. *Perhaps I still can.*

As I dug deeper into my soul, I came face to face with a reality that contradicted the knot in my stomach. The first major breakthrough of my journey. I had uncovered a great deal about my father that I admired, respected, and valued.

Because I never had the chance to see my father's noble qualities, did not mean they weren't there. It dawned on me that my father possessed the uncommon courage to put everything on the line, taking all the punches life threw at him.

Weighted down by his inherent character flaws, my father beat all the odds and fought his way to the top of his profession. A profession where the odds against making it are staggering.

In a world where contenders lined the streets like parking meters (each of the eight major studios had 40 to 70 actors under contract), Leo made no excuses. His philosophy was simple. Win, or die trying.

Leo Gorcey believed he should be the one calling the shots, because he believed in what he knew.

The public voted with their feet and made him a star. Leo never let his fans down. In every one of his films, he delivered. He made them forget their troubles for sixty-two minutes.

That's what Leo did best, and that's what kept his fans lining up at the box office all over the world for ten years.

Dad took on the Hollywood establishment and proved himself the hard way. In picture after picture, Leo put himself on the line. Each time, he came up a winner. Each time, he put it all back on the line.

That's the character he played in the movies, and that's the way he lived. Holding nothing back. For Leo Gorcey, there were no half-measures, and there was no such thing as quitting when he was ahead.

Not only did Dad make it to the winner's circle, but he brought his whole family with him. Leo's brother, David, and his Broadway veteran father, Bernard, had made the breaks that made Leo a star. Leo never forgot them.

As soon as he was in control of his own destiny in Hollywood, Leo invited his father and his brother into the fold. He created the opportunity for Bernard and David to appear with him in nearly every Bowery Boys picture.

Sarcastic digs accusing Leo of nepotism did little to rattle him. He retorted, "If dey can get away wit it in Washington D.C., I can do it in Hollywood!"

As soon as he could afford it, Leo moved his mama Josephine out to California and took care of her. He even moved her along with him and his fourth wife up to Northern California when he retired.

Until the booze got the best of him and disqualified him from the race, Dad always ran to win. And win he did. Not once or twice, but repeating his successes over a twenty year period.

During his peak, Leo took home all the chips, and everything that went along with being a winner.

If he wasn't able to fully enjoy it because of poor personal choices, it mattered little to his fans. Leo's star shone no less bright for the wear and tear on the man behind the legend.

My father carved his name in the oak tree of cinematic history, because he never believed he couldn't.

Success is seldom won for less.

I was beginning to see a magnificent pearl taking shape around the irritating grain of sand in the oyster of my soul.

Perhaps the pain of being Leo Gorcey, Jr., I thought, *has not been for nothing. Perhaps, there is a pearl of enormous value here. But, how do I get at it? Can I endure the hardship of bringing it to the surface? Can I finish this quest?*

I contemplated the cost of moving forward. The weight of new discoveries. More bumps in the road. The overwhelming task of getting the message of these pages published.

Many more days of battling the dark voices whispering in my ear, *You're wasting your time. Not one page of your manuscript will ever be read by anyone except you and your friends. Even if the book is printed, no one will want to read it. Stop now, while you're ahead, and face reality. You'll never make it as an author!*

The pages of my wall calendar were flying by in a head-spinning blur. My fiancée, Krista, supported me with tireless encouragement, even as our savings account dwindled, and we worried daily that we had succumbed to childhood magical thinking.

We often asked each other, "Have we taken leave of our senses?" We worried that we would never see a dime for the months of time we were putting into this project.

Am I just being irresponsible? I'd chide myself, when I was the only one left awake to answer.

I considered scrapping the manuscript and returning to my former occupation as a business consultant.

But if I stop now, I asked myself, *will I hate myself for the rest of my life for giving up?*

Then I had a thought I never dreamed would enter my mind in a million years. *What would my father want me to do?* The question echoed off the walls of my brain like the pealing of cathedral bells at St. Peter's Basilica.

The excitement filled my chest, rose past my throat, and drifted into my brain. I closed my eyes and smiled. I took a deep breath.

The answer came. *Put it all on the line, Son. Hold nothing back. There's no other way.*

Don't get me wrong. I wasn't talking to the dead. I felt like I was in touch with the Source.

Wherever my father got his talent, his will to persevere against the odds, his energizing vision for putting himself out there, I felt like I was connecting with the same creative being.

The father who spoke to my heart was more like the Father of my father. All I know is that when I took that deep breath, and the ones after that, I was breathing in strength, encouragement, and hope from somewhere outside of myself.

A lightness of being came over me.

All right. I said to myself. *Whatever the cost, it's worth it. Somehow, I believe there's a bigger picture here. Bigger than I can see from where I am. Bigger than my dad and bigger than me. And I won't know until I cross the finish line.*

TIDINGS OF COMFORT AND JOY

"**H**ey, Muggs, dis is Huntz."

"I'm under duh depression dis ain't no social call since it's one toity in duh mornin'," Leo muttered into the phone. Even half asleep, the actor's wit was razor-sharp.

"No kiddin', Muggs. I see yuh been workin' on yer powers of inception."

"It's poiception, boid brain. Now wuht duh hell is so important dat you had tuh irrigate my beauty sleep."

"Muggs, Dis is serious. I'm done wit Katzman."

"Waddya talkin' about? Yuh been done wit him since duh last time he floated yer paycheck!"

"Dis time, I'm serious Muggs. No more pictures wit Katzman, and dat's it. By duh way, yuh missed a lousy Christmas party! Dat sonofabitch. He made a big deal about me comin', said he had a special gift fer me...for all my hard work on duh series an' all."

"Yeah, so wuht's wrong wit dat?"

"I'll tell yuh what's wrong wit it. He made like it was gonna' be a few bucks, like a bonus, yuh know?"

"Dat's where yuh came to yer first wrong contusion."

"No, Muggs, I'm serious goddammit. After all duh dough we been makin' fer dese chislers, I thawt it was gonna be a nice fat envelope. I open it up, an' it's empty, except fer dis fuckin' gag card an' a box widda pair uh cuff links!"

"Dat's Sam arright. A reguluh benefracture tuh humanity."

"Yeah. Well, you may tink it's funny, I almost gave 'im an uppercut an' drown duh sonofabitch in his own punch bowl. Anyways, I told 'im I was trough wit 'im an' walked out. Dat's it, Muggs, if you sign wit' him again, I'm out. I'll go do sump'm wit Shemp."

"Arright, Huntz, I'm declined tuh agree witcha'. We'll derange a meetin' wit Jan Grippo in duh mornin'."

"I'm glad you tink dis is so funny Muggs."

"Just sympathize yer watch wit mine an' meet me at Grippo's office at ten in duh mornin', an' bring Angel witcha'"

"Arright, Muggs. Dis bettuh be good, cause I ain't...."

"I know yuh ain't an' neider am I, so get duh hell off duh phone so I can get some shuteye!"

THE BOWERY BOYS

Sure enough, in 1946, when it came time to re-up with Katzman, Leo grabbed the ball and ran with it.

Forming a partnership with Huntz Hall and Jan Grippo, Leo wrestled control of the Leo Gorcey/Huntz Hall franchise away from Katzman.

Leo changed the name of the gang from the Eastside Kids to the Bowery Boys. He also changed his character's name to Terrence Aloysius "Slip" Mahoney, playing up his Irish ancestry on his mother's side.

The new venture carried the name Jan Grippo Productions. Leo was forty percent owner.

The crew at Monogram called Muggsy the Poor Man's Orson Welles.

The nickname played up Leo's new hands-on involvement with the product that bore his name. From now on, Leo would not only star in the series, he would be paid to produce the series and co-write the scripts.

Leo Gorcey was now an owner. A feat that would not be replicated widely by actors until ten years later.

The critics, who had formerly recognized Leo as merely a standout among the other Kids, now hailed him as "A clever actor who gives an excellent account of himself."

Other reviewers nodded favorably. "His comedy timing and handling of gag material are tops. Gorcey gives capable performances with dialogue almost exclusively in his multi-syllabic, malapropism vein."

Still others assigned Leo the title of "Comic genius."

But whether the critics nodded or stuck their noses up at the Bowery Boys, it was no skin off Leo's nose. The films were critic-proof. The dough was rolling in faster than Leo could count it.

On top of the Monogram mother lode of dough, Leo was cleaning up in the real estate market. His investment partner was Max Marks, pharmacist to the stars.

Leo had his hand in business ventures ranging from a doughnut stand, to owning rental properties in the booming San Fernando Valley.

The local rags were quick to pick up on Leo's gold strike.

"Leo, I understand you are now producing and acting in your pictures. You must be rollin' in the dough, eh?"

Dad went straight for the punch. "And just tuh tink! Dey put bank robbers in jail!"

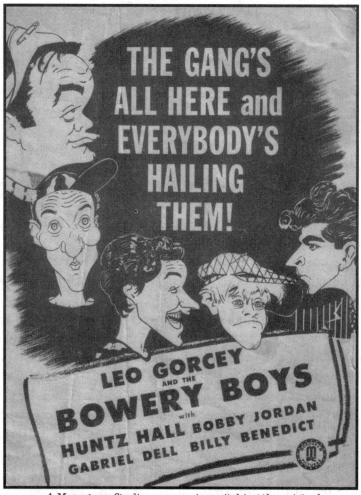

A Monogram Studios promo piece pitching the original
Bowery Boys to theater owners.

NURSE BETTY

Things on the home front in Hidden Hills weren't going as smoothly as Muggsy's career.

Mom had appeared in a number of the Bowery Boys flicks with Dad. By the time I was born, Amelita had racked up eighteen creds in movies. But Dad was not chomping at the bit for any competition in the acting department.

For Mom to break into the big time, she would have had to have gone at it full bore. Instead, she gave in to Dad's "women don't work" chauvinistic mandate. What choice did she have?

Problem was, after Mom gave up the biz to stay home and raise kids, she got bored. So she hired a series of full-time nannies to take care of us. She needed the time to... well, er, drink and carouse with Dad's friends. And the wives of his friends. And one or two of the nannies.

Finally, Dad said, "Enough!" No more amateur nannies.

"Amelita, I want yuh tuh hire a nois!"

"What do we need a nurse for?" snapped The Big 'A'.

"'Cause I'm sick an' tired uh dese friggin' baby sitters comin' an' goin', dat's why. I want a fuckin' professional in here, yuh unduhstand?"

"Yeah. Sure. You're drunk, you bastard."

"Drunk or not, I wanna nois in here...tomorrow!"

The next day, Nurse Betty (her real name) came to the door. Seventeen years old. Recently given birth to a son. She married a serviceman, but said "no" to the life of military base hopping. Instead, she chose the life of a single mom. Not an easy choice in the 50's.

Betty needed a gig to finance her way through nursing school. So into our living room she walked—in her crisp white uniform.

Amelita was aroused. "I love the uniform," Mom cooed. She stroked Betty's arm.

Betty stiffened.

Mom put on her southern Virginia accent and gushed like she was doing a screen test for the Great Gatsby. "Oh, I'm sorry. I guess you're not like that."

Nurse Betty quickly forgave Mom and showed up for work the next day. Her and Mom became buddies.

Betty was the opposite of Amelita. She was reserved, austere, simple. Mom, on the other hand, was...well...a sloppy drunk. A beautiful, intelligent woman. Still, a sloppy drunk, just the same.

Mom felt sorry for Nurse Betty for the fact that all her clothes were uniforms, so Amelita gave Betty a ton of hand-me-downs. That way Mom could make room in the walk-in for a new wardrobe. Somebody had to spend Muggsy's bankroll.

Nurse Betty stayed with us for two years, then took off with her son for Chicago. Our old nanny, Ruby, came back to the homestead. Amelita, meanwhile, was trying to get into the Guiness Book of World Records for the most number of simultaneous affairs while married.

Had Dad been a tad more alert, he wouldn't have let that one slip past him. After all, Amelita was having an affair with him while he was married to Penny. But, then again, if Dad had been more rigorous with his standards, you wouldn't be reading this.

Nurse Betty—1962

A HOME ON THE RANGE

A fan of my dad's once asked, "How is it that a boy from the streets of New York ended up retiring on a cattle ranch in Northern California?"

Well, gather round and I'll tell y'all a story 'bout a man named Muggsy and his passion for the great outdoors.

You've already heard about Dad's fervor for firearms.

Well, Leo loved to hunt and fish. I guess he figured that if he could teach himself the acting business well enough to become a star, he could teach himself to fish and hunt well enough to "Live off duh fat uh duh land!" Believe or not, that was Muggsy's dream!

Don't ask me where he got the idea. All I know is that if Dad could think it, he usually ended up doing it.

Leo actually dug his own swimming pool in the back yard of his first house in the San Fernando Valley. Not because he couldn't afford the pool guys, but because he was outraged by the money they wanted, and he felt he had to prove a point. He did. The Kid's homemade pool cost him a total of $62.50! Including the brickwork!

His friends responded by nicknaming Leo's handiwork, the Gotta Pool. You gotta kill yourself if you're stupid enough to dive off the edge. The Dead End Kid, of course, did dive off the edge and didn't kill himself. He was, after all, invincible.

On one of his hunting and fishing expeditions to Northern California, Leo spotted a nice little cabin on four acres of land, perched on the bank of the mighty Sacramento River. He bought it. Paid cash for it.

After ten years in show business, Dad needed a haven. A place where it was just him, the wilderness, the animals, and a few pals to get soused with down at the local saloon. Which is exactly what he found in Los Molinos, California, population 1250 (42 years later, it's down to1230).

Leo cracked to the press that it was the "traffic" that forced him up to the hills into a part of California that most Southern California folks don't even know exists.

The media fudged the four-acre farm into a four-hundred-acre ranch with several hundred head of cattle.

Leo corrected the error publicly, in a newspaper interview.

What did the Dead End Kid care what his cronies in Hollywood thought?

AMELITA AND
THE TWO BILLS

The Big 'A' stumbled into the Northern California cabin at 2:30 in the morning to the smell of fish. Dad's catch of the day. Thirteen Rainbow Trout, all snagged from the river running through his front yard. He had gutted and cleaned them in the kitchen sink.

Leo was fast asleep, snoring away with his fifth of Hill & Hill on the headboard and his loaded Smith & Wesson .38 on the nightstand.

Amelita, Leo's third wife, went in the bathroom and puked. Then she passed out on the bathroom floor. Two hours later she was feeling her way to the well-stocked liquor cabinet in the den.

She unscrewed the cap off the Gin bottle, dished up some ice from the freezer, and poured herself a Seagram's on the rocks. She knocked back a shot, and started yelling into the air.

"Leo, I've got sump'm tooo saaay! Wake up, goddammit! I...uhhh, have to tell you sump'm...LEO!!!"

Mom fell to the floor to the strains of shattering glass. Dad roused himself, grabbed the .38, and made his way to the kitchen to shoot the hell out of the intruder.

"Oh. It's only you! Wuht duh fuck are yuh doin'? Tryin' tuh get yerself killed, f'crissake?"

"I've got news fer you...you sonofabitch...an' you better listen, and listen good." Amelita was confronting The Dead End Kid while lying on the kitchen floor in a small puddle of her own blood.

"Wuht duh hell is it, Amelita? It's four fuckin' toity in duh mornin'. Can't dis wait till tomorruh?"

"No, goddammit. It's waited long enough!"

"Arright! Say yer piece so I can go back tuh sleep."

"I'm in love."

"Who is it dis time, duh kid dat pumps yer gas, f'crissake. Is dere any body you ain't in love wit?"

"I'm serious, Leo."

"Arright arready. Who duh fuck is it dis time?"

"Bill!" shouted The Big 'A'.

"Bill!" laughed Leo. "Wuht else is new? Yuh been in love wit Bill fer two years. He's married. Leave duh poor son of bitchin' cowboy alone before Evelyn comes ovuh here wit a shotgun and blows yer fuckin' brains out!"

"Not Bill the COWBOY, Bill the DOCTOR!"

"Oh, now yer screwin' duh family doctor? Soives yuh *both* right. Maybe he can figguh out how tuh fix yer fuckin' head while yer at it!" Leo knocked back a shot of whiskey.

"Verrrry funny, Leo. You're a verrry funnnny man!"

"Arright, Dat's it. I'm goin' back to bed. You can sleep on duh kitchen floor."

"You bastard, Leo. Fuck you! Bill's moving in. Get your shit and get out."

The Dead End Kid was speechless. Leo stared bleary-eyed at The Big 'A', all crumpled up on the kitchen floor. Her beautiful jet-black hair was a greasy matted mess. Her face a smeary slick of bright red lipstick, tears, and mascara. Bright red blood oozed from the hand that broke her fall over the shards of the Gin bottle.

Leo staggered into the bedroom, pulled on his khaki pants and flannel shirt, grabbed two fifths of whiskey, and walked back to the kitchen.

On the way out the door, he dragged the avocado green phone to Amelita's side. He dropped it on the linoleum floor and droned, "Here yuh broken down broad. See if yer new doctuh friend makes house calls!"

With that, Leo drove ten minutes to Polly's Motor Court and spent the night. The next day, Muggsy left town. He climbed into his Ford station wagon (one of the first Ford station wagons delivered in the city of Los Angeles) and made the twelve-hour drive back to Los Angeles on the Old 99 Highway.

He drove straight through. He only pulled over to the shoulder of the two-lane, undivided highway for the occasional catnap to rest his eyes.

His flask rode within arm's reach on the front seat. The two fifths of Hill & Hill and a small silver funnel to transfer the firewater to the flask, were safely stowed away in the spare tire well.

The divorce was the bloodiest yet.

Amelita got the ranch in Northern California, one of the cars, $700 a month, and $50,000 in cash—roughly $250,000 in assets and cash. In today's money, it would be more like a couple million.

My sister and I went to the ranch to live with Mom for the summer. But when Dad found out that Mom had dropped us off at a neighbor's house and left us there for four weeks, he was pissed.

Amelita's phone at the ranch rang ten times before she picked it up. "Who the hell is it?" she rasped.

"Amelita, if all yuh want is duh money, I'll pay yuh duh goddamm child support, jist send duh kids back tuh L.A."

A month later, Mom signed over full custody of us kids to Dad. He continued to pay her child support until she married Dr. Bill.

Dr. Bill didn't cotton to the cabin. Accustomed to a higher standard of living, Dr. Bill, whose wife left him when she found out he was sleeping with Mom, bought a nice house on the river for him and Amelita to live in. It was 15 minutes downriver from Leo's ranch.

I'd like to say Amelita and Dr. Bill lived happily ever after. But seriously, what are the chances?

Dr. Bill ended up having his medical license suspended and doing time in the slammer for supplying Mom with narcotics. Mom divorced Dr. Bill and took up with another alcoholic. A local DJ by the name of Sidney.

Sidney was a glutton for punishment. He would obediently walk downstairs to the basement of Amelita's townhouse. Mom would lock him in for days at time. A match made in heaven. Fifteen years after Dr. Bill got back his license to practice medicine, our paths crossed again. My roommate and I were on our way back from Reno. That's where we lost our life's savings.

The Dead End Kid had lost a bundle there too. How much? You don't wanna know. A bundle.

I remembered how to get to Reno from all the time's Dad had taken me there. But I never saw much of Reno. Dad always left me in a cheap motel room while he went off to gamble—for days at a time.

Anyway, I was cruising down the west side of Mt. Lassen when I fell asleep at the wheel. Twenty seconds later my roommate's Chevy Vega was wrapped around the trunk of a pine tree. What can I say? It was 100 degrees out, and the highway was straight and boring. My roommate was asleep in the passenger seat.

We made it on the eleven o'clock news that night—because I'm Leo Gorcey, Jr. So it wasn't me who almost snuffed myself. It was "the son of the famous Dead End Kid."

Anyway, guess who was on duty at the local emergency room that afternoon? Yup. The good Dr. Bill. He did an incredible job stitching me up. You can't even see the scar.

The Doc must have been having one helluva Deja Vu. Dr. Bill had stitched my mom up eight years earlier when she rolled her Lincoln Continental into a bean field.

Was she drinking at the time? What do you think?

Newspaper Photo—The Caption Reads: SIGN OF LEO...
Leo Gorcey, 38, former Dead End Kid, enters Los Angeles Court
to divorce wife, Amelita Ward. He gets custody of two kids.
She gets $700 a month and $50,000 in five payments.

BOYS TO MEN

"**S**omebody send out for Chinese."

The meeting between the Allied Artists brass, Ben Schwalb, Huntz Hall, and Leo Gorcey was grinding into its fifth hour.

Missing was Jan Grippo. His wife's death in 1951 signaled the end of Grippo's presence at Allied Artists. Now, in 1953, Ben Schwalb was filling Grippo's shoes as producer of the Bowery Boys.

Monogram, eager to shed its Poverty Row stigma, changed its name to Allied Artists.

The conference room was reverberating with the sounds of silence. The words had to be said. No one wanted to say them.

Ben took the lead. "Leo, the series needs help."

"Wuht kinda help? Dis is duh best year yet," Leo crowed.

"I know that. No one here is questioning that—least of all, me. I came onboard because I believe in what you guys are doing here."

"Den wuht kinda help?"

"Well, boys, I'll just come right to the point."

"Yeah. Come tuh duh point," mugged Huntz.

"Leo, you and the boys are approaching middle-age. The public is no longer buying you guys as *boys*. We need a new strategy to keep the series alive."

"Wuht else is new? I been tellin' yuh dat fer years!" chirped Leo.

"We've been talking to two veteran comedy writers. Elwood Ullman and Ed Bernds. I want you boys to meet with them. They know the formula frontward, backward, sideways, and upside down. They've done a lot of stuff with Columbia. They're pros at structure. We need to go all-out slapstick. The comedy team of Leo Gorcey and Huntz Hall. Put the age thing to bed. Its the only way we're gonna survive, guys."

Ben Schwalb was a wise man. His plan worked.

Ullman and Bernds pulled out all the stops to come up with

new slants on old bits. The new Bowery Boys slapstick formula was a hit with the fans.

The dough rolled in, hand over fist.

It was official. Leo Gorcey was now toted by the press as the highest paid actor in Hollywood. The kid from New York was earning over $10,000 per week in 1953 dollars. He worked five to six weeks a year.

Which turned out to be way too much free time.

The 'Kid' turned man sporting his St. Christopher medal and Star of David —a clever nod to the religious roots of both his mother and father.

A WOID TO THE WISE

Ed Bernds, who had originally been hired to write for the Bowery Boys series, ended up directing several of the pictures that he and Elwood Ullman had written.

Ed was directing Leo on the set of *Dig That Uranium* in 1955. Shooting had wrapped for the day. Ed and Leo were the last ones on the set.

"Leo, can I have a word with you?"

"A woid? Soitenly!"

"Leo, it's probably not my place to say this, and please don't be offended, but— Well, there was a time, when I first came onboard, that I really thought you worked better—in front of the camera—when you had a few drinks in you."

"Yeah. Well, you were right about dat!"

"Well, I'm not so sure now. I hate like hell to be the one to say this, but I think it's catching up to you."

"Look, Eddie, I been drinkin' duh same amount uh liquor fer years, an' I ain't nevuh missed a day uh woik. I ain't like dose 'sometimes' drinkers dat can't hold deir liquor an' end up staggerin' around an' fallin' all ovuh duh foiniture after a few shots."

"Look, Leo, don't take it personally, okay? I'm just telling you as a friend, I think you should lay off the booze for awhile, that's all."

"Wuht are ya, crusadin' fer Alcoholics Analogous or sump'm?"

"F'crissake, Leo, all I'm saying is why throw your career down the drain?"

"Eddie, I got one little, tiny piece uh advice. I won't tell you how tuh direct, an' you don't tell me how much tuh drink! We'll all be a lot happier dat way!"

"Well, Leo, you can count me out. I told Ben Schwalb, 'No more Bowery Boys pictures.' That's it. I'm done."

"Suit yerself, Eddie."

"It's a shame, Leo. Its a goddamm shame. You've got so much talent."

"Yer goddamm right I do!" Leo spattered Ed's face with spittle.

Ed grabbed Leo by his shirt.

"Goddammit, Leo...."

"Wuht? Yuh gonna take a crack at me? Give it yer best shot Eddie."

Bernds took a deep breath and let go of Leo's shirt. He shook his head and walked off the set.

Ed and Ben Schwalb collided near the stage door.

"Ed, I, uh...."

"Ben, how long have you been standing here?"

"Uh, long enough."

"I need to get out of here."

The two men walked out the stage door.

"Ed, what was that all about?"

"Oh, Leo's drunk. We got into it. He spit in my face."

"Well, I can't say he didn't have it comin' to him."

"Hell, Ben, there wouldn't have been any glory in it. I'm a foot and a half taller than he is!"

THE HAUNTING

"**C**ut!" yelled Bernds' replacement, Jean Yarborough, on the set of *Crashing Las Vegas*. It was Leo's 39th Bowery Boys picture.

"Are you all right, Leo?" asked the director.

"Arright?" Leo slurred. He could barely stand.

"Okay, everybody, take a break," yelled the director.

"Arright...." Leo's bleary eyes were filled with a toxic combination of alcohol, grief and fury.

"Arright?" Leo yelled. "I just saw Papa in dat chair ovuh dere!"

Huntz ran over and waved everyone away from Leo.

"Leo, Leo...you *didn't* see Bernard on the set. Bernard's not here, Leo."

"Not fuckin' here? I jist saw 'im goddammit." Great tears furrowed Leo's ruddy cheeks. "He was just sittin' right dere in dat chair...right dere!"

The drunken actor staggered over and picked up the chair. Huntz followed cautiously.

"He was right HERE, goddammit!" Leo slammed the chair into some casino props.

"No! No, Leo! Put the chair down!" Huntz tried to grab the chair.

Leo swung the chair like a sling-blade at Huntz, grazing the side of his head. Huntz backed off.

"He was here, goddammit."

Possessed with the fury of an F5 tornado, Leo thrashed the set, smashing every prop in sight, until the chair disintegrated into a pile of splinters.

"Papa! Papa! Please...come back, please...."

Leo wept.

Huntz and David drove him home.

Though Leo was visibly drunk in the film, the studio released *Crashing Las Vegas* in April of 1956.

Like the 38 previous Bowery Boys films, *Crashing Las Vegas* was a moneymaker for the studio.

Two months later, Leo turned 39.
He looked more like 50.

With Huntz Hall on the left and his brother, David, on the right, Leo Gorcey broods
in front of the camera on the set of *Crashing Las Vegas*. His mood was no act.

LOUIE

Seven months before Leo destroyed the set of *Crashing Las Vegas*, his father was fighting for his life in a glass-paneled room on the Intensive Care Unit of Hollywood's Leland Hospital.

In the eleven years it had taken Leo Gorcey to blast his way from Broadway bit player to Hollywood headliner, he had never stopped thinking about the day when he would have enough to give his mama and papa a better life.

That day arrived in 1946.

After the release of the first Bowery Boys picture, *Live Wires*, Huntz pitched Leo the idea of a recurring character to act as his foil.

Leo and Huntz went to the drawing board and came up with "Louie Dumbrowski," the charming, gullible malt shop proprietor.

Leo phoned his papa and insisted that Bernard Gorcey sign a contract with Monogram promising to play the ongoing role for the duration of the series. Bernard accepted.

In the Bowery Boys series, Louie Dumbrowski was the sole proprietor of a malt shop, where he was forced to put up with the likes of Slip Mahoney (Leo Gorcey), Sach (Huntz Hall), and their ragtag band of no-accounts, who had voted to make the malt shop their hang out. The strays picked Louie's place, well, because they were able to talk the gullible old shopkeeper into taking their IOU's in exchange for malts and banana splits.

Did the Boys ever pay up? Who knows? But Leo made good on the debt he felt he owed to his papa.

Leo's father inhabited the role of Louie with a passionate caricature of his own temperament—a very short fuse, generous dollops of mugging, a wit like greased lightning, and a charming, but gullible nature.

None of the chops Bernard perfected as a Broadway comedian were wasted. Bernard was a pro. His contribution to the series, far outweighed the credit he was given.

In nearly every Bowery Boys feature, the pint-sized Louie Dumbrowski spouted vain complaints about the Boys' IOU's. He gave in to the smooth-talking Slip Mahoney. And he often bounced all over the globe with the gang on their various expeditions.

Bernard Gorcey learned in New York that he could be living high on the hog one day, and standing in the soup line the next. So to satisfy his desire for a secure income, he put his movie earnings toward the purchase of a small print shop in Santa Monica. Leo kept his father busy feeding him orders for headshots, business cards, and other small printing jobs.

Bernard was driving home from the studio one evening when his car crashed head-on into an Airport Bus at the intersection of 4th and La Brea. Leo's papa took a one-way ambulance ride to the emergency room.

For nearly two weeks, the hearty Russian fought for his life. Bernard was 67 years old when his spirit left the world on September 11th, 1955.

Leo, who had worshipped his papa, was tormented by his father's sudden death.

Every time Leo got in front of the camera to shoot a scene, he thought he saw Papa on the set. His eyes would fill with tears and cast and crew would have to break while Leo tried to compose himself. But it was no use. Nothing could mend Leo's broken heart over the loss of his papa.

The Dead End Kid had bounced back from obscurity to a second life as a celebrity. He had survived 2 financially devastating divorces. He managed to make a comeback and gain almost total financial and creative control over his own movie franchise.

Leo shot from rags to riches, back to rags, and back to riches. The Kid from the streets of New York beat all the odds. He was now assured of his page in the move history books. But could the comedian rise above a third divorce, a whopping $250,000 (in 1950's dollars!) divorce settlement, and the death of his beloved papa?

Slip Mahoney (Leo Gorcey) points a six-shooter at Louie (his father, Bernard Gorcey) while Sach (Huntz Hall) looks on. This was the last film Leo did with his father, Bernard, before Bernard was fatally injured in a traffic accident.

SOMEBODY BUZZ
THE NURSE

The doorbell rang at our home in Hidden Hills. Ruby, the nanny, answered.

Nurse Betty was back from Chicago.

"Boy am I glad to see you, Betty. Come in!"

Nurse Betty was 19. She had her two-year-old son, Jimmy, with her.

"I just got back in town and I wanted to come visit the kids. Are they here?"

"The kids? Oh, they're in the backyard. Its been awful around here Betty, just awful. Here, sit down. I'll fix you some tea. Anyway, Leo's Dad died. Leo had a big blowout with the studio. Amelita's shacked up with a doctor up north. Leo and Amelita are separated...its just terrible what that woman did to him...after he took such good care of her."

"I'm sorry to hear that. How are the kids doing?"

"Well, Little Leo's been a holy terror. Big Leo sent him off to military academy."

"What about Jan?"

"Oh, just quiet as a mouse, as always. I'm kind of glad Ammie's gone. That woman tormented Jan to no end. Disgraceful way for a mother to treat her own daughter. I swear."

Leo's voice boomed out from the den. "Ruby! Where duh fuck are my boxer shorts?"

Ruby yelled back. "I put all the clean laundry on the couch, Leo. I didn't want to disturb you."

Nurse Betty's eyes got big as saucers. "I didn't see his car."

"Oh, it's being serviced."

"Ruby, I'm getting out of here."

"No. Don't go, Betty. He won't hurt you."

Just then, the Dead End Kid walked through the kitchen. He did a double take. *Is that Betty? What's she doing back?* Leo wondered.

Betty avoided his gaze. Leo opened the icebox and chugged half a bottle of milk. He cut loose with a belch that could be heard across the street. Then farted so loud, Ruby's face turned bright red. Nurse Betty just rolled her eyes.

"Coats my stomach," Leo commented as he returned the milk bottle to the fridge.

Leo made his way back through the kitchen and toward the den, to pour himself a drink, now that the lining of his stomach was adequately protected.

On his way past Nurse Betty, he barked, "Go tuh dinnuh wit me tuhnight," and kept walking.

Nurse Betty was in shock. "What did he just say? Was he talking to me?"

Ruby grabbed Betty's hand and leaned across the kitchen table. "You go!" Ruby whispered. "He's really down. He'll be nice to you. You'll have a good time!"

"But...I don't have a thing to wear!" Betty gasped.

"Of course you do! You have nice clothes!"

"No, I don't, Ruby. All I have are uniforms and my sweaters."

"What about all those clothes Amelita gave you?"

"I can't wear Amelita's clothes! He'll know!"

"No, he won't know!"

"Of course he will!"

"Trust me, Betty, he'll never know!"

The next afternoon, Betty's car rolled into the driveway. Ruby didn't drive, so Nurse Betty offered to take us all out for the afternoon.

"Well, how was it with Leo?" Ruby insisted on hearing every detail of the evening.

"It was exactly like you said. He didn't even notice I was wearing Amelita's dress." Betty laughed.

"I told you! Where did he take you?"

"We played miniature golf, then he took me out to dinner,

then he drove me home. A perfect gentleman."

"Didn't I tell you? What else?"

"Well, he said he fell in love with me the first time he saw me walking up to the house for my interview."

"Are you serious?"

"Yeah. He said that's why he used to get so gruff with me, and why he avoided being in the house with me alone."

"Well, God only knows, Amelita was sleeping with every guy under the sun. It's not like Leo didn't know. He thought if he gave Amelita her freedom, she'd stay. There was something wrong with that woman's head, Betty. Before they separated, the boy from the garage came to get Amelita's car to have it serviced...when he brought the keys back, Amelita came to the door—buck naked!"

Brandy laughed.

"What did the boy do?"

"Well, his eyes got big as saucers, of course! Then Leo drove up and the boy turned red as a beet and high-tailed it out of there! Amelita didn't even care. She just stood there with the door wide opened, like she was living in a nudist colony!"

"What did Leo do?"

"Just shook his head and told her, 'Get back in the fuckin' house and put some clothes on!'"

Leo and Nurse Betty started seeing a lot of each other.

"I wancha to go downtown an' get yerself some dressses. Charge it to my account. Get sump'm fer yer son. Get wuhtevuh yuh want."

Betty was in heaven. Lots of miniature golf. Deep-sea fishing every Monday. Dinners out every night except Sunday. On Sundays, Leo would bring home a feast from the local deli and just hang out at home.

The celebrity took the teenager hobnobbing at all his favorite watering holes. Nurse Betty was bowled over every time they would walk into a club and the band, or piano player, would stop whatever they were playing, and strike up Leo's favorite,

Tea For Two.

I could certainly do a lot worse, she thought.

One evening, after a night on the town, Leo missed the turn to Nurse Betty's house.

"Where are we going, Leo?"

"We're goin' home."

"My house is the other direction."

"I know dat. I been droppin' yuh off dere fuh duh last tree months, haven't I?"

"Well then where are we going?"

"Yer stayin' wit me from now on," said the Kid, like he was ordering a chef's salad.

"But, Leo, the baby sitter...."

"Call her an' tell her yuh ain't comin' home tuhnight."

Leo and Nurse Betty woke up the next morning in Leo's king-size bed. Betty rolled out of bed and put on Leo's bathrobe.

Leo took a slug from the bottle he kept on the headboard.

"Take duh wagon an' go home an' get Jimmy an' all yer tings. Yer stayin' here from now on."

"What about my car?"

"We'll get it latuh."

Leo rolled over and closed his eyes. He was snoring before Nurse Betty finished buttoning her jeans.

THE LOST PUNCH LINE

The suits at Allied Artists were leery. It was time for contract negotiations to determine the future of the Bowery Boys series. The suits feared the worst, but hoped for the best.

Leo was obligated to seven more pictures on the existing contract. Then the series was up for grabs.

When Leo arrived at the studio offices, there was enough electricity in the air to light up the strip in Las Vegas. Leo was loaded, and the meeting was short.

Leo wanted to jack up his 40% interest in the pictures in lieu of a salary increase.

One of the suits pounded his fist on the table. "Leo, you're screwing us, goddammit!"

"Fine!" Leo slurred. He stood up, kicked his chair over, and fumed out of the conference room, slamming the door so hard, the racket attracted the attention of two security guards.

"Is everything all right in here, boss?" one of the guards ventured.

The guard was met with a reddened face and a "Get the fuck outta here!"

"Get Stanley Clements on the phone," screamed the Allied Artists boss to his secretary. "And leave a message at the gate permanently barring Gorcey from coming back on this lot! I never wanna see that sonofabitch's face again."

The last seven Bowery Boys films on the existing contract were produced with Stanley Clements taking over Leo Gorcey's spot. When the seventh picture wrapped, so did Huntz. "It's no good any more," Huntz Hall groused. "It's over."

Nurse Betty was busy rustling up some grub for us kids when Dad arrived home from the meeting at the studio.

"How'd it go honey?" Brandy asked.

"I'll nevuh fuhgive myself, goddammit."

"Oh, no. What did you do, now?"

Dad poured himself a stiff one.

"I got duh poifect comeback in duh car on duh way home."

"What the hell are you talking about, Leo?"

"I told duh moicenary bastids I wanted more money. Dey said, 'Yer screwin' us.' I shoulda said, 'Yer well paid fer yer prostitution!'"

"*That's* what you're so upset about?"

"Yeah. I didn't come up wit duh line til I was damn near home."

"What are you planning on doing now?"

"Aaahhh, Fuck duh greedy bastids. Fuck 'em all. Fuck duh whole goddamm town. It's a cesspool. I'm movin' up tuh duh River."

When Huntz and David heard the news, they were livid. In the days that followed, Huntz and David called Leo's house several times a day trying to talk some sense into him.

"Goddammit, Leo, yuh tink yer gonna get laughs from a buncha patatuhs on a farm? Are you nuts? Tink about duh rest of us f'crissake. If you leave like this, yer finished, Leo. And so are we."

"Fuck 'em, Huntz," Leo would scream over the phone. "If duh bastids don' wanna pay me, let 'em find some udduh suckuh."

"What about duh rest of us? You need to come to your senses an' lay off duh booze, Leo. Yer makin' a lotta enemies in dis town."

"Fuck you, Huntz. You always wanted tuh be duh Big Wheel, well, now's yer opportunity. Enjoy yerself!"

David's luck wasn't any better.

"Leo, if we sign for five more years, we'll all be in a better position to quit. That would give the rest of us some time to get some other things goin'."

"Papa's *gone*, David! Don't yuh unduhstand? Papa's gone! It's ovuh, liddle brudduh. Since yuh were a kid in Manhattan yuh been talkin' about becomin' a priest, well now's yer big break."

"Leo, maybe if you backed off the bottle...."

"Wuht duh fuck are yuh talkin' about? Me? Back off duh bottle? I'm bettuh in front uh duh camera drunk on my ass dan any udduh rest uh you guys are sober! You gotta lotta noive tellin' me tuh 'back off duh bottle' liddle brudduh. You an' Huntz wanna woik fer a buncha fuckin' pimps, go right ahead. I say fuck 'em. An' if you wanna stay at dat sweatshop, fuck YOU. An' if Huntz wants tuh stay dere, den fuck him too!"

Leo slammed the phone down, then took it off the hook.

Huntz and David drove out to Hidden Hills to meet with Leo and reason with him. Leo refused to answer the door, occasionally threatening to "blow their fuckin' heads off" if they came on the property.

Hurt feelings crystallized into bitterness and rancor, eating away at their relationships like rust. Leo and David never spoke again.

David became a priest and started a halfway house in Hollywood. I visited him there. He seemed content providing three hots, a cot, and a spiritual pit stop for those less fortunate than himself.

Huntz remained active in dinner theater and television. I met with Huntz Hall several times in the 70's. He got visibly upset when the conversation turned to the subject of the breakup twenty years earlier.

In spite of Leo's bombastic exit from Allied Artists, more film roles would be offered to the comedic actor. Huntz even managed to open the door for Leo to make a comedic comeback in 1964. He finagled him a spot on the *Tonight Show*, with Johnny Carson.

Meanwhile, Leo was ready to go on hiatus—indefinitely.

Leo had turned 38, and he wasn't interested in spending mid-life in front of the cameras.

He was ready for a change.

GREEN ACRES

After Nurse Betty moved into our home in Hidden Hills, Dad backed off a bit on the booze.

I guess being married to a woman 19 years younger gave him a powerful shot of endorphins.

Nurse Betty was nothing like Leo's first three wives. She wasn't in show business. She showed no interest in Hollywood. She didn't drink. She didn't smoke. She didn't sleep around. She couldn't care less about Dad's net worth. She often purchased things for my sister and me out of her own salary, rather than ask Dad for money. She was about as impressed with celebrity as a four-year-old is impressed with peas and carrots.

Betty didn't even know who Leo Gorcey was when she accepted Amelita's job offer to be our first 'governess'. (Dad decided he didn't want any more 'nannies', so he addressed Nurse Betty as the 'governess').

Furthermore, Betty didn't fall head-over-heels for the Bowery Boy when he first took her out.

Betty hung around Hidden Hills because during her first two-year stint as 'governess', she fell in love. Not with Leo, but with my sister and me. Betty came back to Hidden Hills to see us kids. She stayed around because she believed we deserved a better shake than to be without a mother.

Her love for Dad would grow slowly. But it did grow.

One night in 1957, the phone rang. Dad answered.

Long pause. "Amelita, yer drunk."

Another long pause. "You want me tuh do wuht?"

Leo hung up the phone. Nurse Betty yelled from the other room. "Who was that, honey?"

"Amelita!"

"What did she want?"

"She wants to sell my own fuckin' ranch back tuh me!"

Dad wrote the check, and we were on our way to *Green Acres*.

Did Leo care that Dr. Bill and The Big 'A' were living only five miles away from his rustic hideaway? Not for a second. He wanted out of Hollywood.

Now that he had his ranch back, the Dead End Kid packed up the babies and grabbed the old ladies and headed for cattle country.

LOS MOLINOS

I'm eight, my sister Jan is six, my stepbrother Jimmy is four. We're all sound asleep in the back of the Ford woodie station wagon, careening through the night on a 550 mile marathon drive from Los Angeles to Los Molinos.

Los Molinos (Spanish for The Mills) is a sleepy little trailer park town on the East bank of the Sacramento River, about three hours north of Sacramento. It's where serious anglers, like my dad, stalk the Steelhead, the Trout, and the Salmon. But that's about it.

Los Molinos is surrounded by towns with names like Red Bluff, Vina, Corning, Chico, Oroville, and Redding. Redding being the closest thing resembling civilization.

The trailer park town is a fishing and hunting paradise. The pheasant, the quail, the ducks, the bucks—they were all there in their natural habitats waiting to be shot.

There was a 'season' during which it was legal to shoot certain species of wildlife. Shooting them any other time was considered illegal, and carried a stiff punishment, usually in the form of a fine.

The mud puddle of a Northern California berg was home to the cabin and four acres of almond trees Dad referred to as 'The Ranch'.

I woke up groggy and disoriented, dripping sweat under a heap of blankets, pillows, and sleeping bags in the back of the station wagon. I felt worse than if I hadn't slept at all.

Three of us kids were sprawled out, head to foot, in the back of the wagon; packed in there like sardines.

I stared in wonder at the rows and rows of trees that went whipping by the back window of the wagon. Almond trees, walnut trees, plum trees.

Then massive warehouses and sprawling clusters of farm equipment. Some rusted old tractors and ploughs that looked as though they hadn't budged since the gold rush.

I had drifted off to sleep in Los Angeles, and awakened on another planet. But there was a more pressing problem. I had to pee.

"When are we gonna get there, Dad?" I mumbled.

"We'll get dere when we get dere," the Dead End Kid shot back.

The runaway celebrity's glazed eyes were welded to the broken white line down the middle of the worn, two-lane Highway 99.

"Dad, I need to go to the bathroom."

"You'll have tuh hold it."

"How much longer?"

"Till we get tuh duh next gas station."

"How long is that, Dad?"

I strained my eyes over the front seat and through the windshield at the ocean of black. Not so much as a pin light on the horizon. My bladder was aching so bad, my teeth hurt.

"I don't think I can hold it, Dad."

The sound of gravel crunching under the tires woke up Jan and Jimmy. The Ford wagon fishtailed to a stop on the shoulder of Old Highway 99. I could see Dad's crumpled face in the rear view mirror. He looked irritated.

"Hurry up!" he barked.

I rolled out into the freezing cold night and unzipped my pants. A pair of oncoming headlights exposed me like a searchlight in a prison yard. *Could the driver see my exposed genitals?* I turned away from the oncoming car, just in case. But then another car came from the opposite direction. My efforts to avoid exposing myself to all these drivers caused me to pee all over myself.

As I relieved myself I thought, *Isn't it amazing how I can go from feeling so bad to feeling so good in just a matter of seconds?*

I was overwhelmed with gratitude. I turned to thank Dad for pulling over, and the car started rolling forward. I leaped for the back door as the last few drops soaked the crotch of my pants. I dove through the open door of the moving car and into the pile of blankets, pillows, and sleeping bags. Jan howled as I landed on top of her. The forward momentum of the station wagon slammed the rear car door shut just as I reached out to pull it closed.

Fear gripped me as I realized that in his drunken stupor, Dad was about to leave me stranded in the middle of nowhere.

Why did he do that? I wondered. *Is he punishing me for needing to pee?*

I concluded that peeing was bad. To this day, I hold it way longer than I need to.

I kept my mouth shut, afraid to say a word to the madman in the driver's seat. My stomach kept the score. One more blob of stuffed anger.

Dad was laughing. For some reason, he found it amusing.

Humiliation piled on top of shame. Another $500 worth of therapy.

Nurse Betty piped up. "That was really funny, Leo. You could have killed him."

I thank God for Nurse Betty. If it hadn't been for her, my dad would have killed me. As it was, he ended up putting me in the hospital with abdominal pains from all the times he hit me before Betty could pull him off.

Los Molinos is the kind of town no one goes to on purpose. It's not a destination. You drive through it, not to it. People from Los Molinos don't leave.

If someone from Los Molinos is lucky enough to get out, there's a good chance he or she will end up coming back. Coming back and marrying someone he or she knew in high school. Coming back to the comfort of not being in a hurry to do anything.

Los Molinos parents prophesy to their offspring, "Go ahead, get the Big City out of your system. Then you'll come on home where you belong."

Photo Taken in 2002

UNCLE LEE

Dad's first official act after getting us to the ranch without killing us all, was to take us to meet Lee LeBaron. He was Dad's fishing mentor from when The Kid first started coming up to the wilderness, way back in 1943.

Dad insisted we call Mr. LeBaron, 'Uncle' Lee. I couldn't figure out why Dad wanted me to call this guy Uncle, when he wasn't even related to us.

In fact, I remember calling a lot of weird old guys Uncle for no good reason. You know the guys I'm talking about. The used-car-salesmen types who did the same stupid tricks every time they came to visit. "Hey," they'd say, "watch this! I'm gonna make my thumb disappear!"

Just be patient, I'd coach myself, *it'll be over in a few minutes, and I can go back to teasing the cat in the back yard with my stepbrother.*

Uncle whoever would be doubled up, getting such a kick out of himself that my father would have to yell at him to pull him away from me.

"Don't worry, when I'm done talking to your dad, I'll pull a quarter out of your ear!" Who was worried? I certainly was not looking forward to this goofy "Uncle" putting his grubby hands all over my ears. Yuccchh!

Uncle Lee lived with his gray-haired wife in a tiny silver Airstream trailer at the Fishing Camp and Trailer Park that bore his name. I spent many days at LeBarons Fishing Camp over the next 11 years. But I would never learn a single thing about fishing.

Uncle Lee had the look of one of those 110 year-old guys in a *Ripley's Believe It or Not* museum. The Ancient Mariner's hands and face were like old shoe leather. When he smiled, rows of rotting teeth were exposed. But it didn't bother Uncle Lee a bit.

In the 11 years I spent on the Sacramento River with the Dead End Kid, I never once saw Uncle Lee wear anything but khakis. All rumpled up and smelly with fish. To an eight year-old, the man was scary. Which is probably why my dad insisted we call him Uncle. It kept us from running away from the guy.

Dad ordered Jan and I to stay inside the Airstream trailer while he and Uncle Lee went out fishing on the Sacramento River for Salmon, Steelhead, and Trout. Uncle Lee was overjoyed that the famous Leo Gorcey chose *him* as a fishing mentor.

He parked Jan and I in front of his portable black and white TV set. It was about 12 inches in front of our knees. The trailer was tiny.

I wondered how Uncle Lee and his fisherman's wife could live together in a space the size of a large walk-in closet. But they didn't seem to mind. Maybe it's the only place they ever lived in.

First thing I noticed, when Uncle Lee turned on the portable TV with the rabbit ears, was the strip of blue gel taped over the top two inches of the black and white TV screen. I spotted a similar strip of *green* gel taped over the bottom two inches.

Uncle Lee smiled, exposing his rows of yellow teeth. "That's so I can have color TV!" he laughed. "The blue is for the sky and the green is for the grass!"

I thought, *How can this guy stand to have blue and green gel on his black and white TV when he's watching the 'Jackie Gleason Show'?*

Uncle Lee said it worked best when Bonanza was on. Since Bonanza was his favorite program, who cared about the rest?

After Uncle Lee and Dad stepped out of the trailer, I ripped off the Color TV Gel Kit, keeping it close by so I could whip it back on in a hurry when I heard them at the door.

The Dead End Kid holds up his day's catch while Uncle Lee, his mentor, looks on. In the background, the mighty Sacramento River.

BRANDY-LEE RANCH

Dad was a celebrity cowboy, living in a for-real cowboy town. This was no Hollywood set.

He played his new role to the hilt, replacing his entire wardrobe with thousands of dollars worth of cowboy stuff. Dad ordered a half dozen custom-made cowboy suits: matching shirts, jackets, slacks, boots, and Stetson cowboy hats.

Then came the custom designed silver shirt collar tips. Next, the ornate silver and gold belt buckles. And western ties complete with tie clasps—one in the shape of a gun belt and holster, with a teeny little gold six-shooter that actually came out of the teeny little ornate silver holster.

The Dead End Kid was the best thing that ever happened to the Tehama County economy.

Leo's two best friends in the world were not in show business. They were pharmacists. Both of them. One in Los Angeles, and one in Los Molinos.

Don't ask me why Dad favored the pharmaceutical types. Maybe it was because they were so different from him.

After befriending the town pharmacist, Denny Latimer, Dad did what he always did when he took a liking to someone. He gave Denny a new name. Denny's new name was *Tiger*.

Leo made himself at home over at Tiger's house.

Dad would go over to visit Tiger's wife during the day and help himself to Tiger's liquor cabinet. Tiger's white haired mother would chase Leo through the living room in her wheel chair, waving her cane at Leo's head, and cackling, "Leave that liquor alone! You wait until Denny gets home!"

One evening, Dad and Tiger were drinking when Dad announced he wanted to change Nurse Betty's name.

They bandied some names back and forth, but nothing stuck. Then Leo turned his attention to the liquor bottle labels on Tiger's bar.

"Dat's it!" Leo squealed. "I'll give 'er duh name of a drink!"

After rejecting Metaxa, Drambuie, and Courvosier, Leo settled on Brandy. Tiger seconded the motion. From that day until now, Nurse Betty goes by the name *Brandy*.

Now Leo had to create a suitable name for his four-acre ranch. He settled on Brandy-Lee Ranch. Brandy for his wife, and Lee for Leo. I guess Lee just sounded more western than Leo.

Muggsy immediately busied himself at Brandy-Lee Ranch by creating his own version of *Home Improvement*. This was way before do-it-yourself construction was fashionable and before the urban landscape was pockmarked with Home Depot mega-stores.

The Kid shopped at Lassen Lumber.

Leo single-handedly added over 1,000 square feet to the cabin. Then he built a barn and strung some barbed wire fences. Then he bought horses, cows, pigs, chickens, ducks, and sheep.

With a moo-moo here, and a cluck-cluck there, Old MacMuggsy became a full-fledged farmer, harvesting his own eggs, butchering his own meat, and milking his own cows. Leo was 'livin' off duh fat uh duh land!' Another dream turned to reality.

But he didn't stop there. He bought all kinds of farm equipment and harvested the four acres of almond trees every year. For four weeks every year, all three of us kids would sit around shelling almonds until our fingers bled. Then Dad would sell the almonds to the local nut company. Did we share the profits? Hell, no! We were lucky to have any fingers left.

Each almond harvest season, we kids ate almonds until we were nauseous. There was nothing else to do, sitting out there in the driveway, from dawn until dusk, husking almonds and tossing them into 100 lb. gunny sacks that looked like they would never fill up with those itty-bitty, skinny little nuts.

But they did.

After building a second barn, and digging a couple miles of irrigation ditches to water the almond trees, Leo built his own boat dock. He built a flight of stairs going straight down a 30-foot riverbank. One day he fell down the bank with a 26 foot-long 2x6. He damn near killed himself.

Frank Townley, the family doctor, said Leo would have killed himself for sure if he hadn't been so relaxed by the liquor.

After the stairway came the floating dock. Then he bought a little outboard motorboat and tied it up to the dock.

Six years after we arrived, Brandy-Lee Ranch was done. The ninth wonder of the world.

I'd like to say I helped, but all Dad would allow me to do was to hand him the nails.

Now all we had to do was maintain this menagerie. In order to keep the ranch from getting run down, us city kids were introduced to a new word: *CHORES!*

We all had chores. And all us kids stiffened at the dreadful question, every day of our pathetic little lives at Brandy-Lee Ranch. "Have you done your chores yet today?"

We hated chores. We hated the word, chores. We despised any question that included the word chores. To this day, I refuse to live anywhere that requires maintenance, or any kind of upkeep. And I still recoil when I hear someone say the word chores!

A Recent Photo of Latimer's Pharmacy

Our view of the Sacramento River out the window of our living room at Brandy-Lee Ranch. That's snow on the ground—ergo, the reason for the picture!

THE ONE THAT GOT AWAY

The boat dock was finished. Dad no longer had to schlep us down to Uncle Lee's Fishing Camp and Trailer Park to stalk the Salmon, Trout, and Steelhead. We no longer had to be imprisoned in the Airstream while he fished. We no longer had to gag on the stale air. That thick air, that I remember as a kid, was full of "old-people-smell."

Dad could just mosey across his front lawn, patter down to the boat dock, putt-putt across the blue-green water, and weigh anchor at his favorite fishing hole.

Every evening at dusk Dad would bluster, "Dis is duh time uh day when duh fish are bitin!"

Muggsy would order me into the little outboard motor boat, and off we'd go, buzzing up the mighty Sacramento River.

This is the way I remember it, at the age of nine; a typical fishing trip with the retired Bowery Boy.

"Dad, can I drive the boat?"

"Whaddya crazy! Dere are snags all ovuh duh place out here."

"What's a snag?"

"It's a tree growin' unduh duh wadduh. If yuh hit one, we could sheer a pin! It could sink duh boat an drown us!"

"Dad, what's a pin?"

"It's duh fuckin' ting dat holds duh propelluh on...."

"Uh, okay."

Dad cuts the motor, oddly enough, near a huge snag. From his perch beside the Evinrude, Leo spits out, "Quick! Drop de anchor over duh side."

"Uh, okay."

"An stop makin so much fuckin' noise. Yer scarin' duh fish. Do it QUIETLY!"

"But Dad, I was just...."

"Just drop duh goddamm anchor before we float down tuh Yuba City, f'crissake!"

Dad made his "Spit" face and yanked the cord to restart the Evinrude. We motored back upstream for another try. I fumbled with the anchor.

"Get duh hell away from dere and gimme dat fuckin anchor. If yuh want tings done right, yuh gotta do 'em yerself!"

Dad dropped the anchor just in time to keep us from floating down to Yuba City.

He pulled out a tool chest with hundreds of little lures, sinkers, hooks, and rubber thingies that the fish were supposed to mistake for real live bait. I couldn't understand how a fish could be so stupid. But I didn't say anything. "Don't speak unless spoken to." That's what my Dad used to say to us kids. "Children are to be seen and not heard."

The veteran angler started doing all this futzing around at the end of the fishing line. I watched. I had no idea what he was doing and he offered no explanations. I guess he liked it that way. But it just made me never want to go fishing with him. Still, I ended up going every time he asked me.

I can't wait for the day when I can rummage around in my very own tackle box like I know what I'm doing and bait my own line, I thought to myself.

Dad interrupted my daydreaming and handed me a pole with a baited line. His instructions were terse. "Pull back hard on duh line if yuh feel a bite."

Within seconds I was tugging away at the pole.

"Wuht duh hell duh yuh tink yer doin?"

"I got a bite!"

"Gimme dat pole!" Muggsy ripped the pole out of my hands and tugged at the fishing line with his left forefinger.

"Dat ain't no goddamm bite. Duh sinker is just hittin' duh bottom udduh river!"

He shoved the pole back at me with no explanation of how to tell the difference between a bite and a bouncing sinker. I sat there like a bump on a log, dangling the pole out over the water, wondering why Dad dragged me out here on the freezing cold Sacramento River to be miserable.

Twenty minutes of deafening silence crawled by. I made a half-hearted attempt to connect with the Dead End Kid.

"So, Dad, what do I do if I catch a fish?"

"SSSHHHH! Yer scarin' duh fish!"

I wondered how fish could get scared. *They're in the water!* I thought. *What do they have to be scared about?*

Dusk faded to dark. According to Muggsy, it was getting a little *nippy*. Dad unscrewed the top off his flask of Hill & Hill and took a stiff *belt*. I hoped he would say something, but he just turned his back to me and stared out over the water.

I was freezing my ass off. In fact my ass and both of my legs were 'asleep'. I was bursting inside to reposition myself before gangrene set in, but I was terrified that if I moved, I'd 'scare duh fish' and incur the wrath of the Dead End Kid.

I tried shifting my weight to another part of my ass without getting yelled at for 'scarin' duh fish'. The quirky torment of pins and needles shot up and down my right leg. I didn't dare move. What if a Trout or a Steelhead was about to bite?

I remember the pins and needles torturing me to the edge of death. But just when I didn't think I could stand it for one more second, I recovered partial circulation in one leg.

I suspect that had the pins and needles persisted for 30 more seconds, I would have thrown myself overboard before risking moving my leg and 'scarin' duh fish'. My dad was that scary.

Suddenly, my pole snapped forward! I lunged and clutched the rod and reel, tugging with all my might. The pole was bent over almost to the water.

My father's eyes popped right out of his head!

I screamed at the top of my lungs, "I caught a whale, Dad! It has to be a whale! It's so huge!"

Dad yelled back, "It ain't no goddamn whale. Dere are no stinkin' whales dis far up duh river!"

Dad was afraid the line was about to snap. He lunged across the wooden bench separating us, yanked the pole out of my hands, and started reeling in the line.

Dad must have thought he was 'this close' to landing the biggest Steelhead ever hooked on the Sacramento River. He must have imagined that Uncle Lee LeBaron would take a snapshot of the fish hanging by it's dead mouth from the scale on the dock at Uncle Lee's Fishing Camp. My dad would stand next to the behemoth fish and smile ear to ear.

Dad was reeling in the line yelling at the top of his lungs, "Dis one's a real fighter, arright!"

Muggsy worked that rig like a seasoned pro. He was reeling in a little, letting out a little, reeling in a little, letting out a little.

Over the ruckus of Dad's battle with the monster steelhead, we heard the faint sound of hollering about 400 feet down river. We couldn't make out the words.

As the other boat drifted closer, we made out the words. "Your fishing line is caught in my propeller!"

Dad froze and turned beet red.

Sure enough, as the other boat slowly pulled up alongside our little outboard, the fishing line went limp. The other fisherman reached into the water with his knife and cut us free.

I grinned, but not the Dead End Kid. He was about to die of embarrassment. To Dad, looking like a dork was a death sentence. There wasn't enough fortitude in all the earth to hold back the tide of shame that would send my dad into a volcanic rage if he experienced event a hint of feeling powerless, inadequate, or out of control.

Even in this remote little fishing town in the middle of nowhere, Leo Gorcey, the Town Celebrity could not shed his Dead End Kid persona. Not for a second.

We never spoke of it after that day. And I have not repeated the story until now—34 years after his death.

The ones that *didn't* get away!

At Brandy-Lee Ranch: Dad with a string of trout ready to clean in the kitchen sink.

ANNIE OAKLEY
AND WILD BILL

Everyone in Los Molinos loved Muggsy, their Town Celebrity.

Dad had a way of blending in with the ordinary folk. And sticking out like a sore thumb at the same time. The Dead End Kid wanted to be noticed. When he wasn't, he talked about it.

Once a week, Leo would go over to Tiger's house and tell Tiger's wife, Kathy, "I was up at duh Bank of Americuh in Red Bluff dis mornin', and I tink one uh duh tellers is in love wit me."

"What makes you think that, Leo?" Kathy asked while washing dishes.

"I can tell by duh way she looks at me!"

"What way is that?"

"Well, yuh know duh look."

"What look?"

"Yuh can jist tell when a goil looks a soitan way. Yuh know, duh look." Kathy never figured out what Dad was talking about.

Muggsy expected preferential treatment. He always got it. Dad was loaded with blinding charisma. Everyone from the town sheriff, to the doctor and pharmacist all winked at misdemeanors and crimes that would have landed any ordinary citizen in jail. But not the Dead End Kid. Nope. In Los Molinos, Leo Gorcey was King.

When Dad would upset the applecart with his disruptive shenanigans, the townsfolk would just smile, shake their heads and say, "That's Leo for yuh!"

But that's not what they were saying to me in school. I was being threatened daily in the fourth grade. Guys would crawl out of the woodwork. "So, yuh think yer tough 'cause your dad's a big shot movie star?" Then they'd challenge me to a fight out behind the schoolyard.

Most of the time, I didn't show up. But a few times, I got decked anyway. I'd come home with bruises, or a black eye and my stepmother would say, "Leo, we need to get 'Little Leo' out of that school." (That's what they called me—Little Leo).

I switched schools several times to stay in one piece.

To the farmers' kids in Los Molinos, I was an outsider. A smart-ass, know-it-all city kid. Imagine that!

The people who did pay attention to me were the Leo Gorcey fans. The Isn't-there-an-ACTOR-by-that-name? bunch. There wasn't much in between.

While my famous father was off in the local saloons being a big fish, and drinking like one, my attention-getting strategies at home were approaching epidemic proportions. I had now become a seething, bubbling cauldron of anger. When I wasn't torturing animals, shoplifting, or burning things down, I was busy inventing new ways to do away with my sister.

"Jan," I suggested one afternoon, I have a great idea!"

"Yeah, what?" Jan was suspicious. And rightly so.

"I'll be Wild Bill Hickock and you be Annie Oakley. We'll have a Wild West Show!"

"I don't think so."

"Aw, c'mon, Jan, it'll be fun!"

"Yeah, right!"

"C'mon, I promise, it'll be fun."

"Fine. What do you want me to do?"

"Great. Okay, you take this pie tin and hold it up. Right there —yeah. Just straight out like that."

Jan's picture should have been in the dictionary next to the word compliant. She was the prototype of the invisible child. Gee, I wonder why?

I turned and paced off ten yards. Then I pumped some serious air into my pellet gun. I shouldered the rifle and drew a bead on the pie tin. Jan was flinching.

"Keep it right there," I commanded. She complied.

When I was certain I had that pie tin dead center in my sight, I pulled the trigger. Jan let out a yelp that could be heard in Sacramento. The speeding lead pellet had hit her right square on her thumbnail. She was in exquisite pain.

Jan was hysterical. Trying to calm her down was like trying to quench a bonfire with a squirt gun. I squirted away nonetheless.

She went running in to Dad. I followed her. As the screen door slammed itself behind us, I was scrambling for a way to spin the story to keep myself from getting beaten to within an inch of my life.

I never heard anything before or since like the blood cur- dling screams that were coming from my sister. My dad was behind his custom-made cocktail bar, mixing up some alcoholic concoction. Then the Dead End Kid yelled at Jan.

"Shuddup! Shuddup, goddammit, or I'll really give yuh sump'm tuh scream about. Now wuht duh hell are yuh cryin' about?"

Jan sniffled out the story of the pie tin, the errant pellet, and her now black-and-blue thumb. She stopped in between sniffles for intervals of spasmodic gasping. She was still hysterical. Dad yelled some more, in an effort to stop Jan's hysterical screaming and sobbing. "Stop yer fuckin' cryin'. I can't hear a word yer sayin."

Jan started from the beginning and repeated the whole sor- did tale, trying not to cry this time. It was no use.

Muggsy knocked back a shot of whatever it was he was drink- ing and smacked his lips. He gave up on trying to understand Jan's incoherent blubbering. "Leo, wuht duh fuck happened out dere?"

I told him the basic facts about the pie tin and the pellet gun, trying hard to minimize my role in the mishap.

He laughed.

"Soives yuh right yuh dumb broad. Wuht duh fuck were yuh doin' holdin' a pie tin fer dat crazy bastid to shoot at in duh foist place? Yer lucky he didn't take yer fuckin' eye out!"

I couldn't believe my luck. Muggsy was blaming Jan!

Then he came around from behind the bar and grabbed the rifle out of my hand, acting as if he was going to hit me with it, but stopping just short of my head.

"Yuh crazy sonofabitch. I'll tie yuh tuh duh stucco wall out-side an' shoot yer fuckin' arm off wit dis ting." He took the pellet rifle and locked it up. All that night I had nightmares about my dad tying me to the wall and shooting me with the pellet rifle.

A few years of fingernail biting over my pyromania and attempts to kill Jan had my stepmother, Brandy, teetering on the brink. The pellet gun incident pushed her over the edge.

Brandy and Dad had come within an inch of sending me away when I took a knife and carved Zs in every piece of wood furniture in the house, including the baby grand piano. I had been infected by a year of weekly *Zorro* shows. But, shooting Jan was the straw that broke the camel's back.

Brandy and my Dad had given birth to their first and only child together, Brandy Jo. The Jo after Josephine, my dad's Mama, who was now living on the ranch with us.

Fearing for the life of her newborn daughter, Brandy had a heart-to-heart talk with the Dead End Kid. The conversation went something like this. "It's either Leo Jr. or me."

Dad said nothing.

ST. VINCENT'S

Shortly after my tenth birthday, Dad piled me into his tan Mercury station wagon and dropped me off at a place called St. Vincent's School for Boys. It was nestled in a forest of tall Cypress trees in San Rafael, California.

St Vincent's wasn't exactly a school, it was more like an orphanage. The sprawling campus of drab Navajo-white buildings was inhabited by a bunch of boys whose parents didn't want them around because they were *disciplinary problems*. The place was run by priests and nuns.

Some of the boys had no parents—like Joe Davila. I accidentally knocked out Joe's front teeth with a baseball bat during the year I was there. Joe and the nuns never let me forget that one. For the remainder of the school year, I was the 'psycho-baseball-bat-killer-from-hell'. But, hey, was it my fault the guy wasn't wearin' a catcher's mask?

Life at the boys' school was similar to movies I had seen about prison. There was my cellblock. The nuns called it a dormitory. Twenty-eight metal beds parallel parked in perfectly aligned rows on a pea-green linoleum floor with a spit-shine wax job. It reminded me a lot of Ridgewood Military Academy.

Every night at 9:30 p.m., it was lights out. As soon as we were all tucked in, Sister Mary Dominica forced us to recite the entire rosary. There were 10 Our Fathers, 50 Hail Marys, 3 Glory Be's, and 1 Our Father to wrap it up. I suppose she thought she was doing her bit to keep our little 5th grade souls out of Purgatory.

Maybe she was. Who knows?

Sister Mary Dominica recited the first half of each prayer, and all us boys had to answer by reciting the second half.

Sister paced up and down. She was the spitting image of a giant penguin. Her looming shadow darkened the rows of beds as her eyes scanned the bunks for dozing little boys. Woe to the boy Sister caught sleeping. She would sneak up to the boy's bunk and rap hard on the metal frame of his bed with her plywood paddle.

The errant boy would fly two inches above his mattress, suffering shell-shock for the next ten minutes.

Before long, we were like Pavlov's dogs. More like Pavlov's puppies. Conditioned to stay wide-awake until that very last "Deliver us from evil, Amen."

The Rosary was by far the longest part of the day.

Just like in the joint, all of us 180 boys had our meals together in a cathedral-like dining room. "Pass the milk." "Pass the butter." "Pass the mashed potatoes." If a sentence didn't begin with the word "Pass," it was not allowed during mealtime.

Just like in the big house, we were shown one movie each week. Every Friday night at 6:30, we lined up at the candy store window for our sugar fix. Then we were packed into the projection room like sardines on metal folding chairs, to watch the flick.

Our parents sent money for candy, but we were not allowed to keep it. Instead, an account was set up for us at the candy store. When we ran out of money, we wrote letters to our parents and begged for more, mooching Baby Ruth's and Milk Duds off each other until the cash showed up. A $25 check was a small fortune.

Two Sundays each month were designated as *visiting days*. On visiting days the parents who lived within driving distance were allowed to come and take us out for the day, as long as we were back on the grounds by dark.

During my year at St. Vincent's, Dad came to visit me three times. Well, not quite three. On the Sunday morning of Dad's third scheduled visit, I sat alone on the front steps waiting for him to pick me up.

From the top of the chapel steps at the front of the campus, I had a bird's-eye view of the half-mile long road. It was lined on both sides with towering Cypress trees and led up to the circular driveway where the parents picked us up and dropped us off on visiting days.

The kids whose parents bothered to come and see them

would line up on the edge of the driveway like little hitchhikers. I disdained the lowly curb and chose the higher ground at the top of the chapel steps.

I strained my eyes at every single car that entered the drive that day, searching the horizon for Dad's tan Mercury station wagon. One-by-one, I watched as all the other boys got picked up.

Surely, he'll come, I assured myself. Late morning turned to early afternoon. *Surely he wouldn't just leave me here and not even tell me he wasn't coming. Wait! That is Daddy's car right there...That's it! He's here.* I stood up and walked toward the curb. The car pulled up, and out tumbled one of the other boys with his bag of souvenirs from the San Francisco Zoo.

Right color, wrong car.

At 4:30 in the afternoon, I gave up and left my post at the top of the chapel steps. I walked, and walked, and walked. All the way across the twenty-acre campus, through the chest high weeds, over the creek, and then past the out-of-bounds marker.

We boys were severely punished for going beyond the out-of-bounds markers, but I didn't care any more.

There was no path, only thick weeds.

As I ploughed through the weeds, my socks filled up with stickers. The scratches on my arms from the tall star thistle bushes began to itch. I would have to endure the same torment when I came back. I didn't care. The pain was a welcome distraction from the gaping hole of loneliness in my heart.

All the voices I had heard throughout my childhood ganged up on me at once. *You're stupid. You're worthless. No one wants you. No one loves you. You'd be better off dead. You're an orphan, just like those other boys whose parents never come to see them. That's why you're here.*

I winced hard from the pain. Warm, salty tears flowed down my cheeks, dribbling into the dry weeds. I wiped my face with the sleeve of my shirt.

As darkness fell on the open fields around St Vincent's, I quietly wished for a loss of consciousness. I felt my heart swoon into a deep sleep. A sleep from which it would not awaken for a very, very long time.

THE GREAT ESCAPE

My two partners in crime were the most hardened kids in all of St. Vincent's. Martin Eddington from New York, and Jose Gallo from San Francisco. Neither of their parents ever came to visit them.

Martin and Jose were part of the group that stayed on campus all year around. So it wasn't difficult talking them into an escape attempt.

Martin had located the perfect hideout for a clubhouse. It was underneath the foundation of the school gymnasium. It was damp and dark and the last place the priests and nuns would think to look for us.

We kept the place lit with candles we swiped from the chapel. The Catholics are crazy about candles. They put them everywhere. Hundreds of little votive candles were flocked at the feet of the statues of the Virgin Mary and St. Joseph. It was easy to swipe one or two every now and then, and the priests wouldn't even notice they were missing.

Under the gymnasium, we played board games, cussed, laughed, smoked Joes, and planned our escape from St. Vincent's.

On a warm spring day in 1960, the nuns blew the shrill whistle marking the end of morning recess. All the other good little boys lined up at the playground gate to march back into their classrooms.

In all the commotion of gathering up the boys, the nuns hardly noticed me, Martin, and Jose as we scrambled over the chain link fence surrounding the playground. By the time they spotted us running across the adjacent field, it was too late.

I can still hear the nuns yelling after us to come back. The chorus of high-pitched screaming voices faded into oblivion as we ran like the wind. We widened the gap between us and the schoolyard as fast as our eleven-year-old legs would carry us away.

When our lungs were burning so bad we couldn't draw one more breath, and the school yard had completely disappeared over a knoll behind us, we three musketeers collapsed on a carpet of lush green grass, at the feet of a stand of oak trees.

There, we soaked in the warm spring sun.

For those few sacred moments, it could not have mattered less that we had no money, no clothes, other than our prison-like matching uniforms, and nowhere to go. The exhilaration of freedom washed over our senses, sweeping every other thought out of our minds.

We stretched out on our backs, stared up at the sun falling down between the leaves of the oak trees overhead, and savored the glorious silence. Then we fell asleep.

GOT MILK?

We traveled as far as Jose's house on Market Street in San Francisco by picking up empty pop bottles along the road in San Rafael. We had cashed the pop bottles in for the deposits and purchased three one-way Greyhound Bus tickets to downtown San Francisco.

Jose's parents were sound asleep when we arrived at 2 a.m., the morning after our escape. Jose was *persona non grata* at his parents' place. So we picked the lock on his basement door and hoped to get a good night's sleep and re-group in the morning.

We would come and go without Jose's parents ever having known we were there. That was the plan.

Jose's basement smelled of gas and oil. Cobwebs criss-crossed every corner of the basement. It was cold, dark, and damp—like a tomb.

Dumping a barrel full of dirty old rags on the floor, we piled them together and used them as a makeshift quilt. We huddled together on Jose's concrete basement floor, and pulled the rags on top of our shivering bodies.

No Rosary for us. In less than three minutes flat, we were all in dreamland.

At 4:30 a.m., we were startled awake. All three of us tried to shade our eyes against the painfully bright beam of light aiming at us.

Jose's dad marched Martin, Jose, and me upstairs to the kitchen, waving us along with his flashlight.

Jose's parents' apartment was cramped and filled with furniture that looked as if it had been collected from local garage sales. The air was musty and stale.

Jose's mother politely offered me and Martin two plastic tumblers filled with lemonade.

She offered Jose nothing. She shoved her son down on one of the bare wooden kitchen chairs and slapped him across the face. Then she screamed at Jose in rapid-fire Spanish.

Martin and I sat there dumbfounded. We were dying of thirst, but were feeling too guilty to drink our lemonade while Jose was being tortured right in front of us.

Jose's mother turned to Martin and me and asked us, in perfect English, "Are you okay? Can I get you two some more lemonade? Would you like something to eat? Would you like to use the bathroom?"

"No, no, we're fine," we insisted—our faces beet red with embarrassment.

Satisfied that her two guests were comfortable, Jose's mother wheeled around and picked up where she left off with Jose. She yelled at him in Spanish and slapped him all over the head.

Jose's dad was a few feet away on the yellow wall phone, talking in hushed tones to the cops.

On the way back to St. Vincent's, the Highway Patrolman eyed me in the rear view mirror of the black-and-white cruiser.

"Leo Gorcey, Jr.—that name sounds familiar. Isn't there an ACTOR by that name?"

"Yeah," I answered dryly.

"Are you any relation?"

This is just great, I thought. *I'm trapped in the back seat of a police car with bars and locks everywhere. Now I'm gonna be forced to answer questions about my dad for the next hour until we get to San Rafael. I can't believe this.*

"Yeah, he's my dad."

"No. You're kidding, right?"

"No. My dad is the Bowery Boy."

"I grew up watching those movies of your dad. What was that big tall guy's name, again?"

"Huntz Hall—Sach in the movies."

"Yeah. That's right. Sach! Wait'll the guys back at the station hear I had Muggsy's son ridin' with me. They won't believe it. What's he doing these days? Is he still making movies?"

As soon as we got out of the patrol car at St. Vincent's and started walking toward the dormitory, the Highway Patrolman put on his "I'm on official business" demeanor. In seconds, I went from being the celebrity's son back to being the escaped juvenile delinquent.

Sister Mary Dominica herded me, Martin, and Jose downstairs to the locker room. The clacking sound of the long string of Rosary beads dangling from Sister's waist made me nauseous.

Sister's starchy habit cut into her jowls repeatedly as she lectured us about how God was going to punish us for our sins and how the three of us were on our way to hell in a hand basket.

After she put the fear of God in us, she passed out one half of a peanut butter sandwich to each one of us. No jelly, and no milk!

That was Sister Mary Dominica's version of rations—or torture.

Then she sent us to bed, only to wake us an hour later for school.

Two months later, I was released from St Vincent's, and turned back over to the custody of my dad and step mom at Brandy-Lee Ranch. Man, was I glad to get out of that place. Hell itself would have been a relief.

Back at the ranch, not much had changed. The adults were still calling me Little Leo.

The second day I was home, Brandy said to Muggsy, right in front of me, "Have you noticed how Little Leo's changed? I think that year away made a man out of him!"

I knew it hadn't, but I played along.

Why not try and get some mileage out of it, I thought to myself.

GUESS WHO'S COMING TO DINNER?

Dr. Frank Townley replaced Dr. Bill as the Brandy-Lee Ranch family physician. It was Dr. Townley who ordered the blood transfusion for my ailing father three days before the Dead End Kid died at Merritt Hospital in Oakland.

The good doctor was one of Muggsy's regular drinking partners and a big fan of the Dead End Kid. The Doc dropped by several times a week for drinks, conversation, and, well, entertainment.

Muggsy didn't invite many people over for dinner. Having friends over for drinks was one thing, but dinner was very personal. A solemn ritual preserved only for the immediate family.

Dinner at the ranch was the occasion for such uplifting conversation as, "No talking at the table. Just eat your food," and "Get your elbows off the table." And the *coup de gras*: "Where do you think you're going? Did anyone excuse you from the table? Get back over here and sit down until the rest of us have finished."

These were the kind of deep, personal, intimate sharing times Dad wanted to protect from outsiders. But Doctor Townley, well, he was the *family* Doctor. That made him family. So Leo and Brandy decided to have him over for dinner one night.

Brandy went all out. Elegant silk table cloth, silver candelabra, china, the special silverware she kept in that cedar box with the felt lining on the inside. The works.

She had spent the entire afternoon slaving over the hot stove, preparing all Dr. Townley's favorite foods.

Dad had been dieting since moving up to the ranch. After the Dead End Kid quit smoking, he gained over 40 pounds. Through pure will power, and a near Spartan lifestyle, Muggsy lost the weight. And he wasn't about to put it back on.

Problem was, Dad was convinced that what was good for

the goose was good for the gander. He imposed his strict caloric intake and dietary regimen on everyone in the family.

When the Doc showed up for dinner, Dad fixed him his favorite Martini. Leo didn't drink Martinis, but he stocked all of his friends' favorite liquor. And their favorite brands of cigarettes (even though he had stopped smoking).

Dad learned enough bartending to whip up all of his friends' favorite mixed drinks when they came over to visit. His liquor cabinet was stocked with more inventory than most of the local bars in town. If the local liquor store didn't stock what Dad wanted, the storeowner would special order Leo's request from the wholesaler. (That bar on page 147 isn't exactly your typical neighborhood selection of booze your friends keep in the cabinet next to the fridge!)

Brandy had taken off her apron and put on an elegant outfit for dinner, including nylons and heels.

She placed the china serving bowls full of piping hot food on the dining room table to the "ooohs" and "ahhhs" of Dr. Townley. "My God, Brandy, you didn't have to go to all this trouble!"

"Oh, it's nothing, Frank. You've been so good to us."

Frank got a refill and sat down at the table.

The air was filled with the smells of mashed potatoes and gravy, fresh vegetables, sizzling steaks, and hot, buttery muffins. Saliva flooded into Dr. Townley's mouth, as thick aromas of the feast filled his nostrils.

When the Dead End Kid emerged from his bedroom and spotted the serving bowls on the table, he walked over, grabbed them all, and hauled the armload of bowls back into the kitchen.

"Jist soive duh food on plates," he barked to Brandy.

Brandy swallowed her anger and served Dr. Townley his dinner on a plate.

Leo padded back across the dining room and looked over Frank's shoulder. "Dat's too much food!" barked Leo.

Dr. Townley barked back. "Just settle down, Leo. I know how much food I want. I'm a big eater!"

"I said dat's too much food!"

Muggsy walked around to the end of the table, took the hem of the table cloth in both hands, and yanked the table cloth off the table, sending the china, the flaming candelabra, the silverware, the mashed potatoes, steak, vegetables, and glasses filled with drinks, flying through the air and onto the carpet and the surrounding furniture.

Leo steamed into his bedroom and slammed the door behind him.

Brandy blushed. Then she turned stone faced. Finally, she fell to her knees and started to clean up the mess.

POINT BLANK

Dr. Frank Townley gazed down at Brandy on her hands and knees scooping up dinner off the carpet.

"I'm sorry. I'll fix you something," Brandy said.

"Oh, no, don't bother, Brandy. To tell you the truth, I've lost my appetite. Has Leo been behaving like this for long?"

"He's been getting worse over this past year. A few months ago my friend Sue was up from L.A.—it was pretty bad then."

"What happened?"

"Well, Josephine was away for the weekend and all the kids were in bed. Sue and I were just talking. It was about 9 o'clock, and Leo said, 'Time to go to bed! Everyone in your rooms!'"

Dr. Townley bent over from the Naugahyde chair to help scoop up a handful of steamed carrots.

"No, don't do that, Frank. I'll get it. You just sit down and enjoy your drink."

"Are you sure?"

"Yeah. I'll have this cleaned up in a jiffy. Don't worry about it."

"So what happened then?"

"Well, I told Leo, 'No! I want to visit with Sue!' He disappeared into the bedroom to pout. I thought, *Fine. Sue and I can visit.*

"Do you mind if I mix another?" asked the Doc, raising his Martini glass and smiling.

"Oh, go ahead. Leo's probably down for the night."

Had Dad caught the Doc behind the bar mixing his own drink, the shit would have hit the fan. No other guest would have taken the risk.

"So, was that it?" asked Dr. Townley as he mixed another Martini.

"Oh, no," laughed Brandy. "Not by a long shot! A few minutes later, Leo came out of his room with a loaded pistol. He pointed it straight at us and cocked it."

"Holy shit! Are you serious?"

"Oh, yeah."

Brandy did her best imitation of Leo's New York accent. "'I tawt I told yuh to get inna bedroom!' he said to me and Sue.

"What did you do?"

"Well, Sue got up and hurried into the guest room. That was the smart thing to do. I happened to be on the other side of the bar getting Sue something to drink.

"Leo turned around, came behind the bar, backed me up against the wall, and shoved the gun barrel as close to my face as he could get it. He yelled, 'Get in the fuckin' bedroom!'"

"Oh, Jesus, Brandy."

"Well, I yelled right back. 'You'd better shoot, Leo, or you're gonna damn well wish you had!'"

Brandy scooped up the last of the mashed potatoes off the carpet. Frank came around from behind the bar and plopped himself down in the Naugahyde chair.

"Josie can vacuum the rest of that up when she gets home. Anyway, I told Leo, 'You'd better goddamm well shoot'."

"What did he do?" asked the Doc—eyes wide with disbelief.

"He turned and stomped off into the bedroom. There are three doors between the kitchen and our bedroom. He locked all three. I was pissed. So I got the hammer and a screwdriver and took all the hinges off the doors!"

The Doc erupted with a loud belly laugh.

"You're damn right! I was pissed! I'm bull-headed, Frank. My father raised me to never back down from a fight."

"I guess so!"

"By the time I got to him, he'd come out of whatever state he was in. He was laughing! It was weird. I told him, 'Don't you ever, ever aim a gun at me again!'"

"And that was it?"

"Oh, yeah. Leo has stood right next to me and watched me slit enough lamb's throats since we've been living on the ranch to know I mean business!

"I said, 'If I can't get you when you're awake, I'll wait till you're asleep! But I *will* get you if you ever pull this crap on me again!'"

"Did he do it again?"

"No. At least not yet. But then, about three weeks ago, he got up in the middle of the night, turned the floodlights on, bolted outside in his boxer shorts and shot 19 bullet holes in the Mercury."

"Why?"

"He thought the mafia was after him."

"He didn't *know?*"

"No. He didn't realize it was *his* car he was shooting at. When he's like that, he thinks we're all in the mafia. *La Cosa Nostra* he calls them."

"Here all these years everybody's been thinking it was all an act. We thought Leo was just play-acting his Muggsy character...."

"No, Frank...I'm really starting to worry."

"Well, Brandy, I don't think he'd ever hurt you when he's himself. But when he's in that paranoid state...well, he doesn't see *you*. You're the enemy. No one is safe around him when he's in that state."

"So, what do we do?"

"Jeez, Brandy, the symptoms you're describing sound like a brain tumor. He drinks to a certain point and it puts pressure on the tumor. That would make him crazy. What are the chances of getting him over to Corning for some tests?"

"He'll never agree to that in a million years, Frank. Leo hates hospitals. Won't go anywhere near 'em. You'd have to hog tie him and drag him there. Could we have him committed?"

"Are you kidding? He's a movie star f'crissake. No judge around here would commit Leo! It would be like committing Mickey Mouse!

"So, what are you saying, Frank?"

"Well, to put it bluntly, Brandy, Leo's in serious trouble. I'd be surprised if he lives another five years. I hate to say it, but you and the kids could be in serious danger if you stay in this house."

DR. FREUD,
I PRESUME

Brandy and Leo were so impressed with the job the priests and nuns had done rehabilitating me at St. Vincent's, they kept me enrolled in Catholic schools until I graduated high school.

But in my first year at Our Lady of Mercy Academy, I caused the nuns enough concern for my father to take Dr. Townley's advice and cart me off to be evaluated by a psychiatrist.

I was too embarrassed to tell the kids at school that my Old Man was taking me to a shrink, so I took 'sick days', complete with medical excuses from Doctor Townley.

Dad took me to a psychiatrist three hours away in Sacramento.

Why? Well, he wanted the best. And he didn't want word to get around town that he was, ya know, gettin' his head shrunk.

If you were the Dead End Kid, would you?

The anonymity thing became an issue when 'Dr. Freud' insisted that my dad be evaluated along with me, or Muggsy would have to find another shrink. I guess Dad had a genuine desire to get to the root of things, so he agreed to be evaluated.

We went to Sacramento three times, and stayed three days each time, for the 'battery of tests.' That was my first exposure to the now famous Rorschach Test. Man, would I have fun with those ink blots today!

Psychoanalysis was great. I never wanted it to end. No adult had paid that much attention to me in my entire life. But just when I was really getting into a groove with 'Dr. Freud', the sessions came to an abrupt end. No explanation. "We're jist not goin' anymore," I was told.

A few weeks later, I found out why.

While I sat in the car waiting for Dad to come out of The Palomino Room, one of his favorite watering holes, I discovered Dr. Freud's notes. I opened the one-inch-thick file and read until

Dad came teetering out of the saloon and I had to stop.

The gist of the report was that I was imitating my father's behavior. And according to the learned psychiatrist, I had been severely traumatized during my formative years.

I don't know why I cried. I didn't really understand any of it. Still, at 12 years-old, I could feel the words on those pages touching a black hole of pain deep in my soul.

AND THE WINNER IS....

There were two incidents, I now recall, when Dad came through in a big way. Both events played a hand in surfacing my life's passions.

I was desperate for my father's approval. But the problem was that approval in my family was as rare as a field full of four leaf clovers.

When I interviewed my Step Mom for this book, I asked, "What are your thoughts on Muggsy's philosophy of raising kids?"

"Leo was very selfish." Brandy explained, not batting an eye.

"I wanted to spend more time with you kids. He didn't want me to. He wanted my undivided attention whenever he wanted it. Whatever he wanted to do, he wanted me doing it with him. I'd want to take you kids along on outings with Leo, but he didn't want me to."

I guess Dad was too much of a kid himself to be a dad to his kids.

Like many men, I can count the "Attaboys" I got from Dad on one hand.

I played basketball. Dad never made it to the games. I was in school plays. I had to hitch a ride on opening night with another parent. Dad was a no-show at my high school graduation.

I suspect there was room for only one Kid in the Gorcey household. And that spot was already taken.

So you can imagine my shock and surprise when my father showed up to hear me speak at the local Lion's Club Speech Contest.

I was Speaker Number Two. The judges were not permitted to know the names of the three finalists.

The suspense of waiting to hear the judges announce the winner that night was more than I could bear. After what seemed like hours, the emcee mounted the podium and cleared his throat. "And the winner of the 1966 Lion's Club Speech Contest is

Speaker...Number Two!"

My father scared the living daylights out of me when he slammed both fists down on the table. The half-filled water glasses trembled like props in a scene from *Jurassic Park*.

Muggsy knocked my pulse up another few notches when he stood and screamed at the top of his lungs, "HE DID IT! MY SON DID IT!"

Tears of pride welled up in my dad's eyes.

For three minutes, I wasn't stupid. I wasn't a 'hopeless case'. I wasn't the world's biggest screw up. I wasn't an orphan.

For three minutes, I felt loved.

Those few drops of emotional fuel were enough to spark a fervent passion in me for communicating thoughts, ideas, and insights through public speaking and other forms of media.

To this day, I acknowledge that night as a turning point in my life.

My trophy for winning the Lion's Club Speech Contest.
That indentation on the Naugahyde chair, to the left, is where
Grandma Josephine, The Ramrod, sat every day for years.

THE 'STELLA'

When I was 14, I watched and listened in awestruck silence as the Beatles played *I Wanna Hold Your Hand* on *The Ed Sullivan Show*.

That night I stared for hours at the reflection of myself in my bedroom window, playing my little heart out on the air guitar. I played for all those squealing girls in the audience I imagined. The guitar was the magic key that would unlock the gates to the Garden of Eden with the girls. Or that's what I had been led to believe.

The guitar will really make life better, I thought. At last, I had a mission worthy of my passion.

I ran errands with the Dead End Kid one day. We stepped into Hammer and Ohrt Electronics so my dad could buy light switches, and there it was— The Stella hung like a prize on the wall. Don't ask me why an acoustic guitar was on the wall of a store like that. But there it was—in all it's glory.

The Stella guitar is made from wood one step above Masonite. The strings would pass for bailing wire, strung a good two inches above the fingerboard. You have to have calluses on your fingers an inch thick to hold the dang strings down.

I had never laid eyes on anything so beautiful. The Stella was my magic carpet ride to freedom. But the price tag on that baby was a whopping twenty-eight dollars.

From that moment on, I didn't give Muggsy a minute's rest.

That Christmas I rolled out of bed and ran into the living room to see that guitar-shaped box under the tree with my name on the tag. It wasn't there. I circled the tree three times. There wasn't a package anywhere close to big enough to hold the Stella.

My heart got so heavy, I thought it would fall out of my chest.

To head off the gut-wrenching agony of disappointment, my mind raced after logical explanations for the guitar's absence. There could be no possible way my dad and step mom did not know I wanted a guitar. No way.

Within seconds I had the solution. *Relax,* I assured myself, *Dad will bring it out after all the presents have been opened.*

Still, I couldn't hide the just-lost-my-best-friend look. So I got the What's-wrong-Leo? look from every corner of the small living room with the green shag carpet.

My face grew longer and heavier after each package was passed out, unwrapped, torn open, and thrown aside.

Because I was older, most of my packages now held clothes, the ultimate boring Christmas gift for a boy on the verge of puberty. Clothes were a necessity for god's sake, not a Christmas present!

Gone were the tell-tale rattling noises that once brought smiles to my face on Christmas morn. This Christmas, when I shook the boxes, I heard the muffled sound of clothes. The muffled sound that signaled it was time to get ready to act happy.

It took a few seconds advanced warm-up to convince the adults that I was happy to get clothes under the Christmas tree. So I always took a little more time to open the clothes boxes.

Lusting after toys for Christmas and getting hit with clothes instead, was like salivating for a chewy nougat chocolate in a *See's* candy box, and ending up with one of those mushy chocolates I wanted to spit in the garbage as soon as I bit into it.

But if I poked my finger in the chocolates to find the one that was hard and chewy, I got in trouble. "Stop putting your finger on all the chocolates, Little Leo," Grandma Josephine would cackle. "You think the rest of us want to eat candy you already touched! Now take that one! That one you just touched— and that's it. Now pass the box to somebody else. Here, gimme that box!"

I wanted to say, "What difference does it make? I barely touched it! What's the big deal?" But if I said that, I wouldn't be here to tell about it.

"One more word out of that puss of yours, and I'll slap you silly." That's what Grandma Josephine would have said.

The gifts disappeared one-by-one as the trash barrel of wrapping paper overflowed. *How am I gonna sit here for another minute without crying?* I worried.

I looked at Brandy's face. I looked at Dad's face. Not a hint of a look that said they might be getting ready to bring out the big box with the Stella inside. They looked sad. They looked sad as if to say to me, "Why are you so sad?"

I couldn't tell them, of course. What if by some remote chance they were still planning on whipping out the Stella? Then I'd look like the world's most pathetic ingrate. God forbid I should ruin the "We're gonna make you miserable, then surprise the shit out of you" game. Then I'd be the party pooper!

What do I do, I wondered. *Nothin' but wait—I guess.*

As the "Oh, I almost forgot about this one" gifts were being passed out, I scanned the adults' faces one last time. There was no look of comfort there. No look that said, "Just wait a little while longer and we'll bring it out." No look like that.

Christmas was over. The family scattered. I was left alone sitting in front of the tree. I still couldn't believe it. They knew I wanted the guitar. Why did they waste all that money on clothes? How could they *not* get me the Stella?

I couldn't bear it for one more second. I couldn't bear for anyone in my family to see any more of my pain. I decided to isolate. Go in my bedroom, shut the door, and be alone with my sadness.

I shuffled out of the family room, through the dining room and into my bedroom. I walked over to lie down on my bed and lick my wounds.

That's very weird, I thought. *What is that? Something under my blanket...?*

I pulled back the blanket on my bed. I was stunned. I jumped up and down and screamed. I ran out of my room, grabbed every family member in sight and hugged 'em. I found the Dead End Kid and gushed all over him.

My step mom smiled ear-to-ear.

During the gift unwrapping ritual around the tree, Dad had managed to steal into my bedroom and hide the Stella under the covers of my bed. They knew the whole time they were gonna pull the surprise. They just sat there for two hours and watched me stew in misery through the most pathetic Christmas of my life.

God only knows why my dad was so into that surprise thing. I guess he thrived on the drama and the suspense. He got his jollies from the manic mood swings—from long-faced with painful disappointment to hilarious joy and breathtaking exhilaration. No matter. It was all worth it. I got the guitar. That little Stella was my passport to a whole new world. A world set apart from my dad's.

A month later I got my first round of applause from the neighbors when I made my debut in the dining room, singing the Roger Miller classic, King of the Road.

That little smattering of affirmation led to a nine-year career playing in nightclubs, which ended up at the Troubadour in Hollywood.

Then I decided, *Enough of that shit. The last thing in the world I want is to be 40 years-old, staring down at a bunch of drunk guys sloshing a pitcher of beer around and yelling, "Do you know any Led Zeppelin?"*

I am, however, deeply grateful for the Dead End Kid responding to my passion for music. From the day I first cradled the Stella until now, the music has fed my soul. I could not have survived without it.

THE RAMROD

Shortly after Leo moved to Brandy-Lee Ranch, his Mama went through a divorce. Who knows which one?

Leo's brother, David, told a reporter that he thought Josephine was married eight times. "But then," he retracted, "I'm not really sure."

No matter. Grandma Josephine's love life could supply the most prolific of pulp writers with a lifetime of material.

Nannies were in short supply in Los Molinos. Leo was desperate. His Mama asked for the job. *What a great deal,* thought Leo and Brandy, *who better to take care of the kids and keep up the ranch house than the kids' own grandmother?*

Did Leo or Brandy bother to check out this revolutionary concept with another living human being? No. Did they wish they had? Brandy does to this day.

Dad nicknamed his alcoholic, Irish Mama *The Ramrod*. And he gave her free reign. Within a few months, she was running the place.

Grandma Josephine was 62 going on 42. She was in hog heaven at Brandy-Lee Ranch. All the Scotch she could drink, absolute authority over us kids, and the perfect opportunity to weasel her son's affections back from that skinny little upstart, Brandy.

Josephine Condon was raised in Cardiff, Wales by her aunt, who had a boarding house. The aunt worked Jo's fingers to the bone to keep that boarding house spic 'n span.

Josephine kept that ranch house so tidy, we couldn't walk into one room, or touch one thing, or sit down anywhere without the white-haired Ramrod yelling, "Don't touch that! I just cleaned it!" Or, "Don't sit down there, yer ass is filthy! I just cleaned that chair! Now turn around! Look what you just tracked in! I just now vacuumed that carpet! Now go outside and play before I get your father out here!"

Josephine played Dad like a fiddle. She fiddled away, day

and night, cleaning the house, sipping her scotch, laughing at Dad's jokes, and chain-smoking her Kool cigarettes.

Dad, who was accustomed to getting his back rubs from Nurse Betty, was now getting them from Mama Josephine. "Oh, Brandy's busy with the animals," slithered Josie, "I'll do that for you."

Grandma ruled over Brandy-Lee Ranch like the warden of a maximum-security prison. Nothing escaped her eagle eye. One afternoon I walked into the living room, and there sat Josephine on her Naugahyde throne—scotch in one hand and a smoke in the other.

"Are you playing with yourself Leo, Jr.?" asked the warden.

"What?" I couldn't believe my ears.

"I saw stains in your underwear today when I was doing the laundry. You're playing with yourself, aren't you?"

"I, uh...." I didn't know what to say. Some people can make you feel so ashamed of yourself that it paralyzes your throat.

"Stop it, Jo! Leave him alone!" Brandy had walked in and overheard the warden's interrogation.

I hightailed it out of there.

Josephine was convinced that she was one move away from driving Brandy off the ranch and having her celebrity son all to herself.

She was getting her hair done one summer afternoon at the only beauty salon in town, when Josephine hatched a simple plan. While she was waiting for Dad to pick her up and give her a ride back to the ranch, she copied down the license plate of a local farmer's pick up. When she got home, she called Leo aside.

"I know this is going to break your heart, Leo, and I'm sorry to have to be the one to tell you, but I saw Brandy with a man in town. They were together down at the motel. I wrote down the license plate number of the man she was with."

She passed the piece of paper to Leo. But Leo cracked up laughing. Josephine didn't know it, but she had copied down the license plate number of one of Leo and Brandy's friends.

"That's it, Leo," Brandy yelled when he told her what Josephine had done. "If that woman isn't out of this house by the end of the week, You'll be sleeping alone! You can't be married to both of us, goddammit!"

By the end of the week, Leo had moved Josephine out—lock, stock, and barrel. He put her on one of his rental properties in nearby Red Bluff.

The Ramrod—Grandma Josephine!

BABY FOOD

I couldn't sleep. It was 1:30 in the morning, and I was writhing around in my bunk bed with pains in my stomach that made me want to die.

I slept on the bottom because when I used to sleep on top, I had rolled right over the guardrail in my sleep and split my chin opened on the arm of a maple chair. I had to get seven stitches. I was a restless sleeper. So now my brother slept on the top, and I slept on the bottom.

My father came in first, asked me what was going on, then went out to the bar to get a shot.

"What's wrong with Little Leo?" I overheard Brandy ask my dad.

"Ahhh don' know," replied Muggs as he knocked back a shot of Hill & Hill. "Sump'm 'bout his stomach...."

My step mom came in. "Where does it hurt, Leo?"

"All over," I cried.

The pain in my stomach was so bad, I wanted to die. I was hoping I would.

Brandy immediately got on the phone to Dr. Townley. I was hospitalized for three days for tests.

I overheard Dr. Townley and Dad in the hall outside my hospital room. "Well, Leo, I don't know what to tell you. There's one more test we can do, but it's expensive. I mean, I think we should go ahead and do it. I would if I were you."

"Whatevuh yuh gotta do, Doc...."

Dr. Townley instructed the nurse, "Irene, let's go ahead and order that Upper and Lower GI Series on Leo Junior."

Nurse Irene wheeled me down a rat maze of corridors past rooms where groans and cries of agony poured out into the hallway. *Geez*, I thought, *I guess I'm lucky I don't have whatever they have!*

The wheelchair came to a stop inside a small air-conditioned room stuffed with complex looking medical equipment. My see-through cotton gown covered about one quarter of my body, leaving me shivering so hard my teeth chattered.

"Would you like a blanket, honey?" Irene asked.

The love I felt coming from Irene felt so good. Yet, it was so foreign to me. *I wonder what it would be like to have Irene for a mom,* I thought to myself.

"Yes. Thank You," I chattered.

Irene brought me a warm, white cotton blanket and tucked it in all around me. "Dr. Santos will be here shortly," she smiled.

"Thank You," I smiled back.

I wondered if Nurse Irene would consider adopting me.

"You must be Leo Gorcey, Jr?" Dr. Santos shook my hand. "I'm Dr. Santos, Gastro-Intestinal Specialist."

I prayed to God he wouldn't ask me any questions about my dad. This was my time to be sick, and I didn't want to be forced to share it with Dead End Kid. God knows, he got plenty of attention as it was.

I waited a few beats. No head scratching. No "That name sounds familiar...." I relaxed and drew a breath.

I quizzed Dr. Santos like crazy and got a brief overview of what Gastro-Intestinal was. Unlike Dad, Dr. Santos answered all my questions and didn't make me feel like a stupid idiot for asking. I pondered what life would be like if I had Dr. Santos for a dad and Nurse Irene for a mom.

I'll bet they have nice, warm-feeling houses, too, I thought.

Dr. Santos broke into my daydream by placing a tall paper cup in my hands. It was so cold, I almost dropped it.

"Drink up," smiled the Doc. "It's a barium milkshake! Strawberry flavor!"

Cool! I thought, and took a huge gulp. I gagged. "Aucchhh! What is this stuff?"

Dr. Santos laughed. He didn't have to drink it. "It's a liquid chalky substance that flows through your digestive system. It lets me see what's going on in your stomach."

"This is terrible!"

"One more big gulp. Can you do that for me?"

"I guess."

I held my nose and finished off what was left of the nasty stuff. "That's the spirit!" encouraged the Doc.

Doctor Santos grabbed my shoulder and positioned me behind this piece of equipment that looked like a TV screen. "Right...there. Now stand still for me."

He gawked at the oozing barium as it slogged its way, through my stomach, and down through my small intestine.

"All done. I'll call the nurse's station and have Irene take you back to your room."

Dr. Townley called my dad into his plush office and stuck the film of my alimentary canal up on the thingy that lights up the film so that Dad and the Doc would know what the hell they were looking at.

"Well, Leo, everything looks good. I don't see any glaring abnormalities. Judging by the symptoms, all I can tell you from looking at these pictures is that Leo Jr. may possibly have what we call a duodenal ulcer. Thing is, the buggers rarely show up unless the stomach is badly damaged, which your son's isn't."

The duodenal ulcer, I discovered years later, was often used as a catch-all diagnosis for abdominal pains that can't be explained.

When Dad heard about the duodenal ulcer, it made him feel better. Now my pain had a medical term attached to it. Now it could be fixed—treated. The treatment consisted of a bland diet— Dr. Townley's orders.

Having employed the survival technique of disassociating by the age of three, I was deep in denial about the beatings I got from the Dead End Kid. Particularly, the repeated blows to the stomach I endured before Brandy could pull him off me.

I happily bought the duodenal ulcer label, even though I had not the slightest idea what an ulcer was.

The next thing I knew, I was carting little jars of Gerber Baby Food strained vegetables to the school cafeteria in my lunch box.

I thought, *Well, if this will cure my duodenal ulcer, I guess it's worth the embarrassment. What do these other kids know, anyway? They're only in fifth grade...they're not the ones with the ulcer.*

In front of my schoolmates, I'd put on an act like I was enjoying the hell out of that baby food. Like it was the most normal thing in the world to pull up a chair at the cafeteria table, whip out three or four jars of Gerber Baby Food, whip those lids off, and slop down a single serving of strained carrots. Yum, Yum!

When I'd catch my classmates gawking at me out of the corner of my eye, I'd take a big spoonful of Gerber Vanilla Custard and let it dribble down my chin.

I got lots of laughs. And a lot of kids yelled, "You're crazy, man!"

Laughs felt better than tears.

WHAT ULCER?

Years later, I underwent an in-depth medical exam. I told the physician to keep an eye out for the duodenal ulcer. The Doc was impressed that I knew medical lingo.

He called me into his office and tossed a thick file of lab results, X-rays, and charts down on his desk. He took off his lab coat and made himself comfortable. "You're in excellent physical health, Leo."

"What about the duodenal ulcer, Doc?"

"What are you talking about?"

"My doctor told me I had a duodenal ulcer."

"What? When?"

"When I was twelve years old."

"When you were *what?*"

"When I was twelve years old."

"Yeah, I know. I heard yuh the first time. What I'm saying is, twelve year old kids don't get ulcers."

"You mean nothing showed up?"

"No, Mr. Gorcey, I see no signs that you've ever had a gastric ulcer of any kind."

"That's probably because I went on a bland diet for a year."

"Do you know anything about ulcers?"

I lowered my head in shame. No, I didn't.

"Ulcers don't just go away," he lectured.

"But Doc, it was so embarrassing to open up my lunchbox every day in the school cafeteria and take out those jars of baby food. I mean, I had to eat baby food for lunch for a whole year!"

"You're kidding!" The Doc guffawed, "Who in the hell made you do that?"

"Um, my family doctor."

"Baby Food?"

"Yeah. Little jars of Gerber Baby Food. Bland diet, Dr. Townley called it. Strained peas, strained carrots, strained plums, vanilla custard—baby food."

He continued to laugh. "I've been a Gastroenterologist for

twenty-two years, and that's the craziest goddamm thing I've ever heard. Son, I'm sorry for you...that you had to go through that."

"You're sure."

"Mr. Gorcey, you have no ulcer. As far as I can tell, you've never had an ulcer. What are you complaining about? You should be happy! Now, is there anything else I can do for you?"

COUSIN BENNY

I recently ran into my Cousin Benny at a *Bat Mitzvah*. (A *Bat Mitzvah* is like a *Bar Mitzvah*—only it's for girls). I was there on a mission. I wanted to meet the East Coast Gorceys, and search out some of the family secrets.

It was my first time to meet Cousin Benny—the owner of Gorcey's Plumbing and Heating from New Jersey. Plumbing was big in the Gorcey family.

Cousin Benny had the Gorcey glow from head to toe. He motioned to me to join him at his table. I didn't have to introduce myself. "Yer Leo, aren't yuh?" Benny asked already knowing the answer.

"Yeah," I replied, "Howdja know?"

"The Face!" Benny spouted. "You've got the face! You look exactly like your father."

Now white-haired, in his 80's, and full of spit and vinegar, my rotund Cousin Benny bid me to follow him. He grabbed his drink and zigzagged his way across the noisy ballroom. He pushed his way in the direction of the cheese platter, stopped short, turned, and faced me.

"Yuh know why your father was so tough, doncha?" he asked me. His cheeks were flush with his third mixed drink.

"Why?" I asked.

"Because he grew up in New York, that's why! There were *gangs* in New York. He had to *fight* his way up! You get it now?"

Benny's face was exploding with passion. "Anytime the Gorcey boys got together in New York, all they would do is scream at each other!"

Benny gave me the wise-old-sage look. "Who duh yuh think the Bowery Boys were, anyway?" he quizzed.

"A gang!" I yelled back, the added volume in my voice signaling my fourth glass of Merlot.

"Now duh yuh know what I'm talkin' about? Now do yuh understand?" Benny fired back.

I understood.

Satisfied he had imparted the simple but profound Wisdom of the Elders, Benny Gorcey tottered back to his table, drink in hand.

That night I went to see Leonardo DeCaprio in *Gangs of New York*. The Bowery Boys I saw at the movie's Five Points bore little resemblance to my father's gang at Monogram. But I could see what Cousin Benny was getting at.

My great-grandfather, Abraham, immigrated to New York from Russia in the 1890's. Abraham Gorcey begat Bernard Gorcey, who begat Leo Bernard Gorcey, the Bowery Boy. The streets of New York were tough at the turn of the 20th century.

When I went to say goodnight to Cousin Benny, he smiled. "By the way," he said as he gave me a firm handshake, "I've read some of your book. It's good."

THE LAST STRAW

I overheard a lot of arguments as a kid.

My father was addicted to screaming, among other things. I don't know if he screamed to get his point across, if he screamed to intimidate people and get his way, if he screamed because he grew up in New York, or if it was just because he was short. Whatever the reason, The Dead End Kid was a screamer.

And, man, could he scream. What a set of pipes!

One night at the ranch, I was awakened to the nauseating sounds of Dad and Brandy screaming at each other. Apparently, Dad had just slapped her and she was hopping mad.

"Leo, goddammit, you don't hit women!"

"Wuht duh hell are yuh talkin' about? You shoved me!"

"I shoved you because you were comin' at me! I didn't know what you were gonna do!"

"Well, wuht duh hell was I supposed tuh do? Jist stand dere an' let yuh shove me around?"

"It doesn't matter. You don't hit women. There's no excuse for it!"

"Well, dat ain't duh way I was raised. I was taught tuh strike back at anyting dat attacked me!"

"Well, you were taught *wrong*, Leo! You can say anything you want to me, but don't you ever lay a hand on me again."

Dad grabbed his fifth of whiskey and skulked into his bedroom.

That was the last time Dad slapped Brandy. But the violence didn't stop.

A few days later, Brandy heard Jan yelling her head off in the front yard. Brandy came running out of the house to find Dad wrapping a piece of hay baling wire around Jan's neck.

"What the hell are you doing, Leo? Get your hands off her."

Dad hadn't really hurt Jan, but he scared the hell out of her. Jan had left a piece of the sharp wire in the driveway, violating one of Dad's federal prohibitions: "Never leave anything in the driveway."

Jan settled down and Dad went in the house for a drink.

A few hours later, Brandy heard Jan screaming again. This time, when Brandy ran outside, Dad was chasing Jan down the quarter-mile long gravel driveway leading into the ranch, lashing at her with a lead rope.

The lead rope was a six-foot-long piece of rope we snapped on to the halters of our horses to lead them out of the pasture, and back into the barn. Apparently, Jan had not put the rope away in the tack room after using it. This violated another of Dad's federal prohibitions: "Put it back where you found it."

Brandy took off down the gravel road after Dad as he chased Jan and tried to flog her with the rope. She screamed, "Goddammit, Leo, I said leave her alone!" But that was like telling a dog to stop chewing a bone.

Brandy had a huge height advantage over Dad, and caught up with him easily. She wrenched the rope out of his hands, and started hitting him with it! The tables were turned.

The Dead End Kid took off running for the house, with Brandy chasing behind him, whipping the rope at his shoulders.

"You better run, you bastard. If I catch up with you, I'm gonna let you have it!"

Dad reached the back patio door to the master bedroom in the nick of time. He ran inside, slammed the door and locked it.

Brandy returned the lead rope to the tack room. Exhausted, she walked back into the house and collapsed on the living room couch for a snooze. But she was startled out of her nap by the sound of my dad screaming at me.

This far into the day's regimen of drinking, Muggsy was wasted. And Brandy, too exhausted to get up off the couch, yelled at Dad. "I've had enough of this! Leave the kids alone!"

Like a bloodthirsty predator, momentarily distracted from its prey, Leo turned on Brandy. The drunken grizzly bear ambled over to the couch and took a half-assed swing at her.

That was the last straw. As he hunkered over her tall, slender figure curled up on the couch, Brandy coiled both of her knees back toward her body and kicked as hard as she could at Leo's chest. The Dead End Kid's stocky little frame went flying across the living room, and crashed against the master bathroom door.

Leo had the look of a little boy who'd been beat up by the school bully. He got on the phone to his friend, Sheriff Ernie. "Duh broad busted my stinkin' ribs!" Leo whined to his friend, the Peace Officer.

"I'll be right out, Leo. Just sit tight."

ADAM'S RIBS

Sheriff Ernie knocked on the kitchen door. Leo answered in his boxer shorts.

"Oinie, boy, am I glad tuh see you!"

"What the hell's going on out here, Leo?"

"Duh broad busted my fuckin' ribs!"

Ernie watched Brandy wrap an Ace bandage around Muggsy's chest. "You've got to be kidding!" Ernie laughed.

"She weighs 98 pounds f'crissake! Your tellin' me a big tough guy like you?"

"I gotta take a piss," Leo slurred. He tottered off to the bathroom.

"It's a damn good thing you came out, Ernie," said Brandy.

Sheriff Ernie waited for the bathroom door to shut, then turned to Brandy. He spoke in hushed tones, "Ya know, Brandy, I didn't come out here to save you. I came out here 'cause I was afraid you'd kill the guy!"

"Well, I damn near did, I guess! Honestly, I've had enough of his shit, Ernie...this is it...I'm outta here."

"Look, why don't you take the kids and go over to your friend Vicki's house. I'll see if I can talk some sense into Leo."

"That's fine, Ernie, but I doubt if anything's gonna work at this point. He's too far gone."

"Well, I'll stay here with him for awhile, calm him down."

"Frank Townley says he thinks it might be a brain tumor. But Leo will never step foot in the hospital to get it checked."

"When did Frank say that?"

"Just recently...the night he came over for dinner and Leo pulled the table cloth off the dining room table and dumped the whole damn dinner on the carpet."

"Jesus, Brandy, he never said anything about that to me."

"Well, I'm headin' outta here before he comes back out."

"Good idea."

Brandy gathered us up and marched us out the kitchen door,

single-file.

"Oh, and Brandy," Ernie yelled after her, "just pick up the phone and give me a call if you need anything."

"Thanks, Ernie. I may need to do that."

Leo tottered out of the bathroom. He had ripped off his Ace bandage and thrown it on the bathroom floor. He was slathering gobs of white Ben-Gay cream on his aching chest.

"So she really walloped you a good one, eh, Leo?" joked Ernie. "Poor guy!"

"I'm serious Oinie, duh broad kicked duh hell outta me!"

"Ahhh, Leo, a week or two and you'll be right as rain. Maybe you oughtta think about backin' off a little. Brandy's a nice lady."

"Yeah. Nice and fuckin' crazy! An hour ago, duh broad was chasin' me up duh driveway widda rope, beatin' duh hell outta me!"

"Ya probably deserved it, Leo! What the hell were ya doin' to her?"

"I wasn' doin' nuttin', I was jist tryin' to get it trough Jan's thick skull to quit leavin' tings all over duh goddamm ranch, where I could back over 'em an' get a fuckin' flat tire!"

"Well, I imagine if Brandy was letting you have it, she had a damn good reason. I'm tellin' ya Leo, if ya don't back off, she's gonna leave you high and dry. Then what are ya gonna do? Who the hell is gonna raise your kids and run this place f'crissake?"

"Ah, fuck her. Fuck her, Oinie."

After three failed attempts, Leo was able to screw the lid back on the tube of Ben-Gay.

"Jesus, Leo, what the hell is that stuff? My eyes are watering!"

"It's Ben-Gay. Ain't yuh nevuh hoid uh Ben-Gay? Relaxes duh muscles! Yuh oughtta try some on yer bursitis. It'll boin duh fuck outta dose muscles! Yuh'll feel like a million bucks!"

Leo tottered back into his bathroom, retrieved the Ace bandage off the floor, and returned to the kitchen to tend bar for himself and Sheriff Ernie.

Leo poured himself a whiskey, and poured a Chivas on the rocks for the Peace Officer.

"Downna hatch, Oinie!"

"Down the hatch, Leo!"

After watching Leo struggle to wrap his own chest with the Ace bandage, Ernie came around behind the bar. "Here, I'll get that for ya, Leo."

"Yeah, jist wrap aroun' dere tight...."

"Tight enough?"

"Tighter...yeah, jist like dat...now where did we leave off wit dat dart game?"

"I think you had me by 20 points."

"Wuht was duh bet?"

"I don't remember."

"Let's jist start clean."

"Sounds good to me."

The next day, Dr. Townley drove Leo over to Corning Hospital for X-rays. Sure enough, three broken ribs.

The Dead End Kid groused and whined about Brandy breaking his ribs to any of his friends who would listen. He didn't get any sympathy. The townsfolk knew Leo too well. They thought it was hilarious that the shoe was on the other foot—for a change.

The rib-breaking incident was a sobering wake up call for Brandy. She wasn't checked out like Leo's first three wives. Brandy was reasonably present, and somewhat sane. Her only handicap was her youth. Unlike the Dead End Kid's first triptych of wives, Brandy had stood up to Leo.

In their first year together, Brandy had moved out six times on account of being fed up with the Dead End Kid's abuse. Dad took it all in stride.

"All I remember," Leo told Brandy later, "was one trunk and fifty-seven shoe boxes going out the door!"

Brandy stood up to Leo. And it worked. Because Leo knew Brandy meant business. I guess it was her English upbringing.

But now, for the first time in almost ten years, Brandy was scared. She wasn't scared of Leo. She was scared of herself. *If he can push me to the point of breaking three of his ribs,* she worried, *what will I do next time? What if Sheriff Ernie's right? What if I end up killing*

Leo in self-defense? Or worse, what if Leo pushes me to the point where I just snap and shoot him in his sleep, like some of those battered wives I've heard about?

Brandy's mind snapped to the realization that it was over. Not the "one trunk and fifty-seven shoe boxes" kind of over. This was the *over* kind of over. As in she knew she had to get out. And she had to get out *now*. And she wouldn't be coming back.

When she got home from Vicki's house that night, Brandy loaded up her black GMC pick-up. Leo slept while she packed up Brandy Jo and Jan, and moved up to the rental property in Red Bluff.

They stayed on the 27-acre rental property with Josephine while Brandy made up her mind about what to do next.

I stayed behind. I felt loyal to the Old Man. What son wouldn't?

MUGGY'S LAST STAND

As long as Brandy's things were still at the ranch, Muggsy reasoned, she'd have to come back. So he refused to hand over her stuff.

Brandy's stuff was almost everything on the property. All the livestock—horses, cows, sheep, pigs, ducks, chickens. She would have to bring a moving truck and something large enough to transport the animals. And she would need time. At least a day or two.

Brandy decided on a day, and rented a van. She would borrow her friend's horse trailer and transport all the small livestock, piecemeal, with her black GMC pick-up. Leo couldn't stop her. It was her stuff.

Brandy called Leo and told him she was coming out to get her stuff.

"Fuck you," he slurred. And slammed the phone down.

To hell with him, Brandy fumed, *I'm goin' anyway.*

The hired driver turned the moving van onto the gravel road leading up to Brandy-Lee Ranch. Brandy followed behind in the GMC pick-up.

Brandy slammed on her brakes. The van had skidded to a sudden stop in front of her. *What the hell's going on?* She wondered.

She opened the driver's side door and swung her boots out onto the gravel drive. No sooner had her feet hit the ground, than she heard Leo yelling loud enough for all the neighbors to hear.

"Get duh hell off dis propuhty before I blow yer fuckin' heads off!"

Brandy walked around in front of the van. The driver had rolled up the windows and locked both doors. She could see the look of terror on his face. *Poor guy,* she worried, *the kid must be scared half to death.*

Brandy walked past the van and stopped at the entrance to the quarter-mile gravel driveway. Leo wasn't kidding around.

He had a host of pistols, rifles, and shotguns neatly displayed across the entrance to the drive. They were all loaded. And off to the side of the drive were several cases of ammo.

The Dead End Kid stood square in the middle of the driveway, dressed in his Levis, cowboy boots, and Stetson. He had the .44 magnum Cannon cocked and balanced in his right hand. In addition to The Cannon, Leo wore a brown leather gun belt. The holster was tied firmly to his right thigh with a leather string—just like in the gunfighter movies. The holstered sidearm was a .22 pistol. The nine-shot pistol looked more dangerous than it really was.

Brandy marched up and waved the barrel of The Cannon off to the side. "I told you to never point a gun at me again unless you intend to shoot. Are you gonna shoot me, you drunk bastard?"

"If you drive dat truck on dis property, yer goddamm right I will!"

Brandy's eyes were ablaze with fury. "I have a right to come on this property and get my things. Now get out of the way and let us through, or I'll call the Sheriff and you can deal with Ernie."

Leo was drunk as a skunk. "I'm' wahnin' yuh," slurred Leo, "If yuh don't back dose trucks off dis road, I'm gonna blast duh shit of 'em."

The van driver had rolled his window down. He yelled at Brandy to move the GMC pick-up so he could back out. Brandy walked back to talk him down.

"There's no way in hell we're gonna get in here, Mrs. Gorcey," stuttered the driver. "Let's just come back another time."

Brandy glared at Leo. He was fishing his flask of Hill & Hill out of his boot. "All right. Turn the truck around. I guess I'll have to call the damn Sheriff."

Fifteen minutes later, Sheriff Ernie rolled up. Dad was still at his post. Sheriff Ernie climbed out of his cruiser and strode up to Leo. He took off his Ray Bans, shook his head, and said, "Dammit, Leo. This has gone far enough. You have to let her on the property to get her stuff."

"Fuck her, Oinie. I don't have tuh do shit, goddammit! Dis is my fuckin' propuhty. I'm protected by duh United Fuckin' States Constitution, goddammit, and I ain't movin' off dis fuckin' road as long dat truck is in my driveway!"

"Leo...."

"Oinie, yer my friend. I ain't got no beef wit you! But I ain't lettin' dat crazy broad or any cocksuckuh dat's wit her on dis stinkin' propuhty, and dat's final! I don' care if duh whole National fuckin' Guard shows up here wit tanks an' bazookas! I ain't movin off dis road, Oinie, and dat's dat."

Leo took a long swig out of his silver flask. Ernie shook his head and rested his palm on the butt of his revolver.

"You are one crazy sonofabitch, Leo."

Ernie stared at Leo's arsenal laid out across the gravel drive.

"Goddammit, Leo. Why the hell do you have to be so stubborn?"

"Oinie,"Leo drooled, "Duh broad ain't comin on duh propuhty. Period. She can go fuck herself!"

"All right, Leo. I tried, goddammit. I tried."

"Hey, Oinie, yuh wanna *belt*?"

"No, Leo. I don't."

Ernie walked slowly back to his cruiser, climbed into the front seat, and backed out of Leo's driveway. The cruiser's taillights disappeared down the blackberry bush-lined country road.

Brandy-Lee Ranch—the ranch house as it looks today. I didn't dare get any closer for fear of being shot at. The husband of my father's widow once chased me off the property with a shotgun.

SHOWDOWN AT BRANDY-LEE RANCH

One week later, a Tehama County Judge signed a court order for the forced removal of Brandy's things from Brandy-Lee Ranch. The order was to be carried out under the supervision of an armed police escort.

The convoy pulled up to the entrance to Brandy-Lee Ranch. The Dead End Kid stood like The Duke, square in the middle of the road. The arsenal had grown by three or four weapons.

Leo's cowboy boots were firmly planted in the gravel. His Stetson was tilted slightly forward to give him that deadly menacing look. He dangled The Cannon in his right hand.

"I told yuh duh foist time, yuh crazy broad, yuh step foot on dis propuhty an' I'm shootin' yer ass off! Now tell yer stage coach driver an' yer deputies tuh get duh fuck offuh my ranch, or get out de artillery, 'cause I ain't movin' one inch off uh dis driveway!"

"You can't keep me from getting my things, Leo. I have a court order signed by a Tehama County Judge."

"Yeah? Lemme see it."

Brandy produced the paperwork. Leo stuffed The Cannon in the leather gun belt that holstered the .22 pistol.

"So, dis is duh court order?" smirked Leo. "Yuh know wuht yuh can do wit dese papuhs?" screamed Leo. "I'll show yuh wuht yuh can do wit 'em!" He reached into his pocket, pulled out a pack of matches, and lit the order on fire.

"Here's yer fuckin' court order. Bring some marshmallows wit yuh next time! We'll have a barbecue!"

Brandy turned and walked back to the squad car. "Well, he's not gonna let us in."

The Sheriff's deputy got out of his patrol car. As he covered the distance between the squad car and where Leo was standing, he flipped off the snap that held his revolver in place and wrapped his right hand around the pistol grip.

"Mr. Gorcey, I'm Deputy Lacey." Lacey's thin, measured voice betrayed his lack of experience. Lacey was a rookie and didn't know Leo.

Trying desperately to stick to procedure, Lacey rambled through the jargon. "I'm here by the authority of the Tehama County Court and the County Sheriff's Department to enforce a court order to force entry for the supervised removal of Mrs. Gorcey's personal property. We have legal authorization to remove you from the property by force, if necessary."

"Is dat right?" Leo snarled.

"Yes, that's right, Mr. Gorcey. I have another copy of the court order in the car."

"Oh, you got anudduh copy?"

"Yes, we do sir. Now I'm ordering you to stand aside, and allow this convoy to pass."

"Or wuht?" Leo sniped.

"Or we'll have to arrest you for contempt, obstruction, and assault. We'll have to take you into custody, sir."

For a moment, neither man spoke. The only sound was the crunching of gravel under Leo's feet as he took two steps back from Lacey's uniformed figure. Leo rubbed his face as if he was trying to come up with the solution to a complex math problem.

Deputy Lacey gripped his revolver, but kept it holstered. The squawk of the police radio crackled from the patrol car.

"Shit," muttered the deputy under his breath. "Mr. Gorcey, stay put. I'll be right back."

The deputy stretched his arm through the driver's side window and muttered some police jargon into the radio. When he came back, Leo was cradling his double-barreled shotgun.

"Mr. Gorcey, there's no need for this to get messy. Just put the gun down, step aside and allow us to pass."

The Dead End Kid cocked the shotgun and pointed both barrels at the badge on Lacey's chest.

"Ovuh my dead body," spit Muggs. "I told you cocksuckuhs once, an' I'm tellin' yuh again. If dat broad steps one foot on dis propuhty, dere's gonna be a helluva gun battle. Somebody's gonna get duh shit blasted out uv 'em, and it ain't gonna be me!"

"You're making a big mistake, Mr. Gorcey."

"Oh really? Tink again, Wyatt Earp. I ain't duh one wit duh loaded cannon pointed at my chest!"

Lacey yelled over his shoulder for his partner to radio for help.

"Anudduh coupla corpses ain't gonna madduh none tuh me, Wyatt. I got enough artillery here tuh blow duh whole fuckin' Tehama County Sheriff's Department tuh hell an' back!"

Lacey's partner got out of the car and walked over. He was sporting a flat top, wearing Ray-Bans, and chewing Skoll. Dad could see himself in the reflection of the partner's sunglasses.

"Dose are nice shades," cracked Leo. "But dey ain't gonna help yuh much wit a coupla bullet holes trough 'em. Why don't you boys mosey on back tuh duh station an' get a nice, friendly game uh poker goin'. You'll both live uh lot longuh dat way!"

Lacey's partner was cool. "Do we have a *situation* here, Deputy?"

"No, Chuck. Relax. I've got it under control. Did you call for another unit?"

"Yeah."

"Yeah, what?"

"Could I talk to you for a second in private."

Lacey was all jacked up for action. He was plainly annoyed by his partner's request.

"All right, what the hell is it?" Lacey asked, walking with his partner out of Leo's earshot.

"Dispatcher says 'no go'. We have orders to direct all vehicles off the property and report back to the station."

"Are you shittin' me?"

Lacey cast an eye over his shoulder at Leo. Leo smiled back at him.

"They're sending someone local out," muttered Lacey's partner.

"Well, Wyatt, you hoid duh man. Back offuh duh propuhty!" Muggsy yelled.

"How the hell did you know that?"

"I read lips! Now get duh fuck outta duh driveway while you an' yer partner are still in one piece!"

Deputy Lacey snapped the strap back over the hammer of

his revolver. "You're a very lucky man, Mr. Gorcey."

"I tink yuh got it bacwuhds, kid. Yer duh one dat's lucky. Dey wouldda been pickin' up pieces uh yer medulla oblongata out in frontuh Harrah's Club if you'd uh pulled dat piece."

As they walked back to the car, the Deputy's partner looked over his shoulder at Leo and laughed. "What an asshole," he muttered to Lacey.

Lacey got in the car, slammed the door, and barked, "You're the asshole. Yuh think you could'da said that shit any louder? Let's get the hell outta here."

The convoy made a U-Turn and disappeared down the road following Lacey's cruiser.

Leo pulled out his flask, had a little *nip*, and walked down the driveway to the ranch house. He slid behind the wheel of his blue Mercury sedan and drove down to the end of the gravel road. He loaded the arsenal and ammo into his trunk and returned it to the gun cabinet.

A stiff breeze whipped the charred pieces of the court order into the air. They landed in a patch of star thistles a few feet away.

Leo went home and took a nap.

The gravel driveway where The Dead End Kid laid out his arsenal!

THE MOSQUITO

Sheriff Ernie drove up and pounded on the kitchen door.

"Leo?"

He knocked louder.

"Oinie, come on in."

"I don't have time, Leo. Listen, this thing with Brandy...Leo, you can't do this. You have to let her on the property to get her things. She has a court order, f'crissake."

"Hey, fer you, Oinie...anyting!"

"Great, Leo. So you're gonna let her come and get her things, right?"

"Right-O, Daddy-O. No problem. I'll trow a tickuh tape parade in her honor, shoot off a pinwheel or two. Yuh got nuttin' tuh worry about. Yuh sure yuh ain't got time fer a *nip*?"

"All right, Leo. Just one."

Two weeks later, Brandy's convoy rolled up to Brandy-Lee Ranch for the third time. And for the third time, Leo assembled his arsenal at the front gate and denied them entry.

They turned around and went home.

A month after Brandy left, Grandma Josephine moved back to the ranch. Leo was lonely and wanted his mama to keep him company. Anyway, it wasn't working out for Brandy, Brandy Jo, and Jan to live on the rental property with Josephine.

Now it was just me, Grandma and the Dead End Kid—holed up at the ranch.

Grandma was getting older, and I had surpassed my father's height by six inches. So Josephine and I were getting along better. I think Grandma was impressed that I stayed behind to take care of Dad.

Who was I kidding? Who, on the face of the planet could take care of Dad? And, anyway, why were we all taking care of Dad? Wasn't he the adult? Shouldn't he be taking care of us?

Well, he did put a roof over our heads and provide us with

clothes and three square meals a day. That was more than some parents did. And he did rescue us kids from The Big 'A'.

One night, in my sophomore year of high school, Granny and I were talking about how quiet it was at the ranch since the girls left. Dad was asleep in the bedroom. Josephine got up from her favorite Naugahyde chair to go crack open another carton of Kools. Then a gunshot shattered the quiet like a hand grenade going off in a library.

I jumped six inches off my chair. Josephine turned white as a sheet. We looked at each other, then looked toward Dad's bedroom, where the shot came from.

Josephine let out a blood-curdling scream. "Leeeeoooo!"

She ran through the master bathroom, down the hall, and into Leo's bedroom.

I was quadriplegic. I couldn't move a muscle. My brain was burning with fear. I didn't want to know.

Josephine was screaming like crazy. I blocked out the screams and braced myself. I wouldn't even allow myself to think about what Grandma might be looking at in Leo's bedroom.

The distinct odor of gunpowder had wafted into the dining room. After a minute or two, I heard a change in the sound of Josephine's voice. Grandma was still screaming, but now she was screaming *at* somebody.

I crept toward the master bedroom to see if I could make out what she was saying. She sounded angry.

"Goddamm you, Leo, you crazy sonofabitch. Don't you ever do that again. You scared the shit out of us!"

I heard Dad laughing. A huge sigh of relief.

Grandma came out of Dad's room trembling like she had Parkinson's. "A fuckin' mosquito!" she groused.

"A mosquito? What mosquito, Grandma? A mosquito what?"

"The drunken bastard. The crazy sonofabitch was shooting at a fuckin' mosquito."

"Shooting at a mosquito? How could he be...."

"Little Leo, I run in there, and there's your father...sprawled out on his back in his boxer shorts, balls hangin' out, aimin' his pistol at a goddamm mosquito on the ceiling! He says to me, just as casual as you please, 'Duh noise was keepin' me awake!'

"Look at my hands, Little Leo. I'm shakin' like a leaf, f'crissake. I need a stiff drink and a cigarette. Look at me. I'm white as a sheet!"

"Yeah, you don't look too good Grandma...."

"Well, for God's sake, Leo, I was scared shitless he shot himself!"

DOWNNA HATCH

A week after Leo denied Brandy entry to the ranch for the third time, she called. It was late in the afternoon, and Leo was napping.

He grabbed the phone. "Yeah?"

"Leo, this is Brandy."

"Wuht duh fuck duh yuh want?"

"You know what I want."

"Yeah, so dat's wuht yuh woke me up tuh tell me?"

"Leo, I'm coming to get my things tomorrow morning. Are you going to let me in or not?"

"Depends...."

"Depends on what?"

"Depends on duh mood I'm in an' wuht crazy bastid cowboys decide tuh tag along fer duh ride...dat's wuht."

"Leo, just let me get my things, and I'll be out of your hair. Why do you have to make this so difficult for everybody?"

"Because I feel like it, dat's why."

"You can't keep me out forever. Eventually you're gonna end up...."

"Arright, arready. I'm tyuhd...I'm goin' back tuh sleep...do wuhtevuh duh fuck yuh want...."

Brandy wasn't taking any chances.

The convoy had grown by three Sheriff's deputies. They were all armed. They all knew Leo. Deputy Lacey and his partner had been dropped from the detail.

The convoy pulled up to the gravel driveway leading to the ranch house. There was no Leo. No firearms lined up across the driveway. No boxes of ammo piled up on the side of the road.

It was dead quiet. The only sounds were the crunching gravel beneath the patrol car tires, and the shrill call of a peacock coming from the neighbor's farmyard. The neighboring farmers used peacocks as watchdogs.

Sheriff Ernie was driving 'point'. When Ernie was sure Leo wasn't lurking around behind an almond tree with a shotgun, he inched his patrol car slowly down the gravel drive.

Ernie's black-and-white was followed by the van, Brandy's black GMC pick-up, and bringing up the rear, an additional three patrol cars from the local Sheriff's department.

As Ernie's car nosed into the driveway in front of the house, Leo emerged from the kitchen door, smiling ear-to-ear.

"Oinie, I been waitin' over an hour...wuht took yuh so long?"

"Had to round up a little help in case you changed your mind about letting Brandy on the property."

"Ahhh, she can come on duh propuhty...as long as she behaves herself and don't take nuttin' dat don't belong to her."

"Well, that's why we're here, Leo. Brandy just wants her things, then she'll be on her way...."

"Well, why don't you an' duh boys come on in an' take a load off while my soon tuh be fourth ex-wife loots duh place?"

"Sure. All right, Leo."

The four Peace Officers disappeared into the house, bellied up to the cocktail bar. Leo, of course, had all their favorite drinks in stock.

"Arright, boys! Downna hatch!"

The officers raised their glasses and cheered in unison. "Downna hatch, Leo!"

After a few hours of darts and drinking, the van was loaded.

"Hey, thanks for the drinks and the hospitality, Leo."

"Anytime, Oinie. Watch out fer dose puncture vines...I got one in duh right front tire uh duh Moicury de udduh day, came out in duh mornin' and duh tire was flat as a fuckin' pancake!"

"Thanks, Leo. I'll keep an eye out."

The dead end of the street that led to Brandy-Lee Ranch.
In the background, through the trees, is the Sacramento River.

LETTING GO

One of the most important lessons that people can learn
as they move through life is how to forgive.
—Norman Vincent Peale

Forgiveness.

As an adult, I gave ready mental assent to the concept of forgiveness. And what a mind-boggling concept it is! But a concept is just a concept. It doesn't become real until it's acted upon.

As one of my favorite thinkers, C.S. Lewis, once said, "You can't claim to believe a rope will hold your weight until you're hanging from it!"

So it is with forgiveness.

Just the mere thought of forgiving my father, far from the gooey, Hallmark Card appeal of the concept, seemed vulgar, unjust, and unthinkable.

How could I forgive the abuse, the lack of love, acceptance, and validation? How could I forgive the absence of any worthwhile preparation for getting along in the world? How could I forgive the black hole of the agony I had endured from having every one of my physical, mental, spiritual, and emotional boundaries trampled to dust?

How was it possible to forgive the people entrusted with my care? They inflicted so much damage on my soul, for so many years, that my own mind turned on me. I came within inches of throwing myself out of a ten-story window.

How? I cried. *How is that possible?*

And yet, intuitively, I knew the day would come. I knew I would reach the point where my destiny would hang in the balance. Not my next car, not the next wrung up the evolutionary ladder, not the next promotion, not the next million dollars. Those will all pass away.

I knew the day would come when I would stand at the very threshold of eternity with only one thing holding me back from freedom. One thing keeping me from being a free man.

That one thing? *Letting go.* Letting go of the past. Letting go of the record of wrongs done against me. Letting go of resentment against those who did not know what they were doing. Just as I didn't know what I was doing when I hurt many of my loved ones over the years.

That day came. That day is today.

Forgive, and you shall be forgiven, my spirit whispered. *Forgive, and you shall go free. Forgive, and all will be well with you. Forgive, as you have been forgiven. Do it now.*

"No," I cried out loud to no one there. "I can't."

I put down my laptop and fell to my knees, weeping so hard I couldn't breathe.

I'll help you, whispered the voice from my spirit. Then silence.

I pulled up off the floor, opened my laptop, and wrote the following letter to my father, The Dead End Kid.

Brandy Jo, Bernard Punsly, Leo Gorcey, Jr., and Huntz Hall accepting replicas of the Hollywood Walk of Fame Star for *The Dead End Kids*—1994.

DEAR DAD

Dear Dad,

Where do I begin? How do I describe the pain I buried deep in my heart when they lowered you into the ground that day in Los Molinos?

The years of misery so great, it came close to killing me. The tortured cries for you in the netherworld between wake and sleep. The fear that entered my heart when you first came at me with your screams of rage. It was so terrible that I spent most of the energy of my childhood years trying to protect myself from your deadly blows.

Years when I should have been safe to grow, to learn, to discover, to enjoy being a kid. I spent those years crying, trembling, lashing out at you. I secretly cursed you for bullying me into despising myself.

My attempts to put my pain into words have melted into buckets of gut-wrenching tears. They burst from an emptiness inside my heart that cannot be expressed. Only feared.

And you taught me such terrible fear. The fear first invaded my dreams at the age of five.

Where were you, Dad?

All I remember is the noise. You and your drunk friends laughing and talking loud in the living room. I was awake in my bed, paralyzed with fear. I couldn't even cry out. You wouldn't have heard me if I had. You would have told me, "Shut up! Stop crying, or I'll give you something to cry about."

I already had plenty to cry about. I didn't need any more. But over the years, you gave me much more. Your ability to inflict pain on me seemed endless.

By the age of forty, 21 years after they buried you in Los Molinos, the nightmares and anxiety attacks shocked me awake from sleep. I would leap up out of bed, in the middle of the night, and run to the bathroom sink to splash cold water on my face.

Inside my tortured soul, the voice of a child was yelling at the top of his lungs, "Help me! Daddy, please, help me!" But there was no answer. Only a vast emptiness that threatened to consume me.

I could feel the thread that connected my mind to reality unraveling. My mind and my heartbeat spinning out of control. The panic turning to fear; the fear feeding the panic. I was sure the next breath would be my last.

I'd sit cross-legged on the bathroom floor—alone. Everyone else, in my comfortable suburban house, slept soundly, but I was doubled over in terror. I strained for any thought that would stop the fear, just for a second. I had to slow my pulse down before my pounding heart exploded through my chest.

The first time it happened, I was eating an ice cream cone with my youngest daughter. My heart started racing so fast, I thought I was having a heart attack.

Two hours later, there was a doctor in my San Diego hotel room handing me a bottle of Librium. "It's stress," he smiled. "Just take one of these whenever you feel it coming on. They'll relax you." I didn't take them.

The anger I felt toward you for abandoning me, Dad, had no remedy. No pill could make it go away. Can you see now, Dad, why I dreaded the mention of your name, the endless parade of fans, the barrage of questions?

I couldn't tell them the truth! They didn't want to know. Only I knew, and I struggled alone beneath the crushing burden of the terrible secrets about the Dead End Kid. I had to push the secrets down, out of my conscious thoughts, as I strained through piles of polite smiles in response to your adoring public.

I was so angry at you, Dad, for being a drunk, for beating me, for humiliating me, and for making me feel so ashamed just for being alive. Just for existing.

But all my apologies for being a screw-up gave me no relief. There was no penance painful enough to make up for not being enough.

If I could have, I would have beaten you, humiliated you, and made *you* feel the pain. But what good would it have done? You didn't even know yourself where the pain came from. You couldn't find the healing for your own tormented soul.

For years, Dad, I labored to the point of exhaustion trying to fill the hole you left in my heart. I tried anything or anyone that seduced me with the promise to relieve my pain.

But almost without exception, the moment after I embraced these 'lovers', they viciously turned on me. They stabbed at my soul and pierced me with wounds that ached so hard that I begged for death. When death wouldn't come, I tempted fate. I accepted dares to put myself in harm's way.

I came close to death many times, and in the process I discovered a new way to numb the pain of your absence. The adrenaline high of living dangerously—close to the edge. The adrenalin shocked my numb soul to life, like the paddles of a crash cart revive the heart that's stopped.

I became a "danger junkie." I teetered for years on the very brink of self-destruction.

I had such self-hatred. It was still fueled, years after your death, by the tapes of your voice: "You stupid bastard. Don't you ever think? What the fuck is wrong with you? Don't you understand English? If you had a brain, you'd be dangerous. You can't do anything right!"

These were the voices I couldn't stop. These were the voices I tried to destroy before they destroyed me.

People tried to help me. But I soon realized they could never give me what you took with you to the grave. So I chased them away with my rage.

I was desperate and beyond anyone's help.

You were the only one who could help me, Dad. But you were gone, and you would never come back.

I wept for years when the realization dawned on me that I would never hear you say the words, "I love you, Son." I would go to the grave myself and never hear you say, "I'm proud of you, Leo." I cried until I thought my guts would fall out.

I cried more when I realized I would never be able to hug you and weep with you over our losses. I would never be able to tell you how much I loved you and wanted you to love me.

I might have been able to say these things to you in the hospital at your deathbed, Dad. But your mind had gone before I had come. You didn't even recognize me on your deathbed. A wretched shadow of the man you could have been. All my chances for fathering, gone in a single heartbeat.

I felt so lost that day, I don't know how I ever found my way back to the airport. I wish you could've been here, Daddy, to share the birth of my two children. Your two beautiful grand-daughters. You would have been proud.

I wish you could've been here to share my failures and my successes. I wish I could have gone to you for solace, and had you share with me the wisdom of your own lessons about life, and about love. But you couldn't do that.

I wish you could be here now, Dad. I wish I could share this book with you. I wish you could hear what people say about you, about how much they love you, how you brought them so much happiness and inspiration.

I wish I could come over to your house and read some of the chapters to you over coffee, and laugh and cry about your life. And have you give me funny things to add to the manuscript.

If you were here today, Dad, I would tell you, "I love you" to your face. Even if the words made you uncomfortable, I would tell you that I forgive you.

I would laugh with you, again, like I did when I was a kid and you were so funny that my sides would ache from laughing.

I would ask questions and listen to your answers.

I would try to understand you better.

I would thank you for all you did for me. You provided for me even though your own wounds ached so deeply and your only relief was in a whiskey bottle.

I would thank you for showing up at that speech contest.

I would thank you for the Stella, and I'd write you a song!

I'd go fishing with you, and bait my own hook. We'd sit in the boat and talk about everything we have in common, while waiting for the fish to bite. And you wouldn't yell at me, "Yer scarin' duh fish."

I would ask your forgiveness for being such a hell-raiser.

I wish you had been healed enough to enjoy the fruit of all your labor. I wish you had found peace and contentment. I wish you had the opportunities I've had to recover from those emotional injuries and live a rich, full, and satisfying life.

Now that I've poured out my heart to you, Dad, as truthfully as I know how, I can say "Good-bye" to you. I can release you from the jail of bitterness I wrongly sentenced you to, so many decades ago.

Who was I to judge you?

Now, I can truly desire your highest and best, even though you are no longer here. Now, I'm free to love and cherish your memory, along with all your adoring fans whose lives you touched so deeply. And they are many.

I know now that what happened to me in my childhood was not my fault. You were sick, Dad. It was your disease that kept you from loving me the way I needed to be loved.

I forgive you. I forgive you for all of it.

I choose to tear up the record of wrongs I have reckoned against you all these years. I choose to never write in that record book again.

I'll remember you as the father you wanted to be. I'll remember you as the gifted comedian who brought hours of laughter and inspiration to the hearts of your fans, exactly when they needed it.

I embrace you, Dad. I love you and accept you with all your imperfections.

I'm so proud of you. I'm so proud to be your son.

Thank you for all that you gave me, and for bringing me into this world.

I love you, Daddy.

Little Leo

My first promo shot—on the set of *Hold That Line.*

ABOUT THE AUTHOR

Like his father before him, Leo Gorcey, Jr. has been in the spotlight for most of his life. For 17 years Leo worked as a singer/songwriter, actor, teacher, radio talk show host, seminar speaker, and even a licensed minister.

Looking for a new adventure, he turned to a career of copywriting for radio and television. His success at creating scripting and new training techniques for Direct Response consultants led to the establishment of his own marketing firm.

In spring 2002, Leo took a hiatus in Ashland, Oregon. There, he studied Shakespearean theater and began writing *Me and The Dead End Kid*, the roller coaster ride of a story about growing up with his celebrity father, Leo Gorcey. Of his book, *Me and The Dead End Kid*, the author comments:

> "Over the past 20 years, I've been asked one question more than any other: 'How did you survive such a chaotic childhood and come out reasonably sane?' I think *Me and the Dead End Kid* tries to answer that question."

Leo is currently writing the sequel to *Me and The Dead End Kid*, entitled *No Dead End*, due out in Spring 2004.

Leo Gorcey, Jr. makes his home with his wife, Krista, in Laguna Niguel, California.

Contact Leo at his web page: www.LeoGorcey.com

RESOURCES

Alcoholics Anonymous (AA)
>   Phone: (212) 870-3400
>   Web: www.alcoholics-anonymous.org

Al-Anon/Alateen Family Groups
>   Phone: (888) 4Al-anon or (888) 425-2666
>   Web: www.al-anon.org

Recovery Options
>   1-800-NO ABUSE

COMING SOON!

The sequel to . . .

Me and The Dead End Kid

No Dead End

by Leo Gorcey, Jr.